D0777177

Stranded in the Present

STRANDED IN THE PRESENT

Modern Time and the Melancholy of History

PETER FRITZSCHE

HARVARD UNIVERSITY PRESS
Cambridge, Massachusetts, and London, England 2004

Printed in the United States of America

Library of Congress Cataloging-in-Publication Data

Fritzsche, Peter, 1959–
Stranded in the present : modern time and the melancholy of history / Peter Fritzsche.
p. cm.
Includes bibliographical references and index.
ISBN 0-674-01339-5 (alk. paper)
1. Historiography—Europe—History—19th century. 2. History—Philosophy.
3. Historiography. 4. France—History—Revolution, 1789–1799—Historiography.
5. Historians—Political and social views. 6. Europe—History—1789–1900.
I. Title.

D352.9.F75 2004
940.27′072—dc22 2003068560

Designed by Gwen Nefsky Frankfeldt

To Karen

Contents

And only where there are tombs
are there resurrections

—FRIEDRICH NIETZSCHE

Introduction

This book is about our invention and possession of the past. Or rather, it is about the meanings we take from the past and the investment we put in the past. The masonry of former lives has always crumbled, but the historical worldview of the nineteenth and twentieth centuries transformed rubble into evocative ruins. Lost worlds of custom and tradition took on new poignancy, and the unquestioned continuities of history appeared much less straight and orderly. Although the modern era has often been regulated by rationality and science, it also conjured up fantastic stories about national origins and tall tales of lost childhood, along with a passionate longing for the things of the past. It has cast across the landscape thousands of ruins, the marks of what we have come to recognize as history. To survey the dramatic encounters between the present and the past and to get to know the strangers that we have imagined inhabiting other times, briefly take a railroad journey in the early 1800s with Joseph von Eichendorff, a long forgotten Prussian administrator, but a perceptive Romantic writer.

In one of his story sketches, Eichendorff sat a traveler down in a train compartment, a typical nineteenth-century placement. His character looked out the window, reflecting on the jumble of impressions that passed by.[1] "Past the forest, to the right," a half-demolished castle caught his eye. It was far away and stayed in view for a long time, while closer objects vanished from sight. The traveler asked his fellow passengers about the ruin, "its name, origin, and meaning." None of them had precise answers, but they knew the place to be inhabited by a hermit. No one had ever seen the recluse, although one gentleman took him for an "arrogant crank" since he had "not once" sent around his visiting card. "Lighting up her cigar," a lady from Berlin added that the stranger must be "the last romantic," having escaped the turbulence of modern progress for the solitude of the medieval castle.

Eichendorff has deftly sketched the scene and placed readers in a distinctly modern landscape in which the present day of timetables and fashions has rendered the past anachronistic. "People knew the exact hour and minute in which they would arrive in Paris, Trieste, or Königsberg, where I did not want to go, but about the mysterious forest, the very place I wished to visit, I could not learn a thing." While the railway journey enforces the distance from the ruin, it also enables its exploration. The castle remains in view from the train speeding to other places and can thus stir the traveler's curiosity precisely because it is so near and so far away. It thus belongs to an order of things quite unlike the ephemera of the calling card or the cigar which preoccupy the other passengers. The subsequent climb up to the castle, the story's proposed plot, indicates that modernity is not simply determined by the imperatives of the present, but sustains the desire to explore a strange and remote past.

At the castle the traveler found "an old French garden run wild: tree-lined walks and straight gravel paths," even a peacock. As he entered the grounds he came upon the hermit, who looked "perfectly old-fashioned" in his "short green hunting jacket" and "wonderfully full beard." "To me it felt as if I had been magically transported back to the good old days." That the hermit turns out to be Arthur, the traveler's comrade from Luetzow's Freikorps, the irregulars who had fought for Prussia during the Wars of Liberation against Napoleon in 1813–14, is significant. The vast mobilization of the war had plainly unsettled Europe: the castle has been abandoned; Arthur can no longer find his way; travelers in the valley below journey by trains and schedules. For all the fairytale qualities surrounding the castle and its peacocks, Eichendorff takes pains to situate the ruin and his characters in historical time. We know we are in the remarkable period after the French Revolution. The story records a single traveler's feeling of estrangement from a remembered past: the reminder of the *ancien régime* by way of an "old French garden"; the experience as well of postwar unsettlement, which has stranded the veteran; and the heave of industrialization, in which railway passengers speed to Königsberg and Trieste, forgetting about forests and castles. Eichendorff not only records the dramatic transformations of the first decades of the nineteenth century but indicates the new ways that time was experienced as a result: the busyness of the present, the obscurity of the past, and the magical connections that could be made when the past was approached. He also introduces thoroughly modern characters, including the railway passengers who live completely in the fashionable present; the time traveler, who stands in for the century's intrepid historians and storybook readers; and the traveler's quarry, "the last romantic," the fugitive who serves as a witness to the losses and dispossessions of history. It is not the march of time that has produced ruins in this story or stranded people in the present, but the specific course of recent history, and more specifically its apprehension as non-repeatable, irretrievable time. This book will investigate the production of the past and its romance in modern times and suggest the ways in which the past itself is a historical artifact.

A step closer: once the traveler got a better look at Arthur, he saw that the hermit was playing with the "remnants of my homeland" in the company of a boy and girl who, the traveler learns, were the grandchildren of his own childhood companion. Eichendorff suddenly pulls together two elements, the castle and childhood. Both are equally faraway and both are encountered as ruins. By establishing a correspondence between the historical process that wrecked the castle and the glimpse of personal lives of contemporaries estranged from their childhoods and sealed in railway compartments, Eichendorff insists on the mutual definition of public and private time. In an age saturated with history, childhood acquired the same romantic status as the castle ruin, and both became containers to hold the "good old days." The ruins of the past extended into private lives. Whether we are talking about the lost causes that ruined the castle or the childhood pleasures that come up in our memories, the past is disconnected from the present. However, the past is also something that can be recovered in imaginative recollection, in songs, storybooks, and dreams, and in voyages to the ruins. Throughout the nineteenth century the past was an object both of mourning and desire, even as it remained broken and unfamiliar.

"Who says the world has been already been discovered?" inquires the writer Peter Handke.[2] Eichendorff would have agreed with premise of the question. Both in his poetry and in his stories, Eichendorff's narrative elements work to discover and designate an incomplete, wrecked world which is marked by rupture and loss but remains accessible through imaginative second-hand renditions of fairy tales, memories, and other journeyings. The work of the poet or the autobiographer recalling his childhood was to try to see the world as "mysteriously beautiful." Wars and other historical events wrecked the castle and stranded the veteran, but these losses found compensation in the magical aspect they acquired as ruins. "Yes, the world is still full of wonderful treasures," Eichendorff insists, "we just don't see them anymore!" Here he echoes Novalis: "It is only the weakness of our senses that keeps us from catching a glimpse of fairy land." Eichendorff's discovery of distance and his exploration of the past that that distance had brought into view "past the forest, to the right" revealed just this "fairy land" for himself and his public.[3]

The "fairy land" or, as I later suggest, the "household fairies" of modernity, is the subject of this book. I explore the discovery of history, the fragmentation of the past, and the articulation of historical identity amidst newly visualized ruins at the turn of the nineteenth century, and I argue that the early nineteenth-century moment of revolution, war, and industrialization profoundly shaped the way the West thought and still thinks about time and history. Of course, history as a genre existed well before that time. European states had long commissioned chronicles of power, individuals composed their autobiographies, and the Christian religions projected a messianic view of time. But something quite new develops around 1800, in the decades around the French Revolution: the perception of the restless iteration of the new so that the past no longer served as a faithful guide to the future, as it had in the exemplary rendering of events and characters since the Renaissance. As past and present floated free from each other, contemporaries reimagined their relations with the past in increasingly flamboyant ways. The past was conceived more and more as something bygone and lost, and also strange and mysterious, and although partially accessible, always remote. The disconnection from the past was a source of melancholy, something I have tried to capture in my title, but it also prompted a search for new ways to understand difference. Hence Eichendorff's deliberate journey to the unknown castle. At the same time that the distant past no longer offered a complete and visible account of itself, it was therefore available for reinterpretation. History turned dramatic: it offered modern subjects a way to think of their ability to act and influence the world around them in circumstances of contingency; it introduced a whole new range of political actors and political motivations; and it invited people to think of their own lives in a historical, hence politically potential fashion. Elements of the past themselves did not change at all; the castle is no more wrecked when Eichendorff's traveler sees it than it had been before the railway arrived, but the way it was seen changed fundamentally. This was the dramatic result of the French Revolution: an entirely new means to see social experience.

Over the last two hundred years, history has given up its role as counselor and teacher. Historical thinking no longer persuasively summons up situations from the past, and especially from the classical past of ancient Greece or imperial Rome, to illuminate the challenges of the present. The present does not recognize itself as occupying the same temporal plain with Athens, Sparta, or Rome. Men and women today do not see their past counterparts as basically the same, whether living in Periclean Athens or Renaissance Italy or present-day America. What once had been an unquestioned assumption about the intimacy of human beings and the translatability of knowledge across time and space came to an abrupt end in the revolutionary period some two hundred years ago. In the years after the French Revolution, with its unprecedented revision of political action, motive, and cast, historians at the time floundered in their attempts to find an explanation or to fit the revolution in larger conceptual streams. Henceforth, history would be contemplated from the standpoint of epistemological uncertainty, which made historical narratives less authorative, but also more interesting and many-sided. An increasingly strange past came into view and became an object of both public and private desire.

The sharp break between the past and present also expanded the scope and pertinence of historical study. The ideological ambition of the French Revolution, and its reorganization of society meant that history touched many more people and that people were enfranchised to take part in and take advantage of political actions. Modern history was no longer the single, identifiable comprehensive process as understood by the Enlightenment thinkers, invested as they were in the idea of civilization and refinement. By contrast, modern history created a huge stage, enrolled more and more people in its dramas, and found that more and more people took an interest in historical developments. Historical genres, especially autobiographical ones, flourished in the postrevolutionary period as contemporaries saw their lives reflected in and shaped by history.

Moreover, the disconnection between the past and the present made the past an object of intense scrutiny. Insofar as the present moment was characterized by the new, the past appeared increasingly different, mysterious, and inaccessible. Cut off from the present, the past turned opaque, which invited a new, more subtle scholarship to take its measure. More aware of the distinctiveness of their own contemporary present, men and women came to invest the past with its own historicity and to understand it in terms of "time" and "place." This enlarged the scope of history to include the most ordinary artifacts and the most undistinguished subjects that reflected a particular "spirit of the age." Interest in distinctive cultures and customs furthered the enfranchisement, at least in historical description, of many sorts of people, not simply powerful elites. The stylistic distinctiveness of other, former periods invited imaginative journeys backward in time and suggested new possibilities for reconfiguring the present.

Finally, the role of contingency in history expanded as the developmental logic, which made the events of the past cumulative or the resolutions of the present inevitable, was no longer authoritative. All at once, the past was reenlivened with the identification of foreclosed possibilities. Contemporaries came to see what I call "half lives" in the past and to insist on the possibilities of restoring, however incompletely, neglected itineraries. In other words, the disconnection of the past and the present facilitated a wide range of new connections with past histories. Once understood on its own terms, the past was refurbished in startling ways.

The historical view opened up imaginative possibilities for building subjecthood, and both the nation and the individual, and both public and private space, have prominent roles in my argument. These possibilities were premised on the experience and evidence of loss. The losses of the past are irreversible; this is what constitutes the melancholy of history. At the same time, the historical knowledge of losses is shared: people consume and produce historical texts as a way to connect their personal ordeals with larger social narratives. Gathering up poignant testimony and creating empathetic readerships, modern history recognizes the suffering of individuals, however selectively. The melancholy of history contains both these meanings: the sorrowful note of testimony and the sympathetic ear of the listener *and* the organization of occurrences as so much change, wreckage, and loss.

While I privilege the role of the French Revolution and the European wars that followed (1789–1815) in reformulating Western notions of time and history, I do not assert that this historical view never existed before. In fact there is compelling evidence that writers in seventeenth-century England, witnesses to the vast destruction of Catholic sites in the decades after the Reformation, circulated similar ideas about irreparable loss and the eruption of new time. But the scale of events in Europe during the French Revolution, the restless mobilization of new ideas, and the definitive illegitimacy of nonhistorical notions of time throughout the 1800s indicate that the radical moment of innovation was at the turn of the nineteenth century. I am aware that the structure of my argument, with its stress on the "moment of innovation" and its dramatization of the years 1789–1815, reproduces, even if critically, the conceit of modernity which is that history is the relentless iteration of the new.

The experience of loss that connects private ordeals and public dramas makes history pertinent and interesting to the public. Indeed, as I argue in Chapter 1, the notion of the public and the medium of history developed hand-in-hand at the turn of the nineteenth century. Therefore I pay special attention to the genres of representation. I am not only interested in how people thought about the irretrievability of the past or the eruption of the new, but in how this understanding of history transformed cultural practices. Thus, in Chapter 2, I examine the figure of the French émigrés, refugees of the revolution, who not only saw and described their lives in the dispossessed terms of exile, but perceived the world in terms of exile. New ways of thinking about the cultural itineraries of the past are explored in Chapter 3. The discovery of the "half lives" in historical ruins enabled a reconception of national differences and a rejection of political empire. Although the national publics of Europe quickly outfitted themselves with a distinctive cultural heritage over the course of the nineteenth century, the connection to the past remained tenuous and the fragments that were recovered did not tell a complete story. The effort to articulate the difference of the past provides the theme for Chapter 4. Finally, in Chapter 5, I explore how conceptions of history organized private and family life and invigorated autobiographical and commemorative genres.

It is in this last chapter that the far-reaching effects of the historical worldview become clear. I argue that history became a mass medium: Europeans and European immigrants in North America became increasingly aware of and interested in history. These developments were not confined to a highly educated elite nor to the witnesses of war and revolution in Germany and France. The dramatization of historical time that was spurred by the French Revolution came to structure the temporal imagination throughout the nineteenth and twentieth centuries. And the notions of historical change also came to apply to private life and personal development, so that the practices of commemorating, writing, and retrieving the history of family became very widespread. In this way, a historical worldview corresponded to the extension of subjectivity in the modern period. My argument has all the advantages and disadvantages of broad brushwork, but I do want to advance the claim that the social impact and trans-Atlantic scope of the historical worldview corresponds to a dramatic reorganization of modern time and space, so that contemporaries felt themselves as *contemporaries,* as occupants of a common time zone with mutually recognizable personalities, dramas, and processes such as "revolution" or "industrialization." This synchronization finds a faithful expression in the nineteenth-century novel, which pulled together readers as like-minded contemporaries who recognized themselves in the novelist's characters and their lives in her plots. Therefore, while I recognize differences in the particular organization of historical time in Prussia and France and Britain and the United States, I do not find these differences as important as the common endeavor to think historically and to possess the past. This effort was transnational, even as it was constitutive of the idea of the national.

My transnational approach is also true to the shared recognition that the national subjects of the West were bound together in a comprehensive way. It thus allows me to note the complicity between the practices of modern history and the construction of the "West," along with the exclusion of "people without history." Nonetheless, the concept of difference in the past and the empathy for the ruins and wrecks of time enables me to argue that history as a modern genre could be profoundly liberating precisely because it embodied different and alternative subjectivities. For all the synchronization implicit in the idea of contemporaneity, the historical worldview facilitated emphatic exchange and promoted the idea of cultural difference and thus repeatedly returned to the possibility of political change. In my view, history is the only escape from the imperatives of the present.

C H A P T E R O N E

The French Revolution and the Evidence of History

"Thursday the 17th with the market boat to Mainz. Mixed weather"—the sun broke through the clouds as travelers boarded the low-slung vessel. A young couple with two children took leave of their family, an elderly mother and brothers and sisters, who ran back and forth carrying bags and saying goodbyes. On deck, lumber dealers leaned against the ship's boom, complaining about supplies and delivery dates. The touring scene sketched by the thirty-two-year-old Sulpiz Boisserée, a German art collector on his way from Cologne to Mainz in August 1815, is unremarkable but for the raucous, unending debate and commentary that goes on below deck. The talk is not about lumber, and it caught Boisserée's interest as he wrote page after page of description in what amounted to one of the longest entries in his personal diary. *"Unten im Schiff* [below decks]*,"* he noted, "[in] the small, more elegant room in the back," "well-to-do Frankfurters are discussing politics: artisans, tailors or cobblers." One of the artisans is in a "reserveman's uniform with a meerschaum pipe in his mouth" and "speaks to a traveler, a noncommissioned officer, an Italian or Pole, about Napoleon . . . recounts how Frankfurters ran to see Talleyrand: 'He too belongs on St. Helena!'" Boisserée makes his way to "the big cabin," where "someone is reading a newspaper out loud, a Jew is listening and so is a farmer . . . The black-bearded Jew believes that Napoleon will still escape." As for the farmer, he laughs at a story about Blücher punishing the French. "After dinner, a small cabin in the back," Boisserée continues: "a Catholic priest has gathered a crowd . . . he's from Nassau and complains about the Russians, about the Germans, and particularly about the Prussians and their pride. They demand twice as much money, and wheel and deal at the innkeeper's expense—'those are our liberators?'—he snorts his tobacco." The discussion meanders: "Jacobins in Berlin and Vienna . . . a fairy tale about the Peace of Tilsit . . . and back to generalities: France; Napoleon still has his fingers in everything; the French are not doing well; Napoleon is the smartest creature alive, only pride corrupted him." Other passengers recount to the "Italian or Pole," Boisserée can't tell which, stories about serving in the wars in Spain and in Sicily. In the front cabin, an English hussar who lost his leg in "Pamplona '13" chats with some peasant boys, who themselves have recently fought in the wars of liberation.[1]

The description is marvelous. Boisserée wandered from cabin to cabin, catching snippets of publicly informed conversation, pointing out the newspapers, the uniforms, and the mix of travelers, and revealing just how the revolutionary wars created a shared historical awareness. Figures such as Napoleon, Talleyrand, and Blücher, and red-lettered events such as Tilsit or Pamplona, belonged to the repertory of everyday conversations, but their significance was not self-evident; this was argued out among cobblers and tailors, Jews and farmers, Poles and Italians, who do not hesitate to place their own experiences ("Pamplona '13") into the larger picture. What is striking is not simply all the talk about the revolution and the wars, which is taken up again and again, before dinner, "after dinner," cabin to cabin, but also the exchange of opinion and evidence whereby well-known public events are retold in various personalized versions. The travelers participated in a common historical drama by which they organized and connected the events of their time and through which they told their own stories and found that others were interested in them. Carefully setting the scenes—"the small, more elegant room in the back," "the big cabin," "a small cabin," "in the front cabin"—and attentively transcribing the talk back and forth, Boisserée at once drew attention to and enhanced the dramatic qualities of the social exchanges he witnessed. The observer saw people seeing history, and he took such care with his stage effects because he was aware of how novel was this dramatization of experience as the evidence of history.

On that August day on the way to Mainz, Boisserée reported on one of the startling consequences of the French Revolution. This was that more and more people began to visualize history as a process that affected their lives in knowable, comprehensible ways, connected them to the strangers on a market boat, and thus allowed them to offer their own versions and opinions to a wider public. The emerging historical consciousness was not restricted to an elite, or a small literate stratum, but was the shared cultural good of ordinary travelers, soldiers, and artisans. In many ways history had become a mass medium connecting people and their stories all over Europe and beyond. Moreover, the drama of history was construed in such a way as to put emphasis on displacement, whether because customary business routines had been upset by the unexpected demands of headquartered Prussian troops, as the innkeepers protested, or because so many demobilized soldiers were on the move as they returned home or pressed on to seek their fortune, or because restrictive legislation against Jews and other religious minorities had been lifted, which would explain the keen interest of "the black-bearded Jew" in Napoleon and of Boisserée in the Jew. History was not simply unsettlement, though. The exchange of opinion "in the front cabin" and "in the back" hinted at the contested nature of well-defined political visions: the role of the French, of Jacobins, of Napoleon. The travelers were describing a world knocked off the feet of tradition and reworked and rearranged by various ideological protagonists and conspirators (Napoleon, Talleyrand, Blücher) who sought to create new social communities. Journeying together to Mainz, Boisserée and his companions were bound together by their common understanding of moving toward a world that was new and strange, a place more dangerous and more wonderful than the one they left behind.

Boisserée's scene was also a European one. Poles, Italians, and an Englishman were aboard the boat from Frankfurt to Mainz, and passengers recounted experiences in places as far away as Spain and Sicily. They worked in a distinctly transnational frame of reference. And although the maritime scene took place at the end of the revolutionary period, in summer of 1815 after the battle of Waterloo, people referred to events that had taken place many years earlier. The account thus acknowledged both the continental scale of the French Revolution and the force it accumulated over a quarter-century. It was the revolutionary wars across the European map, and the abrasive movement of soldiers and travelers and refugees for twenty and more years, that gave credibility to the picturing of history as a process that destroyed the past and revealed the future. An understanding of how the French Revolution transformed the perception of history and of time only becomes clear if one moves beyond France to all of Europe and moves beyond the years 1789 and 1794, which bracket the familiar history of the revolution from the fall of the Bastille to Thermidor, to include the revolutionary and Napoleonic wars and their aftermath.

Although the precise chronological sequences of the wars does not play a central role in my argument, it is useful to keep in mind the broad developments of the revolutionary epoch. If European observers were not sure of the significance of the fall of the Bastille in July 1789, they became more and more interested in the events in France as the National Assembly debated the new constitution in the years 1789–91. Nothing demonstrated the significance of the revolution more than the tightening antirevolutionary alliance of the monarchies against France in 1792, which led to the declaration of the French Republic and the trial and execution of King Louis XVI. The radical republican experiment culminated in the Reign of Terror in the years 1793–94, and its conclusion in the summer of 1794 usually concludes as well the narrative of the French Revolution. But the republican armies that had repulsed Austria and Prussia in 1792 continued to press into Holland, western Germany, and Italy, staving off repeated Austrian counterattacks and thereby providing French generals (including the young Napoleon) with the victorious battles at Mantua, Marengo, Campo Formio, and elsewhere that are commemorated on the Arc de Triomphe at the far end of the Champs Elysées in Paris. The French Revolution continued to explode across the Continent.

A failed expedition to Egypt in 1798–99 notwithstanding, Napoleon emerged as the most outstanding statesman and gradually imposed a dictatorship on France. A short peace with Austria in 1801 (Lunéville) and then Great Britain in 1802 (Amiens) allowed Napoleon to consolidate his power as consul for life and then as emperor (1804). A new anti-French coalition took shape in 1805, but met with epic defeats: of Austrian armies at Austerlitz in December 1805, and of Prussian forces at Jena in October 1806. With French troops occupying both Vienna and Berlin, the Napoleonic Empire had reached its zenith, establishing peace with Russia and enforcing an economic blockade against Great Britain. Insurrections in Spain in 1808–09 and Austria in 1809 plumbed popular nationalist discontent, but it was only with Napoleon's invasion of Russia in autumn 1812 that the empire unraveled. War against France resumed in 1813, with Napoleon losing on a grand scale in the Battle of Nations at Leipzig in October 1813. The allies occupied Paris in April of the next year, and the emperor quickly abdicated and accepted exile on the island of Elba. However, Napoleon launched a truly dramatic return to France in March 1815, reassembled his armies, marched toward Paris as an astonished Europe held its collective breath, and was finally and decisively defeated at Waterloo, outside Brussels, in June 1815, this time to be exiled on the tiny south Atlantic island of Saint Helena until his death in May 1821.

Time and time again the anti-French coalition formed and marched against Napoleon, and each time the French emerged victorious and stronger, at least until 1812. This gave the French Revolution an extraordinary hold on the European imagination. It was a great drama avidly followed even by Europeans in the Americas, who witnessed a slave revolt in Santo Domingo in 1792, the arrival in the United States of tens of thousands of French émigrés both from Haiti and the Continent, the opening up of western territories thanks in part to the Louisiana Purchase, which the French negotiated to raise money for war in 1803, and republican revolutions across Latin America after the fall of the Bourbon monarchy in Spain in 1808. Americans also came to report on their domestic politics in the political idiom of revolutionary Europe, particularly after the presidency of Thomas Jefferson, who was widely identified with Napoleon. But what really changed in the quarter century from 1789 to 1815 was not just the international balance of power that tilted to favor Great Britain and ultimately the United States, or the prominent new parts that all social classes came to play in national politics, but the way contemporaries understood and experienced history.

What made the past seem so remote and the movement of history so menacing to nineteenth-century observers was the deep rupture in remembered experience that came with the French Revolution. Two intertwined forces were at work in this period: the massive dislocation of revolution and war, and the narration of that dislocation as change or progress, which was seen to extinguish tradition. Without the machinery of narration—the notion of epoch and the sense of new time which structured histories, prefaces, and memoirs—material changes could not have been interpreted as of one piece or identified as an encompassing historical passage that elevated parochial tragedies into more meaningful, legible common fates. And without the restless mobilization of men and women into new economic arrangements, new geographic places, and new political services, the narration would have lost its pertinence, its authority, and its urgency. As a result, in the first quarter of the nineteenth century, material unsettlement combined with a new historical sensibility. Although Europeans had known devastating upheavals before—the Reformation and Thirty Years' War—these were not narrated in terms of fundamental and continual change and so did not drastically alter the temporal identities of contemporaries. "All human beings were subject to general disaster or exploitation as they were to disease," explains George Steiner. "But these swept over them with tidal mystery" and did not revise the way most people thought about history; "it is the events of 1789 to 1815 that interpenetrate common, private existence with the perception of historical processes." Steiner gets to the essence of the changes in these revolutionary years with his wonderful remark that "wherever ordinary men and women looked across the garden hedge, they saw bayonets passing."[2] Steiner is not simply referring to the presence of large mobilized armies, which would not be qualitatively different from the grand armies of the seventeenth century, or even to the *levée-en-masse,* which involved millions of citizens in the wartime cause of the French Republic; rather, he refers to the ongoing dramatization of events in terms of a recognizable and comprehensive transformation which shaped private lives and gave a meaningful social context to the disruption of individual fates by providing narrative form to experience, that is, the story of revolution and of modern politics "across the garden hedge." The most salient attribute of this narrative form was the consciousness of periodicity that distinguished historical epochs and characterized social customs, and sequentialized a view of history as a swift, comprehensive process of transformation in which differences over time assumed overriding importance.

The French Revolution restructured previously authoritative structures of temporality by redrawing the horizon of historical possibility. What made the revolution radical was the very idea of positing a moral community justified in terms of virtue rather than legitimated by custom, tradition, or religion. All the emphasis on economic interests and political ambitions, the argument for bourgeois hegemony or state centralization, which has dominated most social historical accounts of the French Revolution, has tended to slight the utopian vocabulary as something fanciful and dreamy, obscuring the real stakes of the political struggle. In recent years, however, cultural historians have insisted that the presumption that new men and new women could be created and virtuous nations made implied a fundamental change in the idea of the political. "By the end of the decade of revolution," writes Lynn Hunt, "French people (and Westerners more generally) had learned a new political repertoire: ideology appeared as a concept, and competing ideologies challenged the traditional European cosmology of order and harmony." It was the "invention of ideology" that enabled a break with the past, because the revolutionaries held that the social and moral condition of people could be rearranged. Their belief in revolution was itself revolutionary. With astonishing deliberateness, republicans set out to destroy the landmarks of the past: churches, castles, and the graves of the French kings at Saint-Denis. In town after town, church bells were destroyed or silenced, a drastic rearrangement of customary aural space. Ten years after the fall of the Bastille, Napoleon's administrators continued the work of political and religious reform in French-occupied Europe, wrecking hundreds of churches, convents, and monasteries in Cologne and Venice alone. To get a sense of how radical was the French reorganization of time, François Furet compares French with the American revolutionaries who had preceded them by twenty years. Few if any of the principals in 1776 saw it as their mission to "snatch [America] from its past," he argues, or to repudiate the prerevolutionary colonial epoch.[3] Only in France did revolutionaries propose a new calendar, unravel the customary weeks and months, and replace the Christian year 1792 with the republican *L'an 1*. The future could now be imagined as a space of innovation and newness, a place of abundant possibilities.[4]

The most remarkable thing about the revolutionaries was the beliefs they came to hold: that the world was not fixed and that tradition could be rejected. These ideas were expressed in ordinary words and simple sentences, but they led to dramatic changes in social practices because they made men and women conscious of their relations to the world around them and prompted them to examine what they had previously accepted as natural or unchangeable. French revolutionaries dramatized "the instant of creation of the new community, the sacred moment of the new consensus" in ritual and ceremony, and they urged people to present themselves in public as the virtuous citizens they presumably strived to be.[5] The red-white-and-blue ribbons and cockades that republicans wore, and the unpretentious cut to their clothes, soon became markers of loyalty as French revolutionaries grew more conscious of themselves as regenerators of everyday life. Nothing was left unexamined in the effort to remake citizens, a strenuous effort that fully realized not only the pretensions of revolution but its menace. The politicization of everyday life invited republicans to rethink what they owed to others and what they wanted for themselves and, by many accounts, gave a sexual charge to social exchanges, but it also vastly increased the points of contact between the revolutionary state and the individual person.[6] The public presentation of the revolutionary self with ribbons and cockades invited public vigilance, along with denunciations, hearings, and executions. It was the impulse to reexamine the most basic elements of social existence that gave the revolution such power and made it so compelling and interesting and dangerous to Europeans.

The radical nature of the revolution was not immediately clear to all observers, especially sympathetic ones, for whom the achievement of liberty and equality in France in 1789 was often no more than a further installment in the progressive history of enlightened self-governance. "The convulsions are strong," admitted the Swiss historian Johannes von Müller, "but not too expensive for a free constitution. What didn't the English, the Dutch, our own [Revolution] cost!"[7] At least from a distance, the revolution was entirely recognizable. The hundreds of travelers from around Europe who journeyed to Paris, the capital of the revolution, wrote breathless letters back home in 1789, 1790, and 1791, but generally described events in conventional terms of freedom and despotism, which kept them from seeing the ambitious and unregulated nature of the enterprise of fashioning a new moral community. For early travelers, self-professed friends of the events in France, the revolution was radical in the sense that it appealed to basic elements of human nature, realizing in mighty steps commonly shared, if abstract ideas of truth and reason.[8] In the words of the young Friedrich Gentz, later a vehement critic of republicanism and translator of Burke, but in 1790 a young, well-connected civil servant in Berlin's war ministry, the French Revolution was "the first practical triumph of philosophy."[9] For most interpreters, the guidelines of the Enlightenment remained indispensable. Even his imprisonment during the Terror did not deter the Marquis de Condorcet, the well-known enthusiast for the "age of reason," from completing a sunny outline of the "progress of the human spirit." The muddled, but recognizably constitutional order after 1794 tempered but did not extinguish liberal faith in well-regulated government.

Recognizing the French Revolution in this familiar way depended on viewing it as the fulfillment of Enlightenment ideas, but from the beginning there was something strange about the events in France. The radical Montagnard leader, Robespierre himself, insisted that "the theory of revolutionary government is as new as the revolution which brought it into being. It is not necessary to search for it in the books of political writers, who did not foresee this revolution."[10] In this respect, revolutionaries did not so much reach inward to realize the principles of reason, as stretch outward to create a republic of virtue. Enthusiasts spoke repeatedly of a "new epoch" in human history. The dictatorship of virtue which Robespierre led in the years 1793–94 was, of course, the most dramatic attempt to remake the French people. It coincided with intense political activity: Jacobin clubs proliferated in the years after 1789, and especially after the establishment of the republic in 1792. The extension of club life even to small provincial towns indicated the degree to which revolution authorized vernacular political voices. More and more Frenchmen, though far fewer French women, spoke up to express opinions, uphold loyalties, and denounce enemies. Moreover, all aspects of political and social life were examined in the countless newspapers and periodicals and hastily published pamphlets which appeared in public places.[11] There was something of the revolution in the private moment of letter writing, when people expressed their own opinions, revealed their own desires, and challenged paternal authority at home as well as official truths about politics in general. As an introspective and subjective genre, the letter was, in fact, associated with French sentiment and Jacobin indiscipline and ultimately with revolutionary subversion itself.[12] Beginning with the Third Estate's constitution of itself as the National Assembly, the urge to redescribe, rename, argue out, and persuade was the most distinctive characteristic of the revolution.

It was the self-authorization to reimagine the familiar world that proved to be so liberating, and so scandalous. Conservative opponents turned out to be especially sensitive to the audacity of the revolution. Not loyal to the aims of republican politics, and still attached to the privileges of the old monarchy, they saw the promiscuous forms and destructive energy of the revolution more clearly. Conservatives, monarchists, and émigrés were more apt to see the events of 1789 in revolutionary terms, as a fundamental break with the past. Edmund Burke, above all others, recognized the novelty of the revolution, which is why the German poet Novalis dismissed the "many antirevolutionary books [that] have been written for the Revolution" in order to praise Burke's "revolutionary book against the Revolution."[13] For Burke it was precisely the revolution's defiance of "common maxims" and "common means" that made it such a "hideous phantom." It "overpowered the imagination" because its presumption was to innovate even though the "great principles of government" and "ideas of liberty" were, as he ascertained in his *Reflections on the Revolution in France,* published at the end of October 1790, "understood long before we were born."[14] Considering the "chaos of levity and ferocity" across the English Channel, Burke concluded that "everything seems out of nature." The revolution was relentlessly destroying the "present time" in the name of political virtues which "exist only in idea."[15] It was the sustenance it drew from opposing what was supposedly natural, settled, or common that made this particular revolution "the most astonishing that has hitherto happened in the world."[16]

The violence of the revolution derived from its assumption that words and ideas could remake political and social life. Although Burke probably counted himself among those who, at least at first, "could not believe it was possible [it] could at all exist," he had been "overpowered" and forced to acknowledge the hitherto unrecognized power of the revolution's faith in ideas. Nearly two hundred years later, François Furet described this power as "the illusion of politics." "It transformed mere experience into conscious acts," the French historian argued, inaugurating "a world that attributes every social change to known, classified and living forces . . . Society thus recomposed itself through violence." In this statement Furet implies that the political dream is not sustainable and that "real society," or Burke's "matter of fact," will inevitably reassert itself. For many observers this is exactly what occurred in France with the fall of Robespierre. But even as it masked political continuity and overshadowed the play of interests, "the illusion of politics" was real enough; its eschatology of salvation and condemnation justified the Reign of Terror and lingered on in memory. For decades to come, visitors would trace out the words that had spelled out this illusion. Returning to Paris at the beginning of the new century, the great French memoirist, François-René de Chateaubriand, could not help but notice the left-over republican inscriptions: LIBERTY, EQUALITY, FRATERNITY, OR DEATH: "Sometimes they had attempted to efface the word DEATH," he noted, "but the red or black letters showed through the coating of lime." After the Peace of Amiens, in 1803, Sir Samuel Romilly, the British penal reformer, toured the ghostly remains of the revolution. At the Place de la Revolution, he inspected "the very spot" on which the king and later the queen had been executed; along the way, he noted the places still overwritten with "the words, UNITÉ, INDIVISIBILITÉ DE LA RÉPUBLIQUE, LIBERTÉ, EGALITÉ, FRATERNITÉ." Here, too, "OU LA MORT" was sometimes still legible, and it certainly remained terrifyingly legible in written recollections. Even after twenty years, returning émigrés testified to the unsettling effect and hallucinatory power of revolutionary graffiti, "this republican language!"[17] The words did not disappear.

Eighteenth-century notions of orderly progress failed to account for the protean nature of the French Revolution. Despite Thermidor, the revolution did not burn itself out. Thousands of émigrés remained displaced outside the borders of France and the republican regime continued to prosecute the civil war in the Vendée with great severity. Year after year, the revolution failed to find the resting point or the conclusion that so many observers anticipated; it did not do so after Thermidor 1794 (Robespierre's fall) or after Brumaire 1799 (Napoleon's rise), or after the general European settlement with the Peace of Amiens in 1803, or after the emperor's coronation in 1804, or even after the more radical reconstruction of Europe after 1806. Revolution mutated repeatedly into war. French armies ended up exporting ideas of the revolution across Europe. From Dalmatia to Holland, French soldiers and administrators left inalterable changes behind. Not only did the revolutionary forces nurture republican ideas in Germany, Italy, and elsewhere, but they imposed enormous strains on the European monarchies, upset social arrangements between the estates, and finally broke up the old state system altogether. From the perspective of its enemies, long after the fall of Robespierre, France remained a revolutionary, even despotic, and certainly dangerously contagious society.

If the disorder of revolution remained prominent in the fears of its enemies, it was also evident in the disappointments of its supporters. After the Terror, republicans admitted to doubts about the workability of their rational ideas for setting society right. Biancamaria Fontana draws attention to this postrevolutionary, postutopian moment. Not only did "the collapse of the religious and social values of the *ancien régime*" not "automatically result in a new world ruled by reason and tolerance," but the former "unity and compactness (if not coherence) of traditional values" had given way to "a pluralistic universe of competing prejudices and beliefs." It was precisely the "disillusions" in the experience of "newly conquered liberty" that placed postrevolutionary society in a condition of "permanent moral insecurity."[18] The question of what forms to give a fractious political community remained unsettled and unsettling. Observers looked to the future with as much uncertainty as expectation. It is therefore important to take note of the twenty years of unsettlement after 1794, a period in which not only conservatives and émigrés, but also republicans and other Europeans well beyond the orbit of events in France reported on the revolution's repercussion.

It is difficult to overemphasize the extent to which the prolonged nature of the French Revolution disrupted Western conceptions of historical continuity. Commentators repeatedly laid aside well-worn rhetorical templates in which they compared modern with ancient revolutions and tried to fashion a new vocabulary that could convey the unprecedented force of events between 1789 and 1815. This was not a repeat version of the English or the American revolution. Johannes von Müller, after Gibbon the most famous historian in this period, was haunted by the fear that the universal history of civilization he had just completed had been made obsolete by the revolution in France. In a series of heartfelt letters to his brother he reported his bewilderment at the eighteenth century's unpredictable, furious end: *"alles wird so ganz anders,"* he wrote, "everything is becoming so different."[19] Müller's exclamation echoes the intentions of the revolutionaries themselves, and it is itself echoed throughout the next two hundred years. Although fundamental transformations had roiled earlier centuries, modern testimony insists on seeing it just like this: "everything is becoming so different." It is the signature phrase of the modern. Hegel and Marx in the nineteenth century and Walter Benjamin, Herbert Fischer, and Eric Hobsbawm in the twentieth all follow the logic of this emplotment, even if they differ on particulars.[20]

Not all contemporaries believed that historical precedents no longer applied. Many saw French events from Thermidor to Brumaire and the wars against Austria and Prussia in 1805–06 through the perspective of the Roman Republic and the Roman Empire. Napoleon himself gave these parallels plausibility by crowning himself emperor, although his revival of the imperial idea was always more audacious than recognizable. What is striking, however, is how many political commentators appeared to be quite bewildered and disoriented and regarded the unprecedented nature of events to be in fact the defining characteristic of the age. After seventeen revolutionary years, Joseph de Maistre, a deeply conservative Savoyard exile in Russia, could still write: "Nothing resembles this epoch, and history does not provide any datum or analogy as an aid to judgment."[21] Events proceeded outside "the standards of experience," agreed the historian Friedrich Maximilian Klinger, and like-minded statements abound. "The pen quivers in the hand of the historian who takes hold of it in order to try to portray the scenes of a year [1793] which seem to have surpassed human powers of description and feeling and which future generations will hardly believe actually took place," wrote Wilhelm von Schirach, editor of Hamburg's influential *Politisches Journal,* who found no other formula than to repeatedly, if inelegantly reiterate: "Never before" has "such a monstrosity been so wicked"; "never before" were so many "murderous battles fought"; "never before . . . have we seen such broad attacks and retreats."[22] And every year brought new, unanticipated events and developments. Every newly built construction of the revolution had collapsed: "one epoch destroys the other."[23] Readers, too, were overwhelmed: "As of late," wrote Dorothea Schlegel from Vienna, "the newspaper reports have been getting more awful, hugely horrible, we are frightened like children again who are told the fairy tale about the giant who wears seven-league boots and catches up with the poor refugees underfoot again and again." The outlandish imagery of the *Siebenmeilenstiefel* occurs repeatedly in contemporary reports—"one makes sense of the day with the sayings of old women," admitted Ernst Moritz Arndt—an indication at once of the speed, surprise, and consequence of revolutionary events.[24]

Enlightenment conceptions of history also broke down when contemporary observers considered the political drama of an ideological age. What was so remarkable about this revolution was the role of the curbside crowds, the formation of a national audience, and the public nature of the events, as well as the sharply drawn ideological contests. Writing in 1799, Friedrich Gentz summarized the new situation expertly: "Never before in a period of ten years have such a large number of important and intertwined events, such a rapid sequence of extraordinary transformations and restless movement, and such piled-up revolutions taken place. Never before," Gentz caught his breath and continued "have changes of such astonishing variation and with such rich significance in all their social and political aspects occurred on a stage that was so open and accessible, and never have these changes repeated themselves in so many guises and been interpreted from such contradictory points of view." William Wordsworth said much the same thing more briefly when he referred to a "multitude of causes, unknown to former times . . . now acting with combined force."[25] "Never before was the spirit of the times so subject to passions and preconceived ideas"; "everyone has his party," complained the editors of the *Politisches Journal.* In the somewhat stilted language of *Partheylichkeit* and *Unpartheylichkeit,* they put their finger on a key aspect of the French Revolution, namely its dramatization of ideological positions which incorporated contested visions of the future. There was no such thing as a quiet point of objective perspective: "nonpartisanship itself appears partisan."[26] Now that "every reader" had "his own opinion and his own prejudices," in itself a rather revealing recognition of democratic tendencies, this meant that the events of the French Revolution and the Napoleonic Wars were experienced as struggles over the authority and legitimacy of the past, and over the shape of the future, which was increasingly seen as wide open.[27]

What this "multitude of causes" made immeasurably more complicated was the act of writing history itself. Contemporary historians had trouble deciphering the density of events. For historians as much as for writers and artists the French Revolution posed the following problem: "How does a writer or artist represent something he believes to be unprecedented—hitherto unknown and inexperienced?"[28] Observers strained to find appropriate metaphors and models. The "composition of contemporary history" is made difficult, explained Schirach, the German journalist, by "fluctuation in the principles, the decisions, the precautions of the courts and regimes." The fact was that "one almost never has a clear perspective, the political game is always complicated, the movement of events is unsteady, difficult to grasp."[29]

All this stood in sharp contrast to eighteenth-century models, which knew only a finite number of politically active forces. "Behind each ruler," writes Reinhart Koselleck about the cabinet politics of the European courts before 1789, "stood an army and a population of known dimensions whose potential economic power and monetary circulations could be estimated." By this means, the future had been made susceptible to prognosis, which calculated the "finite possibilities" and "arranged [them] according to their greater or lesser probability."[30] This is certainly how Müller had conceived his grand history. He used abstract generalities to give form to individual events, argued in favor of the balance of power, and agreed "with Machiavelli" that history was "un magazin d'expériences" which could efficiently serve political statesmanship.[31] This authoritative but basically static conception of historical subjects and motivations is what made the unexpected series of events that comprised the French Revolution seem completely astonishing, indeed unnatural. In fact, the revolution proved to be sufficiently confounding that many historians at the time failed to complete their work. Müller, for example, admitted that events had overtaken his published conclusions. By contrast, Chateaubriand veiled his confusion in fatalism, acknowledging that "despite a thousand efforts to penetrate the troubles of states," to which he had contributed with his 1797 attempt at *An Historical, Political, and Moral Essay on Revolutions, Ancient and Modern,* "something is missing, *un je ne sais quoi,*" an "indistinct disquiet," a "destitute interior" that tormented the human condition itself.[32] For his part, Friedrich Gentz filled one thick folio volume after another with reflections on the revolution at the turn of the nineteenth century, without publishing them because he found his own explanations inadequate. Gentz was puzzled enough to append astrological epilogues to his political epistolaries. "What do you say to the meteor in Wesel?" he queried fellow conservative Adam Müller, "and to the snow that fell on the 11th of October in Vienna, and in Lyon as well? And what about the flooding of the Danube right during the horrible days of Ulm!" the last a reference to a key battle the Austrians had lost to Napoleon in 1805.[33]

It was the continual production of the new that marked the revolution and left contemporaries disoriented and historians unprepared. In the face of continuing political unrest in Paris and further French conquests in Italy and elsewhere, Gentz remarked in 1799 that the lasting accomplishment of the French Revolution was the "the continual series of revolutions and catastrophes" it had set in motion.[34] Napoleon's wars had accelerated the relentless destruction, "without measure, without proportion, without standard."[35] Mallet de Pan, who had sympathy for political reform, and Joseph de Maistre, who had none, made similar concessions to the basically inconclusive and therefore unprecedently ruinous nature of the revolution. It was not just the scale of destruction but the lack of any sense of direction to events that bewildered people. French victories over Austria at Austerlitz in 1805 and over Prussia at Jena in 1806 came with the complete reorganization of the state system. The destruction of the Holy Roman Empire, the institution of new monarchies, and the redrawing of international borders were experienced as abrupt endings which completely severed the present from the past. "The world is lost; Europe will burn up," predicted the Austrian minister Clemens von Metternich with characteristic peremptoriness.

While this catastrophic rendition of world history did not exclude a chiliastic moment of potential redemption, apparent particularly in the rhetoric of anti-Napoleonic revolts in Spain and Austria, the evidence for chastisement without salvation appeared overwhelming. In the first decade of the nineteenth century, for many of the ranking statesmen and intellectuals who have left letters and diaries, life itineraries suddenly ended in a cul de sac. "The door of hope seemed to me closed forever, to Germany and to Europe," confided Gentz, who left French-occupied Vienna in 1806 for "harsh, tedious exile" in Prague.[36] The shock of entrapment was expressed in unusually physical terms. "An event such as that of Austerlitz," continued Metternich about the year 1805, "is not the crisis of a fever, which often wakes slumbering strengths or gathers scattered powers. The blow has shaken our most vital body parts. We are relieved to be alive at all, and even if can't move our arms or legs, we happily twitch our fingers and stammer our words."[37] This sense of paralysis came with the abrupt failure of the second grand coalition against France. Metternich and others eventually regained their senses, though they also acquired a sense of dread, the shortness of breath that Madame de Staël remembered first feeling when she heard news of Napoleon's coup d'etat in 1799 and which, ten years later, she reported, has "never left me, and I fear it has become the illness of a whole Continent."[38]

It was during the revolutionary epoch that the new appeared to contemporaries as an unmistakable if unknowable force, which upended, uplifted, and destroyed. Inconstancy was the new constant, a presence that seemed to render the exterior world at hand superficial and fragile, and the subterranean forces at work fundamental. "We live in a strange and truly mysterious time," wrote the young aristocrat, Alexander von der Marwitz, to his former lover and intimate correspondent, Rahel Varnhagen, at the end of 1812: "Lightning strikes the soul, omens reveal themselves, and ideas drift through time and like the mysterious appearances of ghosts point to a deeper meaning, the revolution of all things, in which *everything* Old disappears like the ground pulled under by an earthquake, while underneath the ruins volcanoes heave up a new and fresh ground."[39] What is interesting is not so much the accuracy of the remarks, but the absolute terms in which new and old, fresh and corrupt are contrasted, and the explosive sense of time as something sudden, thunderous, and clandestine.

History appeared as an unpredictable gambler, wondrous when it evacuated the French in a few months from central Europe in 1813, but more often malevolent and capricious. Nothing confirmed this lingering sense of uncertainty better than Napoleon's return from Elba in March 1815. History had become a category of the sublime, stranger than a Gothic tale. "Bonaparte in Paris and Emperor again!" an astounded Englishman wrote in his diary. "These revolutions would be too incredible for romance."[40] "No, never shall I forget," recalled Germaine de Staël, "the moment when I learned from one of my friends, on the morning of the 6th March, 1815, that Bonaparte had disembarked on the coast of France." "I thought that the earth was about to open under my feet. For several days . . . the aid of prayer failed me entirely . . . it seemed to me that the Deity had withdrawn from the earth, and would no longer communicate with the beings whom he had placed there."[41] These references indicate how much history had taken contemporaries by surprise. An exhausted Rahel Varnhagen wrote her brother Markus in Berlin: "He is back . . . all the old misarrangements, vexations, bad customs, and mistakes which will now be stirred around. Basta! Everything is going to be different." Rahel felt sympathy for Napoleon, but grew dizzied by the perpetual motion of contemporary history.[42] In a wonderful side note, which reveals how public events manifested themselves in private lives, Rahel reflected: "It will not come out the way I say it will or the way I think it will. If one thinks things will turn up suddenly and violently, they come gradually; if one thinks they will come gradually and smoothly, they turn up unwanted, like the one from Elba, and disturb the world, instead of coming as I had imagined, at the first sign of trouble. Peace and quiet and whatever I had imagined—you shouldn't rely on that at all!"[43]

While there was no doubt that events came one after the other, there was little sense that they followed an orderly, linear pattern, the dominant rendition of history in the eighteenth century. "We are not headed toward the future," which one approaches and foresees, noted Rahel at the end of 1815; rather "the future comes from behind," by surprise, which "is breaking my head apart."[44] As a result, the restoration that followed Napoleon's fall remained fragile and even suspect. The revolution it had supposedly brought to an end lingered in memory as an unsettling presence, evidence for the impermanence and indecipherability of the course of events. Rahel's striking imagery goes even further, for it emphasizes the haphazard accumulation of happenings rather than the work of deliberate actions of people, and therefore serves as a more profound indictment of the idea of progress and perhaps an argument for surprise. It also anticipates Walter Benjamin's "Angel of History," whose "face is turned towards the past." "Where we perceive a chain of events," writes Benjamin, "he sees one single catastrophe which keeps piling wreckage upon wreckage and hurls it in front of his feet." Although Rahel was more sanguine about the possibility of new arrangements following upon bad customs, and Benjamin's emphasis is on the great storm of the expulsion from paradise, like Benjamin she had a feel for the varied layers and hidden possibilities of the present moment. As she had put it: "Basta! Everything is going to be different."

Rahel Varnhagen, Friedrich Gentz, Chateaubriand—these are indisputably educated and well-born witnesses, but it would be a mistake to assume that their insights into the nature of historical time were restricted to their social class. What made the narration of the revolution as discontinuous, explosive time so compelling was the extent of the upheaval throughout Europe. Rahel's premonition of the future coming up from behind resembles Dorothea Schlegel's image of the giant who catches up with refugees again and again. This roadside perspective is entirely warranted. The French Revolution mobilized millions of citizens, soldiers, and refugees, and did so for a period of twenty-five years. Much as the ideology of republican virtue appealed especially to newcomers in French provincial towns in the early 1790s, the discontinuities of historical time made particular sense to waves of unsettled and uprooted people across Europe in the following decades. To be sure, new ways of thinking about history were not suddenly adopted by the mass of Europeans, but these ideas were discussed and taken up well beyond the ambit of salons and courts, and this was due to the revolution's vast ideological and military mobilization. "It is in vain that you hope to escape the calamities of the present age by retired habits and the obscurity of your life," Chateaubriand wrote from his exile in London in 1797; "no one can promise himself a quiet moment."[45] The collective memory of revolution would be "so sharp," the historian agrees, "because so many had participated in shaping it."[46] In what ways are these conclusions on the mark?

The extensive mobilization is rather easily surveyed: the *levée-en-masse* of French citizens, the soldiering across all of Europe, the mustering of home guards, the ebb and flow of refugees and exiles, the tax and capital levies in occupied territories, the dissolution of religious orders, the introduction of the Napoleonic Code, the anguished anticipation and joyous celebration of peace, the commemorations of the victories at Leipzig and Waterloo—all this maneuvered ordinary men and women into the flow of history and made them increasingly aware of the present, taking them away from remembered pasts.

Nothing dramatized the period or spread the revolution as much as war, which extended the ideas of the revolution in at least crude form to millions of people from all classes. Up to 2.5 percent of the French population served in the revolutionary armies of 1794, and at least twice as many did in the years 1813–15; in Prussia the figure reached 6 percent in 1813. Most young men in these places were mobilized. The small British army of 40,000 men in 1789 expanded six fold twenty-five years later; the navy increased from 16,000 men to 140,000 in the same period. Many hundreds of thousands of citizens also took part in Britain's volunteer militias, especially during the invasion scare of 1802–03. In general, death rates were drastic: one in five Frenchmen born in the first years of the revolution (1790–95) was killed in its last years (1806–15); the revolutionary wars killed as many soldiers and civilians, proportionately, as did World War I.[47] From the thousands of Frenchmen who took up domiciles on the left bank of the Rhine to the scarlet-coated British officers who stepped into the lives of the Bennett sisters in Jane Austen's *Pride and Prejudice* to the poor soldiers from France, Saxony, and Bavaria whom townspeople encountered in disheveled clumps as they straggled back from Russia in 1813, the revolutionary wars mobilized and garrisoned and ultimately killed more men than had any other previous war. This gave the military an unprecedented visibility in daily life. No soldiers on a given day; on the next, soldiers marched down the street, had decamped on the market place, and taken up lodgings in private homes. The obligation to house soldiers was such a familiar burden during this period that aunts and uncles greeted visiting relatives with the half-alarmed cry *"Die Inquartierung kommt!"*[48] It would have taken lots of cousins to match the burden placed on towns such as Nürnberg, whose 25,000 inhabitants had over the year 1813–14 to feed and house and otherwise take care of 350,000 men. Not surprisingly, memories of looking at soldiers stayed in mind and they were told and retold in letters, diaries, and memoirs for many decades to come.[49]

Thousands of soldiers and exiles and refugees remained in motion throughout the two decades that followed the first French invasions of western and central Europe, and particularly the

French occupation of the Rhineland after 1792. A chronicler at the time in the small west German village of Dormagen reported on the dead, bloated bodies of French soldiers that floated down the Rhine River each day in July 1793. A few months later, in January 1794: "little groups of Prussians come almost every week through here, going forth, then coming back." The "colossal ball of revolution rolled back and forth" for another half-year before finally coming to rest in October 1794: "now we're republicans."[50] But it was not long before the trials of French occupation emptied Dormagen and other villages like it and filled country roads with refugees. "What with the fear of the French," the streets of Würzburg "are beyond description," reported Heinrich von Kleist in September 1800: "Now refugees, now priests, now Imperial troops, a motley crowd running every which way, questions and answers, and rumors that in a couple of hours always prove false."[51] A few years later, the thrust of Napoleon's war against Austria and Prussia in 1805 and 1806 tossed about countless civilians once more.

When peripatetic Europeans finally took rooms in temporary lodgings, their diaries and letters described the view from the window as columns of soldiers and prisoners and wounded passed through town. "Hardly 10 days from the capital and we are already overwhelmed by uncertainty," wrote Caroline Böhmer from her refuge in a convent in Maulbronn in August 1809: "We had hoped that peace would catch up with us from behind, but we stumbled forward into the war, especially between Augsburg and Ulm, where Spanish cuirassiers, infantry regiments, and the most horrible artillery pieces passed by us all day . . . in Zusmarshausen there was an awful crush: we were walking alongside a column of wounded, then a infantry battalion advanced from the other side just as a herdsman was driving his cattle through town."[52]

German princes, too, crowded the roads ahead of French invaders in 1796 and again in 1805–06. "The numbers of princes and princesses that are now wandering about can hardly be counted," noted the bemused editors of the *Politisches Journal* in the aftermath of the battles of Austerlitz and Jena. That the general *Völkerwanderung* included a *Fürstenwanderung* must have made a strong impression on subjects who had always taken the political order for granted.[53] "Forth and back, in all directions" ran the princes and electors, marveled Goethe's mother to her son in October 1805; "here it is like at Schnitzelputz's house, everything turning in circles."[54] Again and again, references to "seven-mile boots" and to characters such as "Schnitzelputz" indicated not only the mediated, second-hand interpretation of events, but their fairy-tale quality.

Even when people did not leave, conditions of life changed anyway. "Almost 60 per cent of the German population changed rulers during the revolutionary period," calculates James Sheehan. "Among them were the inhabitants of Hausen, a village that had once been part of the Habsburg's western lands and then was given by Napoleon to Frederick of Württemberg in return for his support during the campaign of 1805. . . . Perhaps they believed the political world of 1806 was just another version of the old," he writes. "Like Germans everywhere, however, they would discover that they were now part of a larger world, subject to forces at work far beyond the horizon of their village. Twenty-nine Hausener marched with the Grande Armée into Russia, sixteen—almost two complete age cohorts of the village's young men—did not return." "Terrible cold and lack of bread delivered us to our deaths in Russia" is the sentence written "above their names in the cemetery chapel."[55] There is no doubt that the history of the French Revolution spread to places far beyond Paris, Lyon, and Marseilles. Although settlements in Great Britain were rather more insulated from the fighting, they were nonetheless dramatized by the conflict. "Every town was . . . a sort of garrison," observed George Cruickshank about the mobilization of volunteers in 1806: "in one place you might hear the 'tattoo' of some youth learning to beat the drum, at another place some march or national air being practiced upon the fife, and every morning at five o'clock the buglehorn was sounded through the streets, to call the volunteers to a two hours' drill . . . and then you heard the pop, pop, pop of the single musket, or the heavy sound of volley, or the distant thunder of artillery."[56] This patriotic activity was much remarked upon and, alongside increasingly rigorous wartime taxation, "fostered public awareness among the mass of ordinary Britons," argues Linda Colley in her analysis of how eighteenth-century wars in North America and continental Europe worked to create an encompassing, but relatively recent British identity.[57] The French countryside was full of movement as well, particularly during the military mobilizations in 1792–93, on the eve of the planned invasion of Britain in 1803, and in the two years after 1812. During that year, from "February until the end of May" a young apprentice living across from the French Gate in the village of Phalsbourg remembered "regiments after regiments" pass beneath his window on their way east—"dragoons, cuirassiers, carabineers, hussars, lancers of all colors, artillery, caissons, ambulances, wagons, provisions, rolling on forever, like a river which runs on and on, and for which one can never see the end."[58]

Phalsbourg had seen soldiers before, over many hundreds of years, but the philosopher Georg Lukacs insisted that something was new about soldiering in this revolutionary period. "What previously was experienced only by isolated and mostly adventurous-minded individuals, namely an acquaintance with Europe or at least certain parts of it," Lukacs argued in his analysis of the "inner life" of the nineteenth century, "becomes in this period the mass experience of hundreds of thousands, of millions." Even more important than the fact of travel were the categories in which this travel was understood. These terms were distinctly and specifically historical, so that they revealed "the social content, the historical presuppositions and circumstances of the struggle," and connected up the war with "the entire life and possibilities of the nation's development."[59] What more and more people saw across the "garden hedge" that George Steiner has so incisively imagined were not natural occurrences but political phantasms, audacious attempts to remake, undo, and destroy the conditions of social life itself. For that reason, the revolution pressed itself into the lives of private Europeans with unusual force.

From the outset, the French Revolution was seen as something that demanded judgment. Thus the handful of French troops housed in a middle-class home in Cologne in October 1794 found a ready welcome at the family dinner table—even though their wooden shoes identified them as *sans-culottes*—because "our Herr Vellnagel was a great friend of the French," at least until his tablemates whom he placed left and right at his side addressed him with the familiar *tu* ("the familiar *tu* went public," writes Lynn Hunt about ordinary conversations in the 1790s) and then stole his pocket watch.[60] Even this disappointing instance indicated the ways in which the most ordinary encounters between civilians and soldiers acquired an unprecedented political aspect. As they debated the merits and justice of the revolution's aims, friends broke apart. "Knebel is raving mad," wrote Charlotte von Stein to her friend Charlotte Schiller about the writer: "we had such a falling out that he doesn't want to see me again." Even families divided into ideological camps: "I side w/ Father—against Mother ? Ferdinand" and against the revolution, confessed Regina Beneke, a young woman in Hamburg, in 1794.[61] The arguments went on for twenty-five years, right up to the eve of the invasion of Russia, when Count Pierre Bezukhov and Vicomte de Montemorte disagreed about Napoleon at Anna Pavlovna's soirée in the opening pages of Tolstoy's *War and Peace.* Intellectual itineraries were different enough, averred Chateaubriand, that "those who had lost sight of one another for twenty-four hours could not be sure of ever meeting again. Some went the revolutionary way; others contemplated civil war; others set out for Ohio . . . others went to join the Princes." Chateaubriand, having fled to the United States for the year 1791, knew what he was talking about: he was related through marriage to Lamoignon de Malesherbes, the moderate reformer who was later guillotined, one of whose daughters quit France altogether, while another celebrated the new "heroes of the Bastille."[62]

These conflicts in opinion should not obscure the ways in which the revolution pulled contemporaries into a common orbit. As readers and writers, they reviewed the revolution again and again, and the revolution, in turn, prompted renewed reading and writing. "So much writing and talking," complained Hannah More from her outpost in rural England about the uproar concerning France, revolution, and reform.[63] Indeed, one scholar attributes a good part of the rise in literacy at the end of the eighteenth century to the general desire in Britain to read commentaries on the revolution and to follow the furious debates between Burke, Paine, and Godwin.[64] Newspapers, almanacs, and calendars guaranteed that political events were widely discussed even in the small villages of Germany.[65] Across the Atlantic, American exceptionalism did not keep the French Revolution from being set as a commonplace item into everyday discussion; "whatever is connected with Napoleon promises deep interest," noted the editors of *Godey's Lady's Book,* at the time the most popular journal in the world, as late as 1832.[66] A glance at the periodical literature of this period reveals that American readers closely followed European events. Reading, writing, talking—almost at once, the French Revolution constituted a remarkable republic of letters that stretched throughout Europe and across the Atlantic to North America. In many ways, historical consciousness created the public sphere.

Correspondents not only read histories and commentaries about the French Revolution, which in turn prompted their own reflections, but sought out novels and dramas that would connect their private lives to public events in an affecting emotional or passionate register. "What are you reading?" inquired Rahel Varnhagen in May 1809, in the middle of battles between France and Austria: "for three days, Schiller's *Wallenstein* has been lying on my table." Although set in the Thirty Years' War, the drama possessed an astonishing immediacy: "how every word fits . . . it really is about the same things, the same passions, the same desires . . . the names of the regions and families are almost the same."[67] A stream of didactic novels now forgotten but written by authors such as Jane West and Charles Walker endeavored to safeguard English households from stories that purportedly appealed to French sentiment: the specter of revolution and the misleadings of philosophy figured prominently in the conventional fictional plot of the 1790s.[68] It is not necessary to take seriously the satirical complaint that the English "peasantry now read the *Rights of Man* on mountains, and moors, and by the wayside" to appreciate the ways in which the growing popularity of novels, pamphlets, and newspapers corresponded to an increasingly ideological and contested understanding of the world.[69]

Letters, in particular, became privileged forms for private individuals to remark freely on the public affairs of the revolution; already Helen Maria Williams's *Letters from France* circulated republican opinion in Great Britain between 1790 and 1796. Letters continued to carry on the debate on the French Revolution not only among intellectuals who published responses to Edmund Burke's *Reflections on the Revolution in France* and Thomas Paine's *Rights of Man,* but among ordinary correspondents, who ventured their opinions in writing: "Only you could have brought me to write all of this," confided Agnes von Gerlach to her sister, as she set pen to paper at five o'clock one winter morning in French-occupied Berlin in 1808. As numerous literary scholars have argued, the letter form was well suited to express an insistently personal form of dissent, anxiety, or desire.[70] The criss-cross of letters, written so vigorously and awaited so anxiously, suggests that correspondents shared a common understanding of the implication of events. Readers might experience these only second-hand, but they understood their importance immediately. To refer, as did Dorothea Schlegel, to "an entire historical epoch" that lies "between one mail day and the other," indicates how letter writers participated in the mutual recognition of comprehensive historical transformations.[71] The establishment of this narrative field lent the far-flung hopes and misfortunes of correspondents a poignancy that could be generally shared. Thus the particular moment of the writer—"Today our troops are entering, *right now*"—retained meaning for the reader many days later.[72] This meant that historical narratives provided a socially meaningful context to personal descriptions of public events. Individuals increasingly saw themselves as taking part in historical struggles, and accordingly put value on their own contributions and testimonies. "The Swedish troops are marching through the streets!"—"Now I have to ask you one thing, dear Rahel!" pleaded her husband, Karl Varnhagen von Ense, from war-torn Hamburg in May 1813, "*don't* tear up and burn my letters. It is *these letters,* collected over many years, that will provide valuable details."[73] It was precisely the details, the specific content of Varnhagen's particular experiences in Hamburg, that was valuable as historical evidence. Letters, and other personal testimonies, translated experiences from the private to the public realm and back again, and thereby continually revised and disrupted other, more authoritative narratives.[74] At the same time, this exchange rested on a newly felt sense of contemporaneity which pulled Europeans together into a circle of shared understanding and busy literary activity, one which newspapers attempted to bind in a more permanent way. As Benedict Anderson has pointed out, the nineteenth-century press created an abstract national public in which distant readers came to see themselves as fellow citizens; in similar fashion, early newspapers and other public correspondence made that public historically conscious and able to assimilate far-away events into an overall political scheme.[75] Historical literacy also created that public by giving it a common dramatic frame.

Had events not been dramatized as recognizable historical markers, it would be impossible to understand the shock of the revolutionary moment. Again and again over the course of the French Revolution and the Napoleonic wars observers reacted in common ways to unexpected occurrences. This shock is unrelated to the technical developments of the media, and it is misleading to interpret so-called "flash-bulb" memories of events such as Kennedy's assassination in 1963 in terms of the television age. Rather, the shock of the historical moment is based on personal understanding of what the news means and the knowledge of what it has already meant or will mean to others. It is the shock, the instant, of recognition, so that the dread Germaine de Staël felt about Napoleon's coup d'etat could be construed as "the illness of a whole Continent."[76] In other words, the surprise is delivered in the context of a common understanding that rests on shared temporal and historical categories.[77] Take the example of William Wordsworth, who, when crossing Morecombe Bay to Rampside after visiting relatives one day in early August 1794, "carelessly inquired if any news were stirring." A ferryman transporting travelers from Ulverston cried out in reply: "Robespierre is dead!"[78] Given Wordsworth's detailed response to this event, his biographer Kenneth Johnston regrets not knowing "where William Wordsworth was standing when he heard the news of the fall of the Bastille," which was "one of those world-shaking events that tend to isolate spots of time for everyone."[79] But surely the reason for the presence of a detailed account in 1794 and the absence of a corresponding account for 1789 is not archival accident but the fact that in the intervening years the French Revolution had come to be recognized as a universal drama. Only then could there be a spot of time and only then could history press a claim on even an ordinary band of travelers and the ferryman and on the most casual inquiries in ways that were not imaginable at the time of the fall of the Bastille. Thus the execution of the French king in 1793 and Napoleon's escape from Elba in 1815—news of the *Evenement,* as Rahel Varnhagen put it, moved extraordinarily quickly in March of that year, even without railroads or telegraph—also came as shocks of recognition which illuminated with unusually bright clarity the historical consciousness that Europeans had come to share.[80]

The strangers on Boisserée's market boat in August 1815 shared in just this historical knowledge. Their comments and opinions relied on and advanced a discursive field that facilitated recognition of the revolution as a series of events with public consequences. On the move in postrevolutionary Europe, whether as refugees, soldiers, or entrepreneurs, they were particularly disposed to comprehend the revolution in broad and abstract terms. Public consciousness about the marauding movement of history at the turn of the nineteenth century had the effect of creating a common denomination to individual experiences, so that people could recognize a general cause behind particular effects. Koselleck takes note of this transformation of far-flung events into the protracted "collective singular" of "History" or "Revolution."[81] Yet this process of "singularization" did not lead to unanimity. Rather, it had the effect of making very different testimonies socially meaningful. They were no longer discounted as parochial or unreliable viewpoints but recounted as renditions of understandable and pertinent historical transformations. "Everybody was in history now," comments Mack Walker about the end of the Napoleonic era: "all were present at Armageddon," or at what the philosopher Hegel declared to be the "world court," in which deliberations contemporaries had taken part as historical subjects.[82] As the itineraries and discussions on the market boat indicated, experiences and opinions differed even as they were absorbed in a common frame of meaning. There was unprecedented consciousness of how history interpenetrated individual lives and how, as a result, it gave social meaningfulness or poignancy to feelings of unsettlement. Historical contexts gave the lives of people unprecedented distinctness. At the same time, it was precisely what Lukacs calls the massification of public life at the beginning of the nineteenth century that made the motivations and effects of historical transformations complex and indeterminate. In this sense, history was rendered more invisible. The perception that all aspects of social and political life were assuming new forms, or as the philosopher Friedrich Schlegel put it, the acknowledgment that whatever historical unity there was derived from the suspicion that everything was "movement"—"the epoch is the epoch of movement"—undoubtedly sharpened historical awareness, which was endlessly reexamined in inquiries made at the ferry landing, in debates held below deck, and in the books and newspapers that people bought and read and passed on, and the correspondence they shared.[83] Contemporaries came to see this all-encompassing movement, but since it came with such uncertain and heterogeneous effects, they also made more poetic, interpretive demands on historical writing, and thereby proved open to increasingly ideological or frankly vernacular perspectives. The result was an extraordinary production and consumption of the interpretations of general history.

The radical shift in historical consciousness transformed the French Revolution into the collective singular of generic revolution, dating from 1789 to 1815, one which gave its name to the age: The Age of Revolution. The portraits of Wellington and Blücher, the celebrated victors at Waterloo, may have hung in the antechambers of consulates and embassies with the inscription "To the Saviors of the World," as Alfred de Musset imagined in mid-nineteenth century, but the suspicion that such a safeguarded world had not found rest and would not find rest persisted. For as Musset himself pointed out, when "a nobleman or a priest, or a sovereign passed," the people knew an older truth and perhaps smiled: "we have seen him before now in a different place; he looked very different then."[84] Not only had republican hopes not been crushed, but the future continued to be regarded, in a mixture of anticipation and dread, as a space of fundamental political innovation. There was no undoing the presence of the events of 1789, 1793, 1806, and 1815, a spectacular sequence which for over one hundred years organized historical reflection and historical remembrance. The presence of this history meant that there was no return to the past nor safety in shelter. Thus Hegel admitted in 1819: "I am just fifty years old, and have lived most of my life in these eternally restless times of fear and hope, and I have hoped that sometime these fears and hopes might cease. But now I must see that they will go on forever, indeed in moments of depression I think they will grow worse."[85] At the same time, Friedrich (now) von Gentz saw stretched before him an "Iliad of storms and battles and adversities." He spoke repeatedly of fiends and leviathans overtaking him. Napoleon had died, he wrote in 1824, that much was certain, but "the revolution had incorporated itself into every monster; the revolutionary spirit has traveled around the world in a thousand forms."[86] Concerning unrest in Spain around the same time, Chateaubriand insisted on the fundamental ideological connections between far-flung places: "The fate of Europe hangs in the balance," he maintained: "If the revolution triumphs in Spain, all will be lost. It is necessary to win there, and win completely, or to perish among the ruins."[87] Revolution constituted, in Shelley's words, "the master theme of the epoch in which we live."[88] What did Thomas Carlyle and Robert Southey talk about when they last met? More than a half-century after the storming of the Bastille, the topic was, Carlyle remembered, "the usual one: steady approach of democracy, with revolution (probably explosive) and a finis incomputable to man; steady decay of all morality, political, social, individual; this once noble England getting more and more ignoble and untrue," until it "would have to collapse in shapeless ruin, whether for ever or not none of us could know."[89] This drastic description confirmed how little deference the present paid to the knowledge and experience of the past.

Beginning with Germaine de Staël and the *Considerations on the Principal Events of the French Revolution,* which she wrote in 1817, just before her death, and continuing with scholars such as Thiers, Mignet, Taine, and Barante in the two decades that followed, liberal historians strained mightily to impose structure, pattern, and necessity onto the French Revolution and to narrate the great event in terms of a unifying and rational process. These progressive accounts generated considerable enthusiasm for the moral, political, and social advance of European societies, an optimism that has never entirely faded. Nonetheless, the results were not completely persuasive. The French Revolution could not be so easily digested by historical writing, writes Linda Orr, which "either had to swallow the distasteful, the disgusting parts of the Revolution or cough them up." Historians "had to excise or assimilate into the logic of history the cup of blood, heads bobbing on pikes, and the slash of the guillotine."[90] The very effort of these multivolume nineteenth-century histories revealed the difficulty in snatching the revolution from the mythic present it had created for itself. Optimistic and integrative accounts of the revolution could not quite calm the fears of the terror of history or disperse the impression of the frivolity of its ends.

In Britain, Thomas Carlyle developed another historiographical solution, which fully incorporated the mysterious and protean aspect to the revolution. He tried to create a narrative style that would correspond to the radical contingency of events, and it is Carlyle who, many decades later, best recollects the anxious tone in the letters and diaries of contemporaries in the 1790s. Published in 1837, the furiously written three volumes of *The French Revolution* fashioned new words appropriate to the new subjects that Carlyle identifies, particularly "SANSCULLOTISM"

("What think ye of *me?*"), a "New-Birth of Time," "the Death-Birth of a World."[91] To detractors who objected to these semantic "impurities," Carlyle answered: "If one has thoughts not hitherto uttered in English Books, I see nothing for it but that you must use words not found there, must *make* words . . . revolution *there* [is] as visible as anywhere else!"[92] The appearance of unexpected births and new entities conspired to undo any tidy rendition of revolutionary events. Describing the events of 28 February 1791 ("The Day of Poignards"), Carlyle jumped from Mirabeau in the National Assembly to Lafayette on the streets to royalists in front of the Tuileries: "Such things can go on simultaneously in one City. How much more in one Country; in one Planet with its discrepancies, every Day a mere crackling infinitude of discrepancies."[93] Jules Michelet, too, interrupted the flow of narrative to introduce *chose étrange* or *chose bizarre,* and felt overcome by "vertigo" "watching the prodigious scene of so many beings, yesterday dead, today so alive, creative."[94] Finally, to better convey the "incongruous ever-fluctuating chaos of the Actual," Carlyle deployed the present tense, allowing him to "fling to us specific experiences and comments which puzzle us as to what is happening and why it is pictured in *this* way."[95] For both contemporaries such as Johannes von Müller and subsequent interpreters such as Carlyle, the revolution challenged the authority of the narrator; as a mass popular event, it had invited the involvement of too many different kinds of principals who worked at cross purposes for the eighteenth-century science of politics to provide reliable guidelines. In this way, the endeavor to understand the revolution validated ideas of history as an ongoing process that destroyed the past.

Yet even Carlyle failed to convey how notions such as the "New-Birth of Time" or the "Death-Birth of a World" were taken up by contemporaries to register the upheaval not only of the political universe in an era of republican revolution, but of the social and economic universe in general. A totally mobilized world came steadily into view. By crumpling up the temporal structures of the modern era, the French Revolution made the displacements of the so-called Industrial Revolution stand out. The political revolution encouraged contemporaries to think of industrial improvements as belonging to a single, swift, and comprehensive process which broke fundamentally with the past. Technology became a sure marker of the colonization of the present by the future. Already in 1816 Rahel Varnhagen remarked on this steady intrusion of the new. "Now that the whole world is traveled and known, that the compass, telescope, printing press, human rights, and who knows what else have been discovered, that everyone knows in fourteen days what has taken place . . . how can the old customs endure?"[96] As her itemization makes clear, political and industrial revolutions were two parts of the same swift and perceptible process. Moreover, the utter novelty of industrial machinery made claims for fundamental political reform more plausible. In "The Spirit of the Age," written in 1831, John Stuart Mill announced: "Society demands, and anticipates, not merely a new machine, but a machine constructed in another manner."[97] "This cohort," argues Joyce Appleby about Americans in the early nineteenth century, a comment that is applicable to Britons, the French, and Germans as well, "demonstrated a heightened awareness of 'firstness'—of being the first to have rugs on their floors, to have steamboats and canals, national elections, public land sales."[98] "By the time of the failed Restoration of 1815, at the latest," concludes Reinhart Koselleck about Europe in general, "the consciousness of a transitional period had become the common property of the peoples of Europe, increasingly induced from the social changes resulting from the Industrial Revolution."[99] That historians today argue that technological and economic changes came more slowly in the 1820s and 1830s than the rhetoric at the time suggested, and are therefore misconstrued by the term "Industrial Revolution," only underscores how forceful the new categories of temporality were in creating a compelling view of the world in which the evidence of fragmentation and unsettlement stood out, and broader continuities faded into the background.[100] The French Revolution recurred again and again in the political, economic, and social upheavals that the revolution's new time had brought into view. These detonations across the nineteenth century and across the Atlantic world were not latent reappearances of the trauma of the revolution itself, or even an endless recapitulation of the sacrifices it had entailed, but a new way of thinking about time and about the violence with which it transported contemporaries from the past to the present.

Woven in among nineteenth-century narratives of progress, whether in liberal or Marxist versions, a more melancholic rendition traced out the scars of history. Part of modern experience was a deepening sense of loss, a feeling of disconnection with the past, and a growing dread of the future. Raymond Williams takes note of an "escalator" of historical perspective in which successive generations in the modern era dated the ruin of the past, in this case rural England, to their childhoods or just before, but the genre itself originates from the first decades of the nineteenth century. The highly stylized rural scenes in Victorian literature and painting of this period register what "is no more."[101] They depict a fundamental break in which the destruction of the English countryside was taken to be not so much the result of the passage of time, the recognition of the mortality and transience of all things in a way that upholds the correspondence of past with present and present with future, but rather evidence of a deeper disruption of the temporal and social order itself. By the beginning of the nineteenth century, observers dramatized the part played by enclosures, rural depopulation, and international markets in putting a definitive end to a rural rhythm of which death and decline had been constituent parts, but not overriding features. Social description becomes more drastic, even hysterical. The painter John Constable, for example, returned again and again to "The Valley Farm," Willy Lott's house at Flatford. On his first visits, after the turn of the nineteenth century, Constable painted the scene in a fresh, natural style that evoked a bucolic present. Twenty years later, upon his return in the 1830s, he placed the farm in a fairy-tale setting embellished with dimmer hues, embroidered in golden frills, and darkened by a dying tree in the foreground. In just a generation he had moved Willy Lott from the center to the margins, and turned his farm into an outpost. In Constable's rendition, "Valley Farm" had slipped into the past, which facilitated a sentimental, deeply romantic appreciation of things lost. As Elisabeth Helsinger notes, the site of displacement was the rural scene, whose "known and familiar inhabitants" had become "frighteningly strange to their middle- and upper-class neighbors."[102]

What is remarkable about Constable's portrayal is that it conjures up the marauding effects of time in a distinctly vernacular idiom. It was on a domestic scale as suggested by Willy Lott's farm that the transformations of the nineteenth century were generally accounted. Thus Chateaubriand remembered the "old-time games" by the "fireside" and the "meager resin-torch" that lit up "village evenings," while Ernst Moritz Arndt recalled country roads: "Back then deserts, unbridged currents, pathless forests and snakes, dragons, wizards, monsters at every step, nowadays, highways, express mail, steamships and soon railroads, and inns and taverns and even postmasters in every village."[103] That far less authoritative memoirs written by relatively undistinguished men and women continued to find a wide readership indicates the general interest as well in "old customs and habits, which are now disappearing."[104] Later in the nineteenth century, the popularity of collecting antiques allowed people to possess "the trifles of everyday life."[105] That "hearth and home, rather than scepter and sword," in the words of Raphael Samuel, provided "the symbols of national existence" testified not only to the mass scale of historical awareness, in which even ordinary people recognized the transformations of their time, but, more importantly, to the mundane, customary aspects of the registers of historical change.[106] The vernacular idiom corresponded to a developing epochal consciousness in which representativeness was connected to the context of everyday life. What Sir Walter Scott called *la vie privée* became "the site where historical-cultural difference is inscribed."[107] Examined in terms of their material context and contrasted with one another over time, historical epochs were increasingly regarded as self-contained and distinctive. Of course, the process of historical change that made them appear distinctive also left them vulnerable to transmutation. This was the "age of the spirit of the age," argues James Chandler, a period of transition "when the normative status of the period becomes a central and self-conscious aspect of historical reflection," which is another way of saying that the "age of the spirit of the age" was "the age of discussion."[108]

Whether the world was in the stages of decay or advance, contemporaries such as William Hazlitt, John Stuart Mill, and Thomas Carlyle spoke easily about the "spirit of the age" and the "signs of the time" and quite knowingly—rather in the spirit of having discovered a master code—distinguished reactionaries and progressives, old and new, or what was pregnant with the future and what was anachronistic and past, denoting as they did their present as a distinct and embattled transitory period. Discernible in France, Germany, and elsewhere in Europe in similar terms, commentators on "age of the spirit of the age" explained it in terms of innovation and change and remarked endlessly on what seemed to be the steady intrusion of the new. Journalists set out to inventory exactly what items were passing into obsolescence and which were in vogue. Indeed, the reason the German writer Ludwig Börne settled in Paris was because the city served as the "telegraph of the past, the microscope of the present, and the telescope of the future."[109] The gesture of hailing for the latest news, whether by querying strangers, writing letters, or reading newspapers, could only flourish in an age self-conscious of itself as such, that is, of having taken itself to be a distinctive epoch in which the differences between today and yesterday and between today and tomorrow were dramatized as visible and regarded as pertinent. The terms of this "world picture" enabled the insistently historical imagination of the nineteenth and twentieth centuries.[110] As the philosopher Hans Blumenberg has put it: "Modernity *(Neuzeit)* was the first and only age that understood itself as an epoch and, in so doing, simultaneously created the other epochs."[111]

The delights of popular culture, in particular, made the historical definition of the contemporary moment visible in the marketplace as well as the salon: traditional folklore with its decontextualized and timeless subjects increasingly gave way to quite specifically situated historical plays, novels, and illustrations which owed their popularity in large part to their dramatization of the roles ordinary people played in great public events—often drawn from the revolutionary and Napoleonic period—and to the "authentic" descriptive detail in which they depicted everyday period lives. The material culture of the kitchen, the bedroom, and the tavern, as well as fancy fashions and street scenes, provided remarkably telling markers of historical transformation: just conjure up the displays in the shop window in the film adaptation of H. G. Wells' *The Time Machine.* And by all accounts, the "romantic historicism" of Walter Scott, Victor Hugo, and Alexandre Dumas found a broad audience among increasingly literate Europeans.[112] Even in the most faraway homes, in Frederika Bremer's fictionalized setting in Sweden, for example, the brief inventories of "family cares and family joys" contained Germaine de Staël's *Corinne* and a birthday package of Scott's novels.[113] The Napoleonic Wars provided the poignant scenes for realist fiction from Thackeray to Tolstoy. Fontane has grandparents greeted with "Voilà notre ancien régime."[114] Even children played in this historical space: for one hundred years games, toys, and especially tin soldiers replayed a quarter-century of military movements.

Not so much the events themselves, but their narration and repetition created common coordinates of time and space in the increasingly unified experiential field recognized as history. These coordinates facilitated a remarkable synchronization of nineteenth-century European culture in which events were interpreted as manifestations of a comprehensive process of change, and in which ideas about those events dominated public discourse. Elizabeth Deeds Ermarth comments on the ways that history functioned as a mass medium in this period: "The collection of voices in, say, a novel like *War and Peace* all 'agree'—not in the trivial sense of agreement about particular issues but in the most powerful sense of constructing and inhabiting the 'same' time, which is to say, a medium in which what happens in one moment has influence upon another moment."[115] Historians have not said this clearly, but one of the major consequences of the French Revolution was to create out of the many inhabitants of the territories of Europe the modern species "contemporaries," or as the German language puts it more precisely, *Zeitgenossen,* time comrades, time travelers.

It is a paradox that this synchronization of historical time rested on a very particular premise, which was the acknowledgment of diachronic difference, the idea of the new that distinguished contemporaries, gave them a specific temporal identity not unlike the feeling of generation, and separated or decoupled them from their forebears two or three generations earlier. There is a history of the new, and it prepared people to see themselves not simply as contemporaries, but as inhabiting a particular time and place, a quite particular context, which is familiar and makes preceding epochs and periods unfamiliar. One of the distinguishing characteristics of the nineteenth-century sense of time, then, is the dramatization of change as the restless iteration of the new, and also the insistence that the experience of this change is unique and foundational to the idea of modernity. It may well be the greatest conceit of modernity to claim for itself the special consciousness of transition and indeterminacy. In one stroke it deadened and immobilized history prior to 1789: the Middle Ages, the Dark Ages, the dead ages. And, of course, the immobility which distorted the premodern period worked to accentuate the mobility that supposedly defined the modern sequences that followed it. The conceit served as its own best testimony. Whereas Enlightenment thinkers conceived of the present as the most forward point of a great continuum of progress that pushed on and on, after the French Revolution observers were more apt to think of the present as a point of transition, one which moved away from the past.[116] Historians, myself included, continue to choreograph their narratives in this way. At the same time, the future was no longer conceived as the place where the trends from the past culminated, but as a space in which the new and unexpected would be encountered. As a result there was an increasing gap between what Koselleck usefully conceives of as "the horizon of expectation" and the "space of experience." According to Rudy Koshar, this disjuncture became "the fundamental condition of societal relationships" in modern times: "anticipation of the future worked without deferring primarily to the authority of remembrance."[117] It is this inclination to perceive restless disruption that made the historical imagination such a powerful element in the conception of the self. Never before had men and women lived so alone, noted Alexis de Tocqueville of his contemporaries in the 1820s and 1830s: "They do not resemble their fathers; nay they perpetually differ from themselves, for they live in a state of incessant change of place, feelings, and fortunes."[118] In Tocqueville's view, the burden of modern identity was to live amidst this appropriated unrest and this newly acquired strangeness. Thanks to the mass medium of history, we recognize these nomads as ourselves.

CHAPTER TWO

Strangers

It was not Alexis de Tocqueville but his older cousin, François-René de Chateaubriand, born in 1768, who provided the most complete reports on the displaced people in the revolutionary epoch—strangers or refugees, utterly disconnected from their past lives and thus conspicuously aware of the losses they had endured. "The old men of former times," the French count and diplomat reflected on the society of his childhood at the end of the eighteenth century, "were less unhappy and less isolated than those of today: if, by lingering on earth, they had lost their friends, little else had changed around them; they were strangers to youth, but not to society." It is all different "nowadays," and here Chateaubriand was thinking about the exiles of the French Revolution: "a straggler in this life has witnessed the death, not only of men, but also of ideas: principles, customs, tastes, pleasures, sorrows, opinions, none of these resembles what he used to know. He belongs to a different race from the human species among which he ends his days."[1] In Chateaubriand's view, the revolution had shattered lines of social continuity, casting the present off from the past and thereby creating a "different race," exiles who had become estranged from their own time, that is, stranded in the present, and as a result came to read contemporary history as dispossession.

An aristocrat linked by temperament and marriage to the constitutional monarchists who fell out of favor after the king's flight to Varennes in June 1791, Chateaubriand had every reason to feel threatened by the French Revolution. His older brother Jean-Baptiste was eventually executed, as was his brother's father-in-law, the influential political reformer Lamoignon de Malesherbes, who had befriended young François-René and encouraged him in his 1791 journey to the United States. Once there, Chateaubriand abruptly returned to France after hearing about the arrest of the king, though this was not until many months after the events had taken place, and he subsequently joined the counterrevolutionary forces in Germany before their defeat at Valmy in 1792. He then escaped across the Channel to exile in England. Yet political opposition itself was not the primary source of Chateaubriand's profound estrangement, which was always more than the tribulations of a single French nobleman in the face of republican revolution. What Chateaubriand believed he recognized at work was a comprehensive process of historical destruction that continually pushed the past away from the present. This was the defining tragedy of "our age," "nowadays," the restless production of the new in the present. Chateaubriand distinguished "three different worlds" in just the quarter-century he had lived since 1789: the Republic, Napoleon's Empire, and the Bourbon Restoration. Each of these worlds he regarded "as completely finished as the others," as if "separated by centuries."[2] Although Chateaubriand returned to France in 1801, he never made peace with Napoleon, nor did he do so with the Bourbon monarchy when it was restored in 1814. Like many other émigrés, he felt profoundly, permanently out of place, which is the very place he wrote about for the rest of his life. What he came to realize was not only that one life's span encompassed quite separate pasts, but that life's memory appeared inadequate to fully comprehend any one of the pasts or the passage between them. The result was a deeply personal sense of alienation in which the revolutions of public life broke up the continuities of private life that custom, habit, and piety had once governed. Meditating over "the wreck of empires" in his famous letter from Rome, written in 1803, Chateaubriand came to realize that the observer "himself is a ruin," with "his lukewarm hope, his wavering faith, his limited charity, his imperfect sentiments, his insufficient thoughts, his broken heart."[3] "Man does not have a single, consistent life," Chateaubriand later concluded, "he has several laid end to end, and that is his misfortune." "Friends leave us, others take their place," he added: "there is always a time when we possessed nothing of what we now possess, and a time when we have nothing of what we once had."[4]

This is an eloquent, if gloomy apprehension of discontinuity. Chateaubriand did not feel able to repossess the past, which repeatedly evaded his efforts at recollection. The felt absence of a first-hand connection and resulting apprehension of loss at the moment of second-hand reflection prompted feelings of "misfortune," which are recognizable as the melancholy of nostalgia. Phrasing his observations in a sonorous universal ("Man does not have . . ."), Chateaubriand clearly indicated that his nostalgia was not merely the hurt of a particular François-René, but was sensible as shared experience. At the same time, the declaration is phrased as a revelation: Chateaubriand found the new knowledge of corpses sufficiently revealing to account for it by writing his memoirs. The studied terms of his examination—lives "laid end to end" in handwritten reflection and "laid end to end" again before readers—suggest a perplexity generated by specific circumstances of unsettlement. Although the graveyard he has stumbled upon is his own, it is a newly configured place in which the remains of past lives are registered as ghostly presences that prompt mourning and nostalgia. Chateaubriand's self-reflection exposes the nineteenth-century context of revolution and war in which a modern history of remembrance and nostalgia can be conceived.

For Chateaubriand, the feeling of exile was not a temporary condition, but a distinctively modern fate. The profound effect of the revolution was to reconfigure both time and place. Chateaubriand repeatedly invoked the homelessness of his contemporaries, not just himself: "we are sailing along an unknown coast, in the midst of darkness and the storm."[5] Although the maritime metaphors he favored have an eighteenth-century feel about them, the roiled turbulence of the waters—tides, waves, gales—act with nineteenth-century violence. As he constructs his life, lineages are effaced, communities dispersed, and lives torn apart. The force of history is so violent that it provides his memoirs with their root metaphor, which is exile: "I had scarcely left my mother's womb when I suffered my first exile," he wrote in the first pages, and in the six volumes that followed he told and retold his life as a series of abrupt leave takings.[6] In his telling, his life did not come to a rest. Even after the Restoration in 1814, Chateaubriand faulted the conservatives whose cause he had joined for not seeing that "the times change completely, and one cannot escape either their laws or ravages." "Revolutions come about; they are at our doorstep," he wrote, and it was not only republican conspirators who appeared at the threshold, but technological innovators, social parvenus, bourgeois speculators, and impious believers.[7] Chateaubriand recognized a new time which profaned custom and tradition and divested both of their authority. "There will be no separate revolutions," he wrote in the last lines of his memoirs, only "the great revolution approaching its end."[8]

In the face of this cumulative disorder, however, Chateaubriand did not despair, because he came to fix his identity to the circumstances of contingency. For that reason he identified so strongly with the act of writing, and especially rewriting, and with the elective to fashion and refashion his personal identity. "I believe in nothing except religion," Chateaubriand announced, and so "I distrust everything."[9] He made an awkward republican in America, cut a poor figure as an émigré in England, and infuriated his fellow monarchists during the Restoration. He repeatedly described himself as a swimmer in the course of events who refused to try to reach the banks on either side despite turbulent conditions. "Each age is a river that carries us off according to the whims of the destiny to which we have abandoned ourselves," Chateaubriand explained. "There are those [the republicans] who cross it headlong and throw themselves onto the shore opposite. The others are perfectly happy to remain where they are, without plunging in. Trying to move with the times, the former transport us far from ourselves into an imaginary realm; the latter hold us back, refusing to enlighten themselves, happy to be men of the fourteenth century" at the end of the eighteenth.[10] For his part, Chateaubriand preferred to remain castaway. He cherished the past, but acknowledged its devastation without abandoning its remains. Wreckage swirled around the swimmer, and he found solace in hanging on to this or that piece. Chateaubriand is such a compelling figure because he made rupture the acknowledged pivot of his political and personal sensibilities, of his literary labors, and of his self-estimation. Behind the counterrevolutionary émigré lurks a modern exile who anticipates quite contemporary concerns about displacement in the modern world and the contradictory, amalgamated nature of collective identity.

Chateaubriand constructed his life from the forces of dispersion and the ruins which they left behind. The *Mémoirs d'outre tombe,* which he wrote over the course of forty years, turn over again and again on shipwrecks, revolutions, and accidents which break up the various parts of his life. Saint-Malo, Combourg, Kentucky, London, Rome, Vallée-aux-Loups, and finally Paris—"every one of my days marks a departure"—up until his death on July 4, 1848.[11] Born during a ruinous Atlantic gale on September 4, 1768, he opened his life story with "the tempest that was my first lullaby."[12] He suffered his "first exile" a few days later, when he was removed from Saint Malo to be placed with a wet nurse in

Plancoët. When François-René was ten, a sullen, brutal father cast the family into the far corners of the castle at Combourg: "My sister occupied a closet . . . I was nestled in a sort of isolated cell at the top of the turret . . . [the] man-servant lay in a vaulted basement, and the cook kept garrison in the great west tower."[13] A return visit to Saint Malo as a young man was remembered as leaving him cold and unattached: "already a whole world had fallen into decay."[14] Recollecting his somewhat aimless travels in America in 1791, Chateaubriand found that the powerful impression of New World sights such as Niagara Falls had the effect of obliterating earlier souvenirs of France. "My memory constantly counterposes voyages with voyages, mountains with mountains, rivers with rivers," he realized in horror: "My life destroys itself."[15] The royalist affections that returned him to France in 1792 led him to witness the defeat of the princes at Valmy, and he became gravely ill before finding refuge in England the following year. Looking back on his arrival and impoverished condition thirty years later, when he had returned to London as French ambassador, Chateaubriand found his present, much-celebrated self alienated from its long past counterpart. To gain fame and fortune was "incongruous"; his fellow refugees had long since scattered; even the old cemetery outside his dormer-window off Tottenham Court Road had disappeared beneath a newly laid-out factory.[16] In hindsight, memory was a slight impression that crumbled at the touch into "dust and ashes."[17] Chateaubriand dramatized even personal time in the most catastrophic way.

This crisis of memory is the precondition underlying Chateaubriand's obsession with recollection and commemoration. Again and again he found himself at the graveside. He was horrified at the thought that the revolution had been the "sole bystander" at the registration of the death of his mother, "a poor woman" who, as he puts it, citing official documents, "departed this life at the residence of 'citizeness' Gouyon" in "the Year VI of the French Republic," whereas twelve years later (1786), the death of his father, "the high and mighty Messire," "knight" and "count" and "lord," had been witnessed by notables who recognized his noteworthiness.[18] Those who take away "the bones of their fathers," he wrote in another context, "take away their history"; they rob people "of the proofs of their existence and of their annihilation."[19] The great crime of the French Revolution for Chateaubriand was not to have killed the Bourbons but to have rejected their existence, by destroying the graves of the French kings at Saint-Denis in August 1793. This act outside Paris was the vandalization of the work of God; according to the author of *The Genius of Christianity,* "marks of antiquity" such as the "scathed oak" and the scarred rock were manufactured at the Creation to lend the state of nature its charm.[20] It was thus the ruin of the ruin that distinguished the destruction of modern people from the decomposition of eternal time. Chateaubriand cherished history as an antidote to the modern spirit precisely because it served at once to distinguish and valorize dispossession.

For all his insight into the frail work of memory, the "profound forgetfulness that pursues us" and "the invincible silence that takes possession of our tomb,"[21] Chateaubriand refused to allow the revolution to be the "sole by-stander" of past lives. Its presumption to ignore the dead was as wicked as the insistence of the Bourbons and their supporters during the Restoration that the dead were still very much alive; both conceits failed to recognize the pain of mortal loss, the exile which Chateaubriand saw as central to the meaning of his life. If he demanded respect for the monuments of human ambition and political design, the work of the fathers, he rejected the partisan premise of those ambitions and designs, which tended to turn absolute and immutable, and constituted the sin of the sons. It was a paradox that Chateaubriand honored the impulse but not the consequence of political activity, with the result that he made himself rather unlikable to the royalist political company he kept. And he knew this well: "There are those who resist me, but praise my doctrines, and make themselves the masters of my politics by depersonalizing them, and there are those that settle their affairs with me if I am willing to compromise my principles."[22] It was precisely the contradictions and weakness, but also the tenderness, of men and women that opened the way for the personal, interior faith Chateaubriand espoused. This sense of a ruined lifetime was also the impetus for his literary activity and for his close identification with the fictional character René, who is lost but not obliterated in wild American exile. As a pious nonbeliever, Chateaubriand wrote to express what was no longer self-evident: the attachments of his reverence and the object of his nonbelief. The memoirs, which he affectionately called his "orphan," make distinct the condition of his exile and the self-knowledge of his errancy. It is the displaced individual who, in fact, is best placed to tell the truth about the impurity and the burden of collective history. "The world is not made simple by nature, nor simplified by history," comments Pierre Barbéris; the finished whole of political ambition is contradicted by the testimony of single individuals, by "pariahs in the forests or along the outskirts of the city." There is always "history's remainder," which is the evidence of the outcast individual, the memoirs from beyond the grave.[23]

It would be wrong to think of Chateaubriand as a solitary misfit. He did not write as a straggler in a faraway land. Chateaubriand returned repeatedly to the specific ruins of the French Revolution, although he saw the events in France as a prelude to general dispossessions in the prevailing social and economic order, and he wrote self-consciously as a French émigré, "proscribed, and impoverished," even as he expanded the definition of exile to encompass other people's fates. In his memoirs, Chateaubriand described his life in a specifically historical fashion and emphasized the particular case of "nowadays." It is the imbrication of the private with the public, the recognition that in the new conditions of the present no individuals can promise themselves a "quiet moment," that gave the long-winded volumes their wide appeal. Even an early fragment published in *Revue des Deux Mondes* in 1834 found an appreciative readership: "it depicts not so much the personal history of the author as the particular history of the century," wrote one critic.[24]

What precisely was the connection between the autobiography of Chateaubriand and the history of the century? However personal the terms he used to tell his story—the emphatic first person singular which recounted "my first lullaby," "my first exile"—Chateaubriand's melancholy is inextricably intertwined with the social operations of a broader historical consciousness (knowledge of "our age" to be passed on). It was the availability of a general narrative about the movement of history that gave social significance to the particulars of François-René. As Joan Scott has persuasively argued, the evidence of experience could only be brought forward once a general frame of meaning—in this case, the narrative of the revolution and the movement of modern time—had been constructed to constitute and absorb and circulate such evidence.[25] This is consistent with Maurice Halbwachs's insights into the workings of collective memory. Even the most personal memories depend on the exchange of memories held in common and on the shared value of such an exchange. "It is in society that people normally acquire their memories," insists Halbwachs: "It is also in society that they recall, recognize, and localize their memories."[26] This is not to say that society tends to make memories the same. Rather, my argument is that the social frame serves to distinguish between the kinds of events that are regarded as poignant and socially meaningful and therefore memorable, and those that are regarded as utterly personal or merely circumstantial and therefore not relevant. Thus the widespread recognition of the French Revolution as part of a comprehensive, ongoing conflict over the constitution of society made it possible for all sorts of witnesses to summon up evidence; it multiplied in countless variations which were frankly tendentious, usually unauthoritative, but always telling. Contemporaries came to inhabit "the same experiential space," Reinhart Koselleck points out, but, at the same time, "their perspective was interrupted according to political generation and social standpoint."[27] Each of these perspectives corresponded to a particular, personal version of the revolution. It is worth thinking back on the passengers on the market boat to Mainz in August 1815. They had different experiences and came from different places, yet "below deck" they constituted a common discursive space in which they could tell and listen to one another's particular accounts of Napoleon's Europe. Thus the "singularization" of the revolution manifested itself in the general poignancy it provided to a single person's life story. History is what made lonely François-René so interesting, and it is what made the scribbler Sulpiz Boisserée and the traveling companions he sketched so interested.

The story of Chateaubriand's exile was also compelling because it was frankly nostalgic, an empathetic mode of description which allowed readers to see their lives in new perspective. It well expressed the losses they had incurred during the years of revolution and war. The deliberate rupture of "a single, consistent life" into several, and the melancholic distance at which Chateaubriand gathered up the pieces in his retelling, relied on distinctly modern concepts of historical discontinuity. Chateaubriand's nostalgia is premised on an understanding of historical change that is relentless and violent in character and general in scope; it presupposes a recognition of the demolition of revolution. If yesterday is different from today because a disaster has occurred and misfortune has come to pass, the status of yesterday is not really challenged and yesterday's fortune might well persist in some other place not so afflicted. In the next valley, the world would still be whole, and indifferent. Nostalgia is therefore a product of a shared historical consciousness of general displacement that is able to make parochial misfortunes and individual losses socially meaningful. It provides to lonesome stragglers a common refuge in history, even while it says that their losses are irreversible. Although the virtues of the past are cherished and their passage is lamented, there is no doubt that they are no longer retrievable. There can be no nostalgia without this sense of irreversibility, which denies to the present the imagined wholeness of the past.[28] If this were not so, nostalgia would not mourn the exhaustion of tradition or lovingly attend the bits and pieces that remain scattered about, but, rather, would protest ignorance of tradition's validity, which is the duty of the reactionary. In other words, nostalgia yearns for what it cannot possess, and defines itself by its inability to approach its subject. This paradox is the essence of nostalgia's melancholy. Chateaubriand's memoirs adhere to a formal structure in which the past is constituted as *past.* The historical consciousness on which his nostalgia depends thus creates both intimacy, in that it gives social recognition to the memories of loss, and distance, in that it determines those losses to be permanent.

For all the losses it confirmed, and the distance to the past it verified, the new temporal cosmos Chateaubriand described facilitated new kinds of knowledge. His alienation allowed him to see the world in a more complex and mottled way. Ferdinand Baldensperger, whose 1924 study of the émigré literature is unsurpassed, commented on the nature of this cosmopolitan sensibility. What Chateaubriand, Germaine de Staël, and other French exiles insinuated, he argued, was "a sense of the diversity of the world, one that paid attention to local color, to the picturesque presentation of reality, but also to juxtaposition and dispersion: the dramas and elegies of the emigration played themselves out in an increasingly incoherent universe."[29] Chateaubriand in particular, and the exiles more generally, are thus portentous correspondents for the modern era, well placed to tell about the violence of displacement, the unsettlement of once unassailable certainties, and the contingencies of identity, community, and historical narrative. Precisely because they no longer felt themselves to be at home, exiles, refugees, and other strangers became more self-conscious and "more aware of the assumptions by which they and others interpret social experience." "Exile provokes new forms of interpretation by defamiliarizing the familiar and familiarizing the unfamiliar"—Lloyd Kramer's conclusion about European intellectuals in liberal France in the 1830s applies as well to French émigrés in royalist Europe a generation earlier.[30]

In recent years scholars have paid more attention to conditions of exile and homelessness, which are taken to be as constitutive of social formations as ties to place and home. Diasporic, postcolonial, and other hybrid identities highlight patterns of unsettlement in an age of unprecedented transnational mobility and global exchange. Anthropologists and literary critics have emphasized the conspicuous sense of dislocation and the exigencies of improvisation among migrants, refugees, and other travelers at the turn of the twenty-first century.[31] The French émigrés at the turn of the nineteenth century make up a similar group: they had become strangers in the modern world because the republican community was remade in their absence and on the basis of their exclusion. Even after they returned home, the former émigrés continued to feel out of place. Like Tocqueville and Chateaubriand, they reported on the postrevolutionary world with the eyes of archeologists, following lines of rupture and tracking evidence of unsettlement and displacement. It is worth examining the exiles, unlikely witnesses to the modern world as they may be, more closely.

The first émigrés—the younger brother of the king, the comte d'Artois, the future Louis XVIII, and his court—left France in the first week after the fall of the Bastille in July 1789. A steady trickle of the aristocratic opponents of reform followed them across the eastern border of France. There was little sense of permanent dispossession, however. Like Edmund Burke, royalists reviled the revolution as illegitimate, and since they thought in fundamentally juridical, not historical terms, early opponents gave the revolution little staying power. As it was, the condition of exile had been shared by seventeenth-century Protestants and Frondeurs and was not considered unusual. "One or the other of my wife's ancestors left the kingdom for religious reasons," one early émigré, M. de Bacquencourt, consoled himself: "that's the way the world turns."[32] And the world would turn back: the assumption prevailed that France would return to prerevolutionary moorings. "We expected to spend three months at Tournay and then to return to find everything as it was," remembered the marquise de Falaizeau.[33] In the event, many exiles would not return for another quarter-century. The moment of restoration seemed at hand in summer 1792, however, when the army of the French princes, which included Chateaubriand, joined the counterrevolutionary troops of Austrian and Prussia to invade the new republic. There was no mistaking this royalist force of legitimate return: a self-assured Joseph Thomas d'Espinchal reported that "our princes have expressed a wish that every one of us, whether mounted or unmounted, shall provide himself with a white scarf . . . in addition to his cockade and white plumes." "Brigands, executioners, traitors, revolutionaries!" the royalists shouted across the battlefront; "enemies of liberty, aristocrats, satellites of Capet!" the republicans hollered back in this early skirmish of the long nineteenth-century war of ideologies.[34] In late summer, d'Espinchal noted that "the weather had turned fine, and showed to the best advantage a spectacle that I shall never forget as long as I live: thirty-six or forty splendid squadrons, forming a body of cavalry numbering about 5,000 men, almost entirely composed of the cream of the French nobility, and containing nearly all the *grand seigneurs* of the kingdom . . . These squadrons marched in excellent order, and were mounted as no cavalry was ever mounted before. Their enthusiasm and zeal was indescribable."[35] But the easy victory at Verdun in August turned bad in the muddy rout at Valmy at the end of September. Over the course of a few rain-soaked weeks, the confidence of the princes crumbled: "Now every one went about solitarily, no one looked at his neighbor," testified Goethe in his recollected account, "Campaign in France."[36]

Observers at the time and memoirists who remembered after many years the events in 1792 endowed the defeat at Valmy with great historical power. Goethe accompanied Karl-August, the duke of Saxe-Weimar and, in this counterrevolutionary offensive, the commander of a regiment in the Prussian army, as a kind of "field-poet." His famous remark that "from this place and from this day forth commences a new era in the world's history" recognized the durability of the revolution.[37] Witnesses lingered at the sight of the ruins of the nobility: correspondents repeatedly told about the roads north from Valmy littered with broken pieces, "the debris of broken carriages," "the unburied bodies of dead men and horses."[38] "Our hearts were torn apart every day by the debris we saw and the spectacle of despair and misery it provided," wrote a dispirited Charles de Mercy, formerly bishop of Lucon in the Vendee.[39] The extinction of the nobility as a class appeared close at hand. By the end of 1792 the king had been arrested, and the government decreed the perpetual banishment of exiles and the sale of their properties. Political refugees streamed into Germany and the Netherlands, and they remained in motion as revolutionary armies advanced in subsequent years. "When I left France on the 17th July, 1789," reflected d'Espinchal at the turn of the new year 1793, "I was certainly very far from foreseeing that, after three and a half years of exile, I should be living today with my three boys in a secluded little German village" near Düsseldorf, "and should have, as my companions in misfortune and poverty, the greater number of the nobles and richest landowners of the kingdom."[40]

As many as 180,000 men, women, and children left France in the early 1790s for life in exile. Most of them did so after the massacres of nobles and refractory clergy in the Paris prisons of the new republic in September 1792, and most returned once Napoleon issued qualified amnesties in the years after 1799. The largest share of the émigrés was, in fact, composed of members of the Third Estate, who left as the result of large-scale evacuations in the military zone of Alsace and Lorraine, but servants and other retainers augmented the totals. In addition to counterrevolutionary nobles, thousands of priests quit France in the years after 1792. The clergy, in particular, was faced with the choice of attesting to loyalty to the revolution, and as republican demands grew more insistent, more and more members of the Second Estate fled the country. They made up the majority of exiles in 1792 and 1793. During the summer of 1792, about ten new French names appeared every week in the lists prepared by innkeepers in Konstanz, a southwestern German town that became a central meeting point for the clergy. In the week of 13 September, about ten days after the massacres, the number of new arrivals shot up to twenty-five, including twenty priests, an influx which continued at that rate for some months. By the end of the year, the city registered 835 émigrés, most of whom would stay for at least another two years. Localities in Switzerland, the Netherlands, and Austria witnessed the same thing, an influx which troubled local authorities. Large numbers of strangers disrupted the sheltered localism of these provincial places, and the French exiles long remembered their unwelcome. "Not allowed are Jews, vagabonds, persons without papers, or émigrés" read the sign posted outside one German town—at least according to the testimony of madame de Flahaut in 1823.[41] Paradoxically, the emigrants also represented political danger simply because they brought with them, in ceaseless daily conversations, the propositions of the French Revolution. Already in March 1793 the Bavarian government prohibited the publication of pamphlets and brochures sympathetic to the revolution, and other German governments restricted the movement of refugees and interdicted the flow of foreign newspapers and other publications. In Vienna, police forbade families to take on French governesses or tutors so that "German youngsters and young women will be able to think in German," an imprecise formulation that does not completely hide its antirevolutionary point. If émigrés in Austria and Bavaria were regarded with suspicion for reformist sympathies, their counterparts in Switzerland were taken to be too hostile to France. Having allegedly compromised Swiss neutrality, most were expelled in the summer of 1796. It was only with difficulty that thousands of exiles received passports to cross over to Austrian territory, a journey made all the more perilous by French armies that advanced into southwestern Germany. The refugees were thus kept constantly on the move, and soon scattered across the globe; some 10,000 individuals eventually arrived in the United States, where a half-dozen émigré newspapers appeared.[42]

To imagine the French exiles as a coherent counterrevolutionary body—when in fact no more than 10,000 and probably fewer fought alongside the princes in the summer and fall of 1792—is to miss the force and occasion of their displacement. Hundreds of thousands of families had been forced to leave France after the revocation of the Edict of Nantes in 1598. But the French Protestants, by and large, arrived in foreign communities that provided them with religious and intellectual support and were able to settle down permanently. The French exiles of the 1790s, by contrast, were doubly displaced, physically from their homes in France and ideologically from the ancien régime. At the same time, the continuing force of the revolution, both literally in the form of persistent warfare in the two decades around 1800, and figuratively, as an ongoing social upheaval, withheld from them rest and security. It was with his own exile in mind that Chateaubriand compared the migrations of a bird, who "sets out with its neighbors," "leaves nothing behind," and "returns, at last, to die on the spot which gave it birth," with the man "driven from his native home," who, by contrast, "knocks, but no one opens"; the "proscription which has banished him from his country seems to have expelled him from the world."[43] This was the bitter revelation of the defeat of the counterrevolutionary armies in 1792, and the long time of exile and reflection in the years that followed: one was not simply banished from one place (Paris or Lyons) but expelled from familiar coordinates of time and space altogether. The experience of the French émigrés was defined by the fundamental suspicion that they would not resume the course of their old lives and were, in fact, lost forever.

The dispersion of the emigrants and the distance they felt from the old regime corresponded to the prolonged nature of the revolution, which continually threatened to overtake the exiles: "What catastrophes! What heaped-upon ruins!" wrote Abbé Martinant as he recalled fleeing one German town for another in summer 1795. Over the next months, Martinant fled south from Augsburg to Konstanz, and eventually back east to Hof, but even there, in July 1796, "I made haste to leave, fearing once again the invasion of the French."[44] Thousands of priests, nobles, and other opponents of the republic shared Martinant's fate as they crowded border towns and suffered the suspicions of local inhabitants, who viewed them as harbingers of revolutionary disorder or else as obstacles to peace with France. After Valmy, emigration had become banishment, and individual feelings of loneliness or isolation emptied into a sense of general dispossession. Chateaubriand repeatedly referred to himself as "a Jew without a homeland."[45] As late as 1812, Auguste de la Ferronays could still take stock of his life "without country, without home."[46] This sense of separation was attenuated by the fact that the émigrés left behind family members: "My mother and my sister, one is in Paris, the other in Brittany; my two sons are in London, we're in Hamburg," lamented madame de Falaiseau in a 1798 letter to her nephew.[47] Even if memoirs were embellished after many decades, the point remains that exile came to stand for a rupture far greater than the alternations of fortune implicit in Bacquencourt's imperturbable view of the world. When in autumn 1792 one anonymous correspondent commented dispiritedly, "time passes," it was without anticipation of an eventual rehabilitation; it served as a severe measure of losses incurred.[48]

The emigrants eventually returned to France, most during Napoleon's reign, some not until the Restoration of the Bourbons in 1814, yet their return was ambiguous. Their memoirs described a postrevolutionary world still not set right. While their properties lay in ruins or had been sold off, alarming traces of the revolution remained, particularly the still-visible graffiti of republican virtue—*". . . ou la mort"*—that showed through the coats of whitewashing lime: the old order had not been fully restored, nor had the revolution been entirely destroyed.[49] Despite a ferocious outcry, nobles whose lands had been sold as *biens nationaux* after 1792 were not indemnified until 1825 and then only in the form of an annual pension, which did not undo the revolutionary act of disinheritance or provide security to their heirs. Although most émigré nobles did recover some property, pieces which either had not been sold or had been transferred to relatives, many continued to think of themselves juridically and sentimentally as a distinct class of entitled survivors. They thereby invited others to treat them as anachronistic relics. This is certainly the view of Honoré de Balzac, whose novels give a sweeping version of the upheavals in French society between 1789 and 1848. Balzac placed the most refractory emigrants in what he aptly named *The Gallery of Antiquities,* and described one old-regime household in *Lily of the Valley* as follows: "family silver without uniformity, Dresden china which was not then in fashion, octagonal decanters, knives with agate handles, and lacquered trays." The narrator admits to his delight in these "quaint old things."[50] The nobleman of the valley, the comte de Mortsauf, is himself a wreck, inalterable in his opinions and old before his time. In Mortsauf, Balzac represented a readily identifiable character in early nineteenth-century society: the man of the postwar Restoration dressed up in the court dress and fancy wiggery of the ancien régime.[51] There was no return to contemporary society for those caricatured as antique, quaint, or otherwise out of place.

The word the exiles grabbed at again and again to describe their fate was "shipwreck," *naufrage.* It no longer described the horrible end or the lucky survival of an individual sailor or even the chancy crossing of the icy Zuidersee which hundreds of émigrés managed by night and storm in winter 1795, but rather calls attention to the dramatic breaks in the life stories of people who never felt quite at home again. The imagery of earthquake, which Friedrich Schlegel preferred, indicated the same thing: the vertiginous sense of movement and destruction.[52] But earthquake suggested a single, ruinous, almost freak episode of nature against culture, whereas shipwreck implicated society, the miniature arrangement of orders and roles on board the ship that broke apart around the individual, and so it is the more telling word to grasp the consequences of the revolution. Chateaubriand examined his life through the wrecks of social formations, and similar imagery was used by a succession of other emigrants: Louis-Joseph-Amour de Bouille recollected in his memoirs the "debris" of his life; La Ferronays in 1837 referred to his "tormented existence."[53]

If well-born émigrés took stock of their experiences during war and revolution and later recollected their lives in terms of dispossession, they also repossessed their lives in unexpected ways. The shipwreck of exile brought them to new places which entailed a reappraisal of many of the certainties of eighteenth-century salon culture. Aware of their alienation from developments in France and their fragile position in society, a number of the returnees proved to be unusually open to differences in custom and culture in the world around them. Exiled and on the run, they were forced to become, in Mallet du Pan's felicitous phrase, "cosmopolitans despite themselves."[54] This cosmopolitanism was anything but the *mondaine* disdain for the undeveloped indigenous world beyond the court, the salons, and academies of metropolitan

France. Confidence in the triumph of a single European civilization—a notion expressed, for example, by Rivarol who, earlier in the 1770s, reported back on a world which was, as "the times have come to indicate, French"—diminished as "the picturesque instance, the popular spectacle, the eccentric custom" came into view.[55] Germany, in particular, appeared to more and more French exiles as an enclosed, almost medieval society into which the ideas of the Enlightenment had hardly penetrated. The "gothic" world across the Rhine looked as distinct and whole as the grave Catholicism of Spain. Even England appeared more autochthonous to the émigrés and less like France. What had come into view was not so much the underdevelopment of Germany or Spain, but the particularity and robustness of separate national traditions. The marquise de Marcillac, who left France in 1791, wrote at the time of the Spanish uprising against Napoleon that "far from being known as the ugly duckling of Europe," Spain "achieves self-respect by being itself, conserving and transmitting to its descendants the customs of its fathers."[56] If Enlightenment thinkers had projected across time and space the coordinates of universal development, émigré observers were more apt to identify discontinuity and incongruity. Having dramatized a revolutionary break in their personal lifetimes, they were more able to accept the simultaneity of completely different life experiences. In light of this acknowledgment of difference, the entire cosmology of nineteenth-century thought needs to be reconsidered. The exiles resisted the grand modern idea of progress and assimilation because it effaced the evidence of their past lives, and cherished incommensurability and anachronism because through them they recognized their present-day survival.

It was Germaine de Staël, daughter of Jacques Necker, Louis XVI's well-regarded reform minister, who tackled the issue of national traditions head-on in her famous travelogue about Germany, and perhaps most economically in her Italian novel, *Corinne.* "Without exile," argues Charlotte Hogsett, one of Staël's most perceptive critics, she "would probably never have traveled extensively. From childhood she had considered Paris to be the center of her existence."[57] But Staël, like so many others, ended up making several border crossings over the course of her life, which forced her to revaluate the epistemological status of the border between Paris and everywhere else. Staël eventually became, as she herself put it, "a stranger in her native land," an alienation which encouraged her to explore the condition of nativeness.[58] In the novel *Corinne,* published in 1807, she undertook a sustained exploration of national identity, which ultimately keeps the two lovers, Oswald and Corinne, apart. The worldly affections between individuals founder on the principle of national difference. Oswald cannot be happy in Italy, or Corinne in Scotland, as she herself recognizes: "Habits, memories, circumstances create some kind of web around us that even passionate love cannot destroy." And it is these selfsame habits and memories of home that give unity and grandeur to the national literature that Corinne patronizes. Against the French aristocrat who with the certainty of Rivarol knows that "we have the real classical authorities"—"Bossuet, La Bruyère, Montesquieu, and Buffon"—Corinne insists that "the literature of every country reveals a new sphere of ideas." Staël's border crossings in fiction thus served to introduce "all the countries where there is something unique about their manners, dress, and language," and she saw "the civilized world" imagined by Rivarol and his kind as "very monotonous."[59] Sadly, the different and "foreign ways" are established in a way that is binding: in *Corinne,* at least, the lovers separate as the claims of the household and the authority of the father are reaffirmed. In this way, national liberty comes at the expense of individual liberty. This violence against the individual is the price paid for the articulation of the principle of difference that defies "the classical authorities" and provides in a recuperative way the heritage necessary to resist despotism in the form of Napoleon and his supranational empire.[60]

France, too, looked different from the perspective of exile. For all her efforts to repicture Germany and Italy, the "two nations out of fashion in Europe," and give "them back the reputation of sincerity and wit,"[61] Staël was also writing about France: Corinne's sacrifice—she returns to Italy to die of grief—reflects Germaine's own pain of exile from France. "To cross unknown countries, to hear people speak a language you barely understand, to see human faces that have no connection either with your past or your future," she commented in *Corinne,* "means loneliness and isolation without peace or dignity."[62] No cosmopolitan despite her sensitivity to national traditions, she believed she belonged in France, and in the indigenous ways that her foe Napoleon precisely did not. "He had no French recollections in his heart," Staël insisted.[63] "I was born on the banks of the Seine," she explained, "where his only claim to citizenship is his tyranny. He saw the light of day on the island of Corsica, practically within Africa's savage sway. His father did not, like mine, devote his fortune and his sleepless nights to defending France from bankruptcy and famine; the air of this beautiful country is not his native air; how can he understand the pain of being exiled from it, when he considers this fertile land only as the instrument of his victories. Where is his *patrie?*"[64] In an odd way, Staël kept Corinne and Oswald from committing Napoleon's crime, which was that of trespassing. (Of course, Napoleon did more than trespass on France, he trespassed on Europe; and while France and Germany represent one order of difference, they are both inscribed in a more profound order of difference in which Europe is distinguished from Africa.)

Staël's discovery of *patrie* across the Italian and German borders is symptomatic of a repatriation of sentiment during the emigration. The defiant insistence of aristocrats that home was where the *fleur de lys* was flying or the letters of the Académie de France were read, which applied in the first years of exile, gave way to a more material and sentimental evocation based on personal memories and family intimacies. According to Baldensperger, "home is the place of the most heartfelt, spontaneous memories."[65] Exiles cultivated the memories of what they no longer possessed and thereby created a sentimental narrative of interior loss and imaginary nationhood rather than a political or juridical statement of entitlement. It might be easy for "privileged families," with their culture and education, to forget their sufferings, observed Isabelle de Charrière, "but I will not try to forget everything; the most sweet memories are wrapped up with the most sad. Like the exiled Jews, I do not want to stanch my tears or stop crying for my unhappy country." Charrière repudiated the aristocratic presumption of self-worth in order to explore the fate of exile, which permitted a more vulnerable, but also more individualistic and introspective perspective.[66] Just to see a distant bit of France on the voyage to England, for example, was deeply moving to Auguste de la Ferronays. "Ô ma Berte!," he wrote to his wife in 1810, "arriving here, we saw the coast of France! I cannot tell you what this sight meant to me. It is a feeling so painful, so sad, but also so sweet. There it is, our country, the peculiar object of all my desire!."[67]

For exiles, home is less a particular place than a longing. Undistinguished but emotionally vibrant verses celebrating the sweet attachments of homes littered the hastily published newspapers of emigration. Losses were tallied up in the London-based *Mercure de France:*[68]

> Quel charme de revoir sa chaumière tranquille
> De passer tout à coup des impures vapeurs
> Qui s'élèvent sans cesse et nagent sur la ville,
> Dans un air embaumé du doux parfum des fleurs!
> Qu'en ouvrant sa maison, on aime à reconnaitre
> Le cri de ses verous longtemps restés muets!
> La table, les gazons, le cadran, les bosquets,
> Combien de souvenirs leur aspect fait renaitre!
> Quel l'oeil avidement court d'objet en objet!. . . .

[What charm to see this tranquil cottage again / All of a sudden to leave the dirty fumes / Which rise continuously and float about the city / And enter a balmy air filled with the soft scent of flowers! / The joyous memory, in opening the house, / Of the creaking locks silent for so long! / The table, the lawn, the clock, the grove. / How many memories their sight brings back! / Our eyes eagerly drink up everything they see.]

Exiles frequently gathered their families together to sing about their memories and attachments in simple, affectionate verses:[69]

Du beau pays de ma naissance
Ces cruels m'ont forcé de fuir;
Et pour jamais loin de la France
Je dois végéter et languir,
Pauvre émigrant

D'une famille trop chérie
Le souvenir perce mon coeur;
Ah! loin d'elle il ne'st dans la vie
Pour moi ni repos ni bonheur,
Pauvre émigrant.

[The beautiful country of my birth / These cruel ones have forced me to flee / And forever without France / I must vegetate and languish. / Poor emigrant! / Of a family so cherished / The memory pierces my heart; / Oh! Without her there is nothing in life / For me, neither rest nor happiness, / Poor emigrant.]

Almost every day, reported Falaiseau from London, emigrants met in their hotels to sing, to reminisce, and to recount their stories.[70] Their correspondence and newspaper articles elaborated the sentimental narrative of loss. For one example, François-Charles de Modène, in exile in Konstanz, longed for a cookbook to prepare meals that would remind him of home; happily, he acquired *Cuisinière Bourgeoise* in August 1795.[71] What was love of country, Chateaubriand asked? "the smile of a mother, of a father, of a sister . . . the young companions of our childhood . . . the care bestowed upon us by a tender nurse . . . the village clock . . . the churchyard yew," an itinerary of local places and personal memories that would later quite faithfully form the basis of Chateaubriand's memoirs.[72] For the exiles, quite particular personal memories and domestic attachments increasingly formed the idea of the nation.

The artifacts and souvenirs of exile were preserved as carefully as the memories of home, in a way that made the condition of separation a fundamental basis of identity. As one can gather from the prefaces to the huge memoir literature that flourished under the Restoration, family circles cultivated memories of the emigration and guarded the handwritten letters and journals, and it was sons and daughters, or more often nephews and grandchildren, who undertook the publication of these pieces.[73] The household was thus both the focus of and the point of transmission for memories of exile. Nearly seventy years after the revolution, Tocqueville wrote to his wife about "an old family, in an old house that belonged to its forefathers, still enclosed and protected by the traditional respect and by memories dear to it and to the surrounding population—these are the remains of a society that is falling into dust and that will soon have left no trace."[74] It was the domestic sphere that preserved and made visible the souvenirs of the ancien régime. What this domestic scene, from London hotels to Modène's kitchen to Tocqueville's old house, indicates is that the emigration was largely conceived as a sentimental narrative of loss, nostalgia, and remembrance and only secondarily related to the politics of the revolution. Exile facilitated a view of the past as loss, one which was felt personally, and which inspired an equal measure of piety and despair.

The imagery of exile was expressed in the first-person singular. It was not representatives of the estates who spoke up, but individuals stranded in the present. Although many of the most eloquent exiles of the 1790s left France as well-connected representatives of the first estate, they ended up recalling the emigration as solitary individuals displaced from embracive social milieus. The emigrants proved to be keenly aware of how the twists and turns of world history had marked their physical bodies, separated their families, and caused immense personal distress. Alexis de Tocqueville's father, for example, woke up one day to find that his hair had turned white; Alexis's mother never recovered her mental health. In Balzac's world, Mortsauf suffered fits and seizures.[75] (The face of Joseph Görres, former revolutionary, German nationalist, and for many years an exile in France, was described by contemporaries as "a battlefield of defeated thoughts.")[76] The huge textual archive of the emigration is in itself a testament to this introspective, personal, almost Rousseauvian voice. Exiles produced an extraordinary number of personal documents such as letters, diaries, journals, and memoirs. Of course, the separation from family and friends disposed the émigrés to write, and days when the post arrived were always occasions to gather and to gossip. For Germaine de Staël, exile was but "a tomb where the post arrives."[77] But the act of writing was more than a function of distance or separation. It offered a way to reconfigure the alienated self, to recollect the "debris" of a lifetime, as Louis-Joseph-Amour de Bouille put it. In her primer for the education of *les petits émigrés,* Stephanie de Genlis recommended "a book of souvenirs. This Swiss and German invention is quite wonderful: one can write about all the people you love and your own thoughts, and sketch as well the pattern of landscape, flowers, and portraits. I have sent one to my sister, and I not only included some pieces of ribbon and plants from our garden, but gave her locks of our hair." The miscellaneous nature of the scrapbook and the scattered thoughts, remembrances, and souvenirs it invited revealed how even undistinguished exiles depicted an unsettled world and made sense of their historical situation. Indeed, many emigrants regarded their autobiographical texts as "fragments."[78]

To write about life as an ordeal was to perceive and name and put into a larger context events that otherwise would have gone unremarked. It was to "turn consciousness inside out." The very terms of alienation, notes Michael Seidel, provided new perspectives from which to testify.[79] Crossing the border of France, then, was always very much a crossing of the boundaries of the self. "Six years ago," Germaine de Staël remembered as she was writing her book on Germany in 1809, "I was on the banks of the Rhine, waiting for the boat that was to take me to the other side; the weather was cold, the sky dark, and everything seemed to be a fatal omen . . . There was on our ferry an old German woman, seated on a cart; she refused to get off of it even to cross the river. 'You are very calm,' I said to her. 'Yes,' she answered, 'Why make noise?'" For a moment, Staël censored her own self pity: "these simple words struck me; in fact, *why make noise?*" Yet she realized that "even if generations were to cross through life in silence, unhappiness and death would observe and attack them nonetheless."[80] Contrasting her crossing with that of the old woman, and her noise with the woman's silence, Staël indicated that exile is political and has cause and context. As part of a larger historical narrative, it prompted Staël to raise her own voice and readers to respond to it. "The misfortunes of my country are so intimately tied to my own," testified madame de Ménerville in much the same way, "that I can not pass it over in silence." Subtitling her reminiscences "The Daughter of a Victim of French Revolution," Ménerville wrote because she understood the etiology of her distress.[81] The first-person singular was a distinctly personal voice, but it relied on the collective operations of historical sensibility that made it possible and necessary to speak out.

What is remarkable about this early literature of exile is the popular resonance it found. "Nearly the entire world," concluded the *Journal littéraire et bibliographique de Hambourg* in 1799, "regards the emigration as an inexhaustible source for novels."[82] Why was this the case? To a large extent, accounts of the emigration had all the elements of the adventure stories that had been popular in the eighteenth century. The escapades of the plucky madame de La Tour du Pin certainly contributed to the enduring appeal of her memoirs.[83] But the hardships of exile also appealed to readers across Europe who had themselves suffered the calamities of war. "In all the novels which deal with the French Revolution," observed Agnes von Gerlach from French-occupied Berlin, "it is always the case that unhappiness separates families and divides lovers, and now I find this to be the case."[84]

After the wars had come to end, the production of autobiographical texts continued unabated. Indeed, the French Revolution generated an outpouring of memoirs equaled only by the survivor literature of World War II, notes Marilyn Yalom. Of course, the Holocaust and World War II are traumas of a different order, although the five million dead in the revolutionary and Napoleonic wars certainly warrant a comparison with the death rates for civilians and soldiers in World War I. But the point is that dispossession around 1800 invited prolific self-reflection about loss in the present and about remnants of the past. For more than one hundred years, friends and relatives assiduously cultivated the émigrés' opposition to republicanism, handing down stories about displaced royals and anguished exiles, preserving handwritten recollections, and editing published versions. "The passages that were read to me were either touching statements of loyalty or declarations of the happiness to have lived back then," remembers Philippe Ariès about his own royalist family circle as late as the 1920s.[85] That the nineteenth century became a "century of memoirs," as madame de Fars Fausselandry proclaimed already in 1830, on the first page of her autobiography, was owing to the insistent press of public events on private lives and the pertinence of the reconsideration of those lives in the light of historical change. In the gestures of recollection, the exiles assumed the role of special victim; their eyewitness accounts presupposed a personal, testimonial relationship to public history and marked out a collective identity. Nonetheless, the particular misfortunes of the exiles resonated with a much wider range of readers, for whom "hybrid chronicles that track[ed] the convergence of an individual destiny with national destiny" corresponded to a general sense of displacement in what was quickly short-handed as "the age of revolution." Literary scholars argue that memoirs found readers precisely because readers recognized the historical nature of the hardships of their own lives. Memoirs reenacted the founding premise of the nineteenth century's favorite literary form, the novel, which was that the story of private people pertained to the general unsettlement of society.[86]

The publication and circulation of so many hundred accounts of exile made the world look completely different, because these writings scattered across its face the ruins of its people. The literary embellishment called "Frenchman's Island" on Lake Oneida, New York, wonderfully illustrates this archeological rendering of the modern world. The original "Frenchman" was Louis Des Watines, a nobleman who had left France before the revolution and settled with his family on the lake's westernmost island in 1792–93. He cleared the land but soon discovered that someone else had title to the island, and so he returned to the mainland. After a few years of unsuccessful financial dealings in New Rotterdam, today Constantia, New York, he sailed back to France in 1799. Although Des Watines was apparently an unpleasant man, his stay on what became known as Frenchman's Island caught the imagination of neighbors who savored the idea of "our French Robinson." That Des Watines' wife gave birth to a daughter in an Indian camp across from the island only sharpened their curiosity. This tale of a life "amongst savages" gained additional power when the German novelist Sophie von La Roche transformed the unlucky, unlikable Des Watines (about whom she had learned from her son Fritz, who had settled in the United States) into a gallant French exile who had fled the guillotine with his young wife. La Roche dramatized the tension between the well-born origins of the Frenchman and his lowly state on Lake Oneida. She also juxtaposed the farm on Frenchman's Island to the American village on the north shore and to the Indian settlement opposite, thereby upholding the differences that separated the aristocratic Des Watines from the rude commercial enterprise of the colonists and realigning his exile with the endangered "free" natives. The real Des Watines was quite unlike La Roche's Frenchman, whom the turns of fictionalized history forced into the wilderness and, once there, transformed into a "cosmopolitan despite himself." As retold by La Roche, the story poignantly recapitulated the fate of French émigrés. It also admired the contours of the new life the Des Watines had made: the attempt to farm, the happiness of family, the affinity to the endangered natives. Published in 1798, La Roche's book was successful enough to appear a few years later in a condensed version for young readers. Thanks to this popularization, the physical remains of Des Watines' homestead acquired the aura of a meaningful ruin which stood for both the misfortune and resilience of the exiled nobility. It attracted numerous pilgrims over the years, including Tocqueville and Beaumont in the 1830s. And they found what they were looking for: "fragments falling into dust," precisely what evoked the losses and ruptures and absences of the forty years that had passed since the revolution. It was the perspective of the exile that prompted La Roche, Tocqueville, and Beaumont to look for and to find the ruin of Frenchman's Island.[87] That estrangement and homelessness emerged as such dominant themes in the nineteenth century is due in large part to a literary tradition elaborated by the French emigrants. They encountered the new century from the interiorized, obsessively subjective perspective of displaced persons.

Frenchman's Island is a key site in the geography of the modern time. However distant it seemed from events in Europe, even the United States came to constitute a "symbolic, desolate landscape of the postrevolutionary world."[88] Whereas the eighteenth-century imagination populated America with virtuous colonists and "noble savages," accounts after the revolution exposed a troubled side to the idyllic republic. According to Harry Liebersohn, "it was a bitter quarter century of seeing the world upside down that prepared Continental travelers for a sense of identification with the nobility and suffering they observed among Native Americans." At the same time, travelers were less apt to celebrate Anglo-American mastery of the wilderness and more likely to see its corruption. In other words, "the crisis of the nobility provided a starting point for generalized insight into historical defeat."[89] Arriving in the United States in spring 1791, and recollecting his journey several years later, Chateaubriand described a wrecked place. Entering Philadelphia for the first time, the young Frenchman was shocked to find that republican virtue had given way to cosmopolitan vice: "elegance in dress, luxury in equipages, frivolity in conversation, inequality in fortunes." "There was nothing to indicate that I had passed from a monarchy to a republic," from Old World to New. Well north of Albany, along the Hudson River, evidence of decay was still visible, for there "in the midst of a forest appeared a sort of barn": inside, Chateaubriand found "a score of Savages," "their bodies half bare, their ears slashed," but also a "little Frenchman, powdered and frizzed"; he was "making the Iroquois caper to the tune of Madelon Friquet," a popular song at the time. Instead of hearing the "shouts of the Savage and the braying of the fallow-deer," he walked through the Adirondack forests only to make out "the habitation of a planter" just beyond "the hut of an Indian." By the time he made his way down the Ohio River, Chateaubriand had grown weary at the sight of new settlers pressing into Kentucky from Virginia. In "wilds where man [once] roved in absolute independence," he asked, "will not slaves till the ground under the lash of their master . . . will not prisons . . . replace the open cabin and the lofty oak . . . will not the very richness of the soil give rise of fresh wars?" Chateaubriand recognized the poignant sign of degeneration in the New World: the tragic figure of the Indian who "is no longer a Savage in his forests, but a beggar at the door of a factory."[90] Indeed, Chateaubriand identified his own fate with that of the Indian; both had suffered a historic defeat and were condemned to live amidst the ruins of what once had been a noble existence. In a flash of recognition, Chateaubriand on the Ohio River, like Des Watines on Lake Oneida, approached the Indians on the far shore as contemporaries who shared with him the strange time of exile. He thereby overturned the grand assumptions of evolutionary history which placed Frenchmen and natives at quite different developmental stages and withheld from each the possibility of understanding or empathy for the other.[91] Aware of his own ruined state, he recognized the devastation of modern history and consoled the victims it left behind.

For many of the well-born travelers who followed Chateaubriand—Alexis de Tocqueville, for example, or Prince Maximilian of Wied-Neuwied—the departure to the New World revealed itself to be a journey back to the Old World, a return to the ruins of their own social formations. They proved to be acutely sensitive to the force of historical destruction in the United States because they had witnessed it at home. The gunshot that Tocqueville heard in the Michigan woods, for example, shattered any notion that there was a wilderness, a place outside of history. "The noise of civilization and industry will break the silence of the Saginaw," and the irresistible push of "the great European settlements" will eliminate these scenes of "primitive splendor," he wrote.[92] And Neuwied was astonished at how little the white settlers knew or cared about the native Americans they had displaced.[93] Americans themselves were, of course, less apt to scrutinize development on the frontier in terms of the ruins it produced. Indeed, Tocqueville marveled at their practical faith in progress. For him, Americans saw "humanity as a changing picture in which nothing either is or ought to be fixed forever"; they thus had little sense of the tragedy of history. But others saw matters differently. James Fenimore Cooper's *Leatherstocking Tales,* for example, describes an arc of development which begins with the "almost impenetrable forest" in *The Last of the Mohicans,* continues on to the "stumps and stubs" and forest fires of *The Pioneers* in Templeton, and finally arrives at the desolate landscape of *The Prairie.*[94] Richard Slotkin somewhat offhandedly points out that "Cooper never loves his Indians so much as when he is watching them disappear," but that is because he partially assumes their point of view in order to reveal the extent of devastation and displacement. Cooper and others constituted "boats against the current," as Lewis Perry insists in his study of culture in antebellum America: an eloquent, if understated sense of drift and uncertainty questioned the broader "faith in the flow of progress."[95]

Not all émigrés emerged from exile as witnesses to change and difference in the world around them. But the fact that La Roche's story of Frenchman's Island, Chateaubriand's journey to Albany, and Cooper's carefully dated scenes in Templeton ("The close of Christmas day, A.D. 1793") all occurred more or less at the same time and place is suggestive of the extraordinary reconfiguration of Western history in the wake of the French Revolution, and of the ways in which the experience of the French exiles could be used to express more general misgivings about the nature of change and the direction of progress in the West. Although the émigrés indisputably opposed many of the aims of the French Revolution, they stood for much more than the politics of revolution or counterrevolution. The highly stylized encounters between Des Watines and the camp across the shore, or between Chateaubriand and the capering Iroquois, operated on a more fundamental level. Held together in a common American frame, French exiles and Native Americans testified to the tragic nature of social and economic change. In contrast to the big books about progress and mastery and empire, their accounts introduced a version of modern history that was more alert to loss and dislocation, to the scars of progress, and more suspicious of the pieties of the present day. Suzanne Nash notes that representation of postrevolutionary society in terms of "what it had lost—as debris or ruins, quagmire or sewer" as much as in terms of "the solidity of its foundations" was in large part due to the imagination of exile.[96] Travelers—or, more likely, readers—went to Frenchman's Island because they felt an affinity with the strangers there.

The imagination of exile produced a world composed of strangers, dispossessed and uprooted people like Des Watines, the capering Iroquois, or René. Indeed, the revolutionaries themselves frequently found themselves stranded by the twists and turns of political events, and their errancy during this period could also have served this argument. The imprisonment of the king in 1791, the declaration of the republic in 1792, the reign of terror the following year, the occupation of Switzerland in 1798, Napoleon's coup d'etat in 1799, and finally his coronation as emperor in 1804, each in turn alienated erstwhile sympathizers. The personal anguish of William Wordsworth in the face not only of Robespierre but of "this melancholy waste of hopes o'erthrown" in Robespierre's aftermath is well known, and was the basis of his reappraisal of the relations between the self and society.[97] Some years later, Joseph Görres, who, like Wordsworth, would become an abashed foe of the revolutionary impulse, felt completely disoriented once Bonapartists rebuffed his efforts on behalf of Rhenish republicans: "the whole beautiful building destroyed, its grounds razed." "A flood of iniquity has flooded my inner self," he wrote to his fiancée after his return from Paris in 1800: "now I have to settle in a new land, must build a hut to protect you and me from life's storms."[98] The constant efforts to build, dismantle, and resurrect the revolutionary community generated a constant stream of outcasts who felt betrayed or excluded. As a result, notes Pierre Barbéris, historical formations were regarded as now legitimate, now illegitimate, depending on the perspective of the viewer.[99]

Remnants of the old regime, the republic, and Napoleon's empire littered the nineteenth century. They are all jumbled up in the childhood reminiscences of Ernst Renan, for example. He recalled the unmarried daughter of an impoverished noble who remained in "mid-air," unacceptable to middle-class suitors and too well-born for peasants. "It seemed as if she had been brought into the world with the destiny of not finding a place for herself in it," comments Renan, alert to the newly wrought possibilities (and literary theme) of no longer finding such a home. And then there was uncle Pierre, who, upon hearing the news of Napoleon's return from Elba, climbed up a castle tower to fly the red-white-blue flag of the republican cause. "A few months later, when the opposite cause was triumphant, he literally lost his senses. He would go about the streets with an enormous tricolor cockade, exclaiming: 'I should like to see any one come and take this away form me,' and as he was a general favorite townspeople used to answer consolingly: 'Why, no one, Captain.'" Renan also remembered an old man wrapped in a threadbare coat who died alone among his books among which was found "a packet containing some faded flowers tied up with a tricolored ribbon. At first this was supposed to be some love-token, and several people built upon this foundation a romantic biography of the deceased recluse." But Renan's mother told him otherwise: "I am sure that he was one of the Terrorists. I sometimes fancy that I remember seeing him in 1793."[100]

In many ways, Renan's villagers are icons of modern times, because they are represented in terms of their homelessness in the present. They are strangers. One hundred years ago, Georg Simmel, the founder of the sociology of modern life who lived and worked amidst the rapid development of industrial Berlin, defined the stranger as someone who "arrives today and stays tomorrow." The stranger is not simply an unknown person, a foreigner from the outside, but is also the protagonist of change because he stays, and by his presence he forces local residents to confront him: he unsettles them. Simmel's definition goes beyond a simple opposition of insiders against outsiders in order to put stress on the element of time in which the stranger makes tomorrow different from today. My argument here is that the reconfiguration of time in the aftermath of the French Revolution is what in large measure conspired to create strangers out of exiles by stranding them in new historical circumstances in which the present was cut off from the past. Nonetheless, as Simmel suggested, these strangers stayed and they raised disconcerting questions about yesterday, today, and tomorrow. If historical circumstances continually produced conditions of estrangement, strangers in turn stood out as reminders that the circumstances were themselves newly arrived, or contingent. As Zygmunt Bauman puts it, the stranger reveals "the 'mere historicality' of existence:" "The memory of the *event* of his coming makes of his presence an event in history, rather than a fact of nature."[101] In other words, strangers exposed the historicity of the world, and historical transformation, in turn, produced more and more strangers. Strangeness relied on this perception of history.

Because strangers exposed the ruins of previous historical epochs—the *ancien régime,* the republic, and the empire—their presence sharpened a sensitivity to historical flux and historical destruction in general, one we share to this day. Chateaubriand, as we know, imagined the "great revolution," and Tocqueville asked himself repeatedly "whether the *terra firma* we are seeking does really exist, and whether we are not doomed to rove upon the seas forever."[102] This was the *mal-du-siècle* with which writers and artists in the 1820s and 1830s identified. Their most famous spokesman, Alfred de Musset, embellished on the melancholia and aimlessness of his peers: "Behind them a past forever destroyed, but with the still smouldering ruins of centuries of absolutism; before them the dawn of an immense horizon, the daybreak of the future; and between these two worlds something like the ocean . . . something vague and floating, a rough sea full of wrecks."[103] Musset did not claim to know which elements "vague and floating" belonged properly to the world left behind or the world ahead, but he arranged time in terms of matters slipping and matters congealing. The confusion between what was coming and going made the in-between state all the more precarious. At the time, it was not resolved, after all, whether the word liberty was a "dim recollection" or "shadowy hope," and perhaps the truth of it is not resolved today.[104] In his novels Stendhal too repeatedly raised the question of what was the nature of historical possibility and the strength of postrevolutionary arrangements. On the one hand, Lucien Leuwen, posted at Nancy, introduces the reader to a stagnant and corrupt life in which "Napoleon is gone and forgotten, or all but forgotten; his memory lingers as a vague nostalgia among the veterans gone cynical and corrupt in the service of the Restoration."[105] Everywhere veterans have made their peace, police are armed, and cloisters rebuilt. On the other hand, Nancy's monarchists constantly look over their shoulders, half-expecting another future to sweep them away: "And if it was suddenly announced that a Republic had been proclaimed in Paris, who would protect him against the local populace?"[106] When political bets in Paris are hedged, an observer exclaims: "Oh heavens . . . do you think the republic so near?"[107] In *The Red and the Black,* Stendhal pokes fun at masters who pay their servants extra in case "the terror of '93 returns."[108] The character Julien himself, trying to make his way in the world, furtively reads the newly published histories of the revolution. Living in the shadows of 1789, 1793, and 1815, it was not clear whether current history taught the lesson of restoration or reversal or whether it advised young men to take up the priest's profession or the soldier's, to serve the Church or the nation.[109] What the hedged bet in Paris, the extra tip in Verrières, or the furtive glance in Nancy indicated was the outline of the ruins of the present. The strangers and exiles spoke up in unmistakable inflections of the conditional tense, charging their time in equal parts with premonition and anticipation.

CHAPTER THREE

Ruins

In the aftermath of Napoleon's victory over the Austrian Empire at Wagram in 1809, which confirmed his victory at Austerlitz in 1805, the foundations of the new French order in Europe had never appeared more permanent. Former critics of the French Revolution rushed to make peace with the imperial regime, seeking audiences with the emperor and accepting official positions. Napoleon's tours of Germany in 1807 and again in 1808 were nothing less than triumphal. "Rich and poor, nobleman and commoner, friend and foe all rush out," wrote Philippe de Segur, a member of the emperor's entourage. "With alert curiosity these masses fill the streets, roads, and public squares, waiting through the day and even through the night to get a glimpse" of Napoleon.[1] In Weimar, the "procession passed by our lodgings," recounted Caroline Herder. "I tried to get a good look at Napoleon and, as if on purpose, he looked up at the window and greeted me. The impression on me was: I have seen a genius."[2] Audiences with Napoleon honored leading intellectuals such as Goethe and Johannes von Müller, a one-time foe who got the post of minister to Jerome Bonaparte, King of Westphalia. Not surprisingly, scientists at the University of Leipzig bestowed the name "Napoleon" to a newly discovered cluster of stars in the constellation of Orion.[3] Remaining opponents of Napoleon had never been more isolated. Permanently exiled from France, contemplating a new life with August Wilhelm Schlegel in the United States, Germaine de Staël believed that Napoleon was determined "to deny any refuge in the whole of Europe—even a desert—to proscribed people."[4] From Vienna, Dorothea Schlegel despaired to her husband, August Wilhelm's brother, Friedrich, who was attached to Habsburg headquarters: "how tormented, derided, suppressed, and crushed under foot we are . . . we are treated with such horrible arrogance by the victors of Wagram and Enzersdorf . . . what hopes remain of all the things we had a right to? Where is hope in this world?" "What future remains for my sons," she asked plaintively, "other than comply with the laws of evil."[5]

In a voice of gloom Dorothea Schlegel confessed to Sulpiz Boisserée that she felt completely cut off from the past. "Time has now become so fluidly rapid," she wrote. "It is not possible to keep up; between one mail day and the other lies an entire historical epoch. I feel like I am watching the most diabolical card tricks." Again and again, over the last fifteen years, French armies had appeared across the border, forcing luckless refugees to pack up and flee, or to make unwanted accommodations with new rulers. Like many of her contemporaries, Schlegel believed that the gambling play of revolutionary politics had radically cut her off from the past and stranded her in the revolutionary present.[6] Unsettled as she was, however, Schlegel took comfort in the antique landscape of the faraway Rhine Valley she had visited some time earlier. "Towers, spires, capitals, and columns"—all "evoked memories" of "past greatness." Thanks to these recollections, she "forgot the present," at least for a time. Dorothea Schlegel went on to contrast the ruins along the Rhine with others she had seen along the Danube, which were "confusing" and "raw" and kept her from forming a meaningful picture of its past. She concluded the letter by thanking the young art collector for reminding her that "monuments and art objects" still existed amidst the present-day destruction of war and revolution.[7]

What is remarkable about this communication is Schlegel's consciousness of ruptures of continuity and her insistence on the articulation of the past. She feels at once disconnected from previous mail days and connected to ancient Rhenish ruins, and is uneasy both about the prospect of a present which is forgetful (one without "monuments and art objects") and a past she cannot decipher (Danubian ruins, which are "confusing"). Keenly aware of the ruins of the present, she shows renewed appreciation for the ruins of the past. Left unspoken are the national values attached to present and past: the ruins of the past that she sees are German and the destruction in the present is French, so that Schlegel sets up an implicit contrast between German memory and French forgetfulness. And she differentiates between ruins on the Rhine and ruins on the Danube. It is clear that she sees ruins historically and distinctly rather than according to eighteenth-century aesthetics—that is, not as markers of a generic and inevitable capitulation of art to nature, nor as the decay of all things, nor as an admonition against this worldly vanity—but as specific representations of national tragedy.

Schlegel did not perceive Napoleon's empire and the French occupation of Austria as the inevitable installment of universal Francophone culture, but as the profound jeopardy of cultural dispossession. To her, French rule was something alien. In an earlier letter, Schlegel had surveyed the immobility and demoralization around her. Her great fear was that her sons would go into exile and "leave behind their mother's grave in a wasteland inhabited by barbarian hordes."[8] Schlegel sees history at work on an international scale, and it appears as a dangerous force that menaced both her home and her grave.

Schlegel's reference to her unvisited grave indicates that what is at stake in the global operations of war and empire is memory.

History would bring either her oblivion in the empire, or her memorialization in a place not occupied by the French, presumably in a national culture her sons would preserve and memorialize. She associates the idea of Germany with her own tended grave, just as the idea of Germany has, to her mind, rescued the ruins on the Rhine from the forgetful, eternal present of the French Empire. It is the national form that gives Schlegel her idea of home. And it is the imperial form which threatens the distinction of culture, the presence and commemoration of the past, and the cultivation of self. Schlegel anticipates the nineteenth century's obsession with national difference, its origins and exclusions.

Although Schlegel is concerned to rescue memory of the nation from the eternal present of empire, she also sets up an opposition between the Rhine and the Danube. Both places have ruins, but she only recognizes the historical depth of the Rhine, while the sights along the Danube, which she identifies near Budapest, are "tartaric wild," remnants of forces that "dominate the land but do not give it form." The Danube is no longer contained in Schlegel's opposition between German history and French empire, but is a more fundamental East-West divide between savagery and civilization, between Oriental prehistory and the European refinement of historical form. The reference to the Danube that Schlegel smuggles in thus anticipates the ways in which history in the nineteenth century was constituted in opposition to a nonhistorical "other" in the form of the non-West, the traditional, and the "premodern." Staël had done much the same thing by placing Napoleon and Corsica in proximity with Africa.

The things that Schlegel sees and fails to see in 1809 point to a long-term, profound reorganization of time and space that enabled a new consciousness of history and a new sense of national feeling and a field of difference structured along the axes of nation and empire and East and West. Observers reimagined the past in terms of the momentous break in historical continuity that they postulated in the present. The losses were manifest in the debris of ruined lives they saw around them, and the hopes they had for themselves they nourished through the counterfactuals they projected onto the past. In other words, the ruins of the past were taken to be foundations for an alternative present. The result, then, was that nineteenth-century contemporaries took ruins to be the debris of quite specific historical disasters, not simply the general devastation of time, and they anxiously attended to the preservation of these dated and provenienced ruins. These remains pointed to the specific work of culture as opposed to nature, a distinction which became fundamental to the newly emergent Romantic conceptions of the past. Contemporaries looked upon a landscape littered with the ruins of other worlds (not the disrepair of their own) and scarred by the traces of calamity and destruction and conquest (not simply misfortune or obsolescence). Sites like Frenchman's Island or the crumbling castles along the Rhine were taken out of natural time and placed in historical time, a process of denaturalization that suddenly revealed scars of political and religious displacement.[9] The stony ruins along the Rhine thereby acquired German provenance.

Shifts in the perception of time thus had the effect of changing the sense of place. Formal insights into the action and mutability of the historical process and into the production of ruins provided evidence of abrupt endings and new beginnings, and thereby encouraged the efforts of contemporaries to "make" or resist history in the present. In this way, the manifestation of historical loss corresponded to an acquisition of wealth, because markers of rupture and contingency indicated possibility and variability. "Culture is the unsettled night in which the revolutions of yesterday sleep," writes Michel de Certeau about this modern perspective, "but fireflies and even majestic nocturnal birds can be seen crossing the darkness. These flights trace the chance of another day."[10] As "majestic nocturnal birds," ruins reidentified the variety of subjects available in the vicissitudes of history. Indeed, some years later, as

Dorothea Schlegel witnessed the fall of Napoleon's empire and the anticipated liberation of Germany, she believed she saw the birds in flight to "the new dawn of wonders."[11]

The willful destruction of castles, manors, churches, and abbeys, the sites of the feudal and religious authority that republicans were determined to clear away, and the historical terms of the dislocation felt by so many Europeans, whether they sympathized with the revolution or not, fashioned across Europe a vast landscape of ruins. Contemporaries repeatedly pointed out the ruins of the present, suddenly recognizing the familiar ruins of ancient Greece and imperial Rome in the demolished structures of their own time, and seeing the force of destruction to which antiquity testified in the eventfulness of contemporary history. "I cannot better depict the society of 1789 and 1790," concluded the ever-observant Chateaubriand, than "by likening it to the collection of ruins and tombstones of all ages which were heaped pell-mell . . . in the cloisters of the Petits-Augustins: only, the ruins of which I speak were alive and constantly changing."[12] An enthusiast of the French Revolution such as Constantin-François Chasseboeuf, comte de Volney, traveled to Egypt and Mesopotamia and saw the ruins of Bourbon France reflected in the debris of ancient empires. By contrast, a more skeptical observer of the revolution, Hubert Robert, who was in fact imprisoned for a time in 1794, surveyed the spectacular demolition work of the revolutionaries themselves in such paintings as *La démolition de Saint-Jean-en-Grève, Les ruines de l'Abbaye de Longchamp en 1797,* and *La violation des caveaux royaux à Saint-Denis,* and imagined the wholesale destruction of the Louvre in the near future. Another victim of the Terror, Jean-Baptiste Cousin de Grainville, was among the first modern writers to recognize "the last man" as a contemporary.[13] Of course, the French revolutionaries were not the first to wreck a church, but the fact that nineteenth-century observers loitered around the particular sites of revolutionary destruction indicated how recent history had come to be dramatized as a series of abrupt endings and new beginnings. For exactly one hundred years, the square on which Liège's Saint-Lambert cathedral had stood before being destroyed by the French in 1795 was kept empty, testimony to the villainy of the republicans, the suffering of Catholics, and, later on, the national cause of the Belgians.[14] In hundreds of towns and cities across Europe the marks of the revolutionary conflagration stood out: outdated republican inscriptions, fading graffiti, cannon balls lodged in stone walls, the groove marks left by Napoleonic swords. After the French Revolution, ruins were more proximate and more dense, and they evoked more precise and terrifying sentiments.

To be sure, the ruins of modernity were not conjured up all at once. The eighteenth century was fascinated with ruins to an extent that appears to jeopardize any argument that insists on the distinctively archeological knowledge of the nineteenth century. But the differences between ruins in the eighteenth-century country garden and those in the nineteenth-century world view are fundamental. Beginning in the 1720s, ruins settled into the imaginary landscapes of aristocratic Europeans. For the most part, they were rendered as a part of nature that had reclaimed the works of humanity, and as such they insinuated the frailty of the edifices of society. A constituent part of the general appreciation for the picturesque, the crumbling form enhanced the extreme and unfinished or variable aspects of nature. "Garden-ready" *(gartenfähig)* was also "picture-ready" *(bildfähig),* and broken bridge spans, collapsed edifices, and crumbling walls served the same function as craggy rock formations and overgrown grottos to indicate irregularity and contrast. Indeed, artificial ruins were often embedded in spaces of untamed nature, up against the corrosive action of streams and waterfalls, half buried or covered with vines and brush so that nature appeared to have over taken the works of men and women. One contemporary landscape designer referred to the ideal image of "slowly drowning in the floods of time."[15] While the ruin in the garden suggested the impermanence of human effort and human pride, and taught the moral lesson of humility, it also testified to the restorative and ameliorative power of nature over human sin. What the ruin evoked in any case was the power of nature and the subordination of all worldly things to the cycle of death and birth, degeneration and regeneration. The prevalent mood was melancholy, but still in harmony with otherworldly designs and superhuman forces. Functioning in this way, ruins appeared old and faraway but lacked historical specificity. Moreover, the status of the ruins remained unchanging: old stones were part of the natural order. The eighteenth-century landscape configured both the opposition of art and nature and the ultimate reintegration of art into nature.[16]

Outside the garden, there was little concern for protecting or conserving actual ruins. Medieval heritage was almost completely neglected, and at the few sites such as Tintern Abbey which elicited general interest, visitors preferred the scene to be in disrepair, exposed to natural elements as far as possible. As Ian Ousby points out, eighteenth-century travelers often expressed disappointment in the face of the insufficient wildness of the ruined place.[17] Otherwise, antique ensembles in Europe were more or less interchangeable. They summoned up general feelings of the transience of all things. As a result, no single location merited any special effort at preservation. Of course, Europeans had long collected antiquities, mostly Greek and especially Roman items, but they did so in order to retrieve exquisite pieces, exemplary specimens rather than recovered relics, in Stephen Bann's important distinction.[18] For this reason casts of ancient artifacts were regarded as telling as the original pieces. Otherwise, the ruins of Greek and Roman settlement themselves were not considered interesting or even imperiled, and were not protected.

Discovered in 1748, Pompeii is a good illustration of the way the eighteenth-century ruin was approached for its exemplary quality rather than its mysterious otherness. Hugh Honour points out that "where the site had at first been regarded as no more than a mine from which precious objects might be extracted," later, in the nineteenth century, it came to be "seen as an historical terrain to be explored and mapped out in detail, with as much regard for broken pots and fallen stones as works of art." Indeed, it was none other than Chateaubriand who wondered why all the "household utensils, implements of divers trades, pieces of furniture, statues, manuscripts, & all of which are promiscuously carried to the Portici Museum." "Why not," he asked, "have left these things as they found them, and where they found them? Instead of their removal, they should have been preserved on the spot: roofs and ceilings, floors and windows, should have been carefully restored . . . would not this have been the most interesting museum in the world? a Roman town preserved quite entire, as if its inhabitants had issued forth but a quarter of an hour previous!" What Chateaubriand proposed was the method of excavating ruins *in situ* in order to make sense of context, the particularities of time and place which distinguished this place from all others.[19] This situatedness of Pompeii fascinated Germaine de Staël as well: "in Rome, it is mostly the remains of ancient monuments that are to be found, and these monuments recall only the political history of past centuries; in Pompeii, however, it is the private lives of the people of ancient times which are set before you just as they were." This "just as they were" is the mark of a new historical sensibility that scrutinized differences, like those that made distinctive the Italian and German places that Staël surveyed.[20] "The distinction is similar to that between the Neoclassical artist's selection from Antiquity and the Romantic's attempt to retrieve a moment of the past," continues Honour; "both looked back, but in different ways and for different purposes." Attention shifted "from the merits of works of art which might assist in the creation of recreation of the 'true style,' to the clues which buildings, paintings, statues, domestic utensils, petrified foodstuffs, and calcinated figures of men and dogs might provide for the recreation of the past which would extend knowledge of how people lived and felt in the first century."[21] Concern with context and curiosity about "how people lived" indicated a rather more complex relationship to the past than had been seen before. In the nineteenth century, the past was increasingly reorganized according to temporal and spatial differences.

The example of Pompeii indicates the growing historical rather than aesthetic interest in ruins, which were taken more and more as evidence of past, and possibly very different, life worlds. "Against the stereotypes of classicism," writes Stephen Bann, history in the nineteenth century came to have "a particular value. It served, in the simplest terms, as a principle of difference." No longer part of a natural cycle of degeneration and regeneration, ruins were increasingly regarded as the sites of particular and knowable historical events. In other words, the production of ruins was the result of specific economic or political disasters and not the general work of nature. Important precisely because it had a historical context, the ruin in the era of the French Revolution was turned into an object of reanimation; it was rediscovered, unearthed, preserved, and studied for its messages. The nineteenth-century ruin was no longer the stonework half-buried in the grottos of the enclosed garden, but half-exposed debris partially exhumed in the open field of literary and scientific study.

What is striking about the discourse of the ruin in the early nineteenth century is the extent to which the ruins of nature were now carefully distinguished from the ruins of history. In his inimitable, reductive style, Chateaubriand distinguished this "second class" in *The Genius of Christianity:* "they exhibit nothing but the image of annihilation, without any reparative power. The effect of calamity, and not of years, they resemble hoary hair on the head of youth. The destructions of man, are besides, much more violent and much more complete than those of time: the latter undermine, the former demolish." At first, Chateaubriand saw this violent demolition as part of a divine order: "when God, for reasons unknown to us, decrees the acceleration of ruin in the world, he commands time to lend his scythe to man." And yet, on second glance, the unknown reasons and the unbidden command are taken to be the more specific work of the French Revolution, for a few lines later Chateaubriand leads the reader behind the Luxembourg palace. Together they witness "a church the roof of which had fallen in . . . the doorways blocked with upright planks." They stroll "among the sepulchral stones of black marble scattered there and there upon the ground; some were completely dashed in pieces, others still exhibited some vestiges of inscriptions." "Wild plum trees" grew amid "high grass and rubbish" in the inner cloister. "And in the sanctuary, instead of that hymn of peace formerly chanted in honor the dead, was heard the grating of instruments employed in sawing the tombstones." "It was reserved for our age," meaning 1789, "to witness what was considered as the greatest of calamities among the ancients"—"we mean the dispersion of their ashes."[22] Not the ruin, but the ruin of the ruin is the hallmark of modernity.

The distinction between the work of nature and the work of history, and the antirevolutionaries' insistence on what might be called the catastrophic theory of ruins, which relied on the difference between the ancients and the moderns, was elaborated throughout this period. Already Edmund Burke placed the destructive ambition of the French Revolution "out of nature," and William Wordsworth, reappraising what he called the "impossible individuality" of the revolutionary self, distinguished the "sovereignty" of the revolution in its unnatural, unsupportable ambition, "pollution tainted all that was most pure." What Wordsworth had in mind, comments Laurence Goldstein, was not "the oblivion that passing time inflicts," but "apocalyptic catastrophe."[23] The devastation wrought by society remained in view a generation later. In the 1830s, Victor Hugo distinguished three different kinds of *lésions* on the cathedral of Notre Dame de

Paris. In the first place, there was the work of time, the wind and rain which wrinkled the outer skin of stone and gave it a rough-edged beauty. More horrible were the effects of "political and religious revolutions, unleashing blinded crowds, [that] have scarred the building with brutalities, contusions, and fractures." It was left to taste and custom to inflict the worst injuries, however, for, as Jean Maillon puts it, "it is vanity that tries to restore good taste with one-thousand ornaments."[24] In this more perilous case, the sway of fashion rather than force of political opposition threatened to obliterate the antique, though both, fashion as much as politics, depended on the operation of temporal sequences of historical change to reposition the artifact.

The catastrophic interpretation of modern history assimilates biblical and Christian elements in important ways. "While the main line of change in the prominent classical patterns of history, whether primitivist or cyclical, is continuous and gradual," argues M. H. Abrams, "the line of change in Christian history is right-angled: the key events are abrupt, cataclysmic, and make a drastic, even an absolute, difference." The "stark drama" of the Christian story plays itself out in "the extremes of destruction and creation, hell and heaven, exile and reunion, death and rebirth, dejection and joy, paradise lost and paradise regained," but these were increasingly understood more in historical and inconclusive terms and, in this case, *pace* Abrams, are not so easily resolved in a new harmonious order to come on earth.[25] Nonetheless, Abrams is certainly right to see a new "right-angledness" to postrevolutionary history. If, as for Friedrich Schlegel, "classical is what can be studied in terms of cycles," then "the classical and the revolution are the poles of the historical," where the revolution stands for unrepeatable, heterogeneous time and produces the ruins of revolutionary causes and counterrevolutionary alternatives.[26] In this view, ruins in the early nineteenth-century imagination were not located in the natural time of pre- and posthistory, in which nature reclaimed history, but in history, and they carried the specific marks of even quite recent and specifically referenced historical events and are often carefully dated ("The close of Christmas day, A.D. 1793"). As a result, the ruins in view became more distinct and less ancient; they traced the ruptures of the medieval era, the Reformation, and the Counter Reformation, and revealed the prevalence of thisworldly suffering and thus the contingency of historical process. They indicated the possible futures that had been foreclosed on in past defeats. At this level of specificity, ruins also became more national, providing evidence of indigenous settlement beneath foreign conquest and imperial occupation. The work of archeological recovery in this period aimed at the reconstruction of the multilayered contexts that historical victories had effaced. Antiquarian activity prospered along the fault lines of conquest: Germanic settlements beyond the Roman *limes,* Protestant strongholds in Catholic France, Irish or Scottish national culture in the uneasily United Kingdom.[27]

Once the ruin was understood in a historical frame, its meaning changed dramatically. History was no longer regarded as the operation of fundamental, general rules, but the result of the "antinomies" and "counter-working tendencies" that Karl Mannheim regards as characteristic of Romantic interpretation.[28] Ruins suddenly provided evidence of counter lives. The fragmentary nature of the ruin, "the accidents and particularities of its broken profile, become the marks of its individuality and therefore autonomy."[29] Ghosts appeared in the same way: as the residue of historical disaster. "The Gothic topos of the haunted house resonates with half-repressed memory of . . . cultural defeats," notes Katie Trumpener, who links "particular haunted places" with the "compression and concretization of historical time," the tumbledown Irish and Scottish castle in the aftermath of English conquest, for example, or the abandoned Tory house in republican New England. Ghosts told stories in the forgetful present about the hurtful past by way of unsanctioned details.[30] They scribbled across the clean slates of victory. It is my contention that the historical frame provided to ruptures, disasters, and defeats a testimonial power that the antique curiosities in a princely cabinet never possessed. Rather than signs of death and decay when seen from the classical eighteenth-century perspective, the fragments of the past were still partially alive. They possessed a sort of half-life, the power to inspire and frighten.[31] Although history threatened the ruin of the ruin, the fragment also spoke through history in a way that the silence of nature's reclamation had not permitted.

Given its evocative potential, the ruin came to be treasured for its ability to speak for an alternative historical scheme: this is already clear in Dorothea Schlegel's letter to Sulpiz Boisserée. In a more historically self-conscious age, therefore, the changing styles of landscape architecture rearranged the placement of old stonework in the garden: by the beginning of the nineteenth century, ruins were apt to be more reconstructed and more detailed so as to make more distinct their historical provenance, and they were relocated out of nature's shadow into the open. A new generation of German princes built for themselves medieval castles replete with fortifications, moats, drawbridges, and the like. In Günter Hartmann's words, "what had formerly been a landscape of ruins evolved into a landscape of the Middle Ages."[32] The stress on the historical specifity and national provenance of the ruin also shifted attention from the carefully groomed ensembles in the garden to actual fragmentary debris in the countryside. Previously neglected ruins were closely studied, mapped, and classified, inserted into historical sequences, and maintained as commemorative sites that contained historical information. Since they were increasingly regarded as the remnants of vast political and religious confrontations, ruins became the objects of strenuous preservation efforts which sought to protect the spirit of the past that the stones allegedly contained. "It is difficult to comprehend a situation," comments Susan Crane, "in which a physical object, often of rather significant proportions and durability (such as a Gothic cathedral), is presented as something ephemeral and fleeting, and where the ephemeral, fleeting sensation of historical perception is described as having solidity and depth. This is however an accurate characterization of the inversion created by the rhetoric of early nineteenth-century German historical collecting and preservation."[33] What is crucial here are not the ruins themselves, for they did not change, but the new historical field in which they were seen and apprehended. Like Simmel's stranger, the ruins appeared all at once, and they stayed in view. They were rendered visible by new structures of temporality based on disorder and rupture, concealment and half-life, that emerged with the revolution in France. The power of ruins in the nineteenth century was to depict the violence of historical movement without imputing necessity to its direction. They challenged the absoluteness of the present with the counterfactuals of the past. In this sense, classical modernity does not uphold a pure linear conception of time but a more hybrid tradition that included right angles, gaps, and displacements.

Precisely what message about the past the ruins held was not completely clear, though; certainly not as transparent as the natural rhythm of life and death they had designated one-hundred years earlier. As monuments to unnatural deaths and defeats, leftovers from another time, ruins became more remote and impenetrable. According to Michel Foucault, in *The Order of Things,* modern "European culture is inventing for itself a depth in which what matters is no longer identities, distinctive characters, permanent tables with all their possible paths and routes, but great hidden forces developed on the basis of their primitive and inaccessible nucleus, origin, causality, and history. From now on things will represent only the depths of this density." The aim of antiquarian work, then, was to reach these depths and origins, and it corresponded to the hermeneutic method of the nineteenth century in which literary and scientific interlocutors had to interpret what the ruins meant and for whom they spoke. The stress was on what Benedict Anderson aptly terms "reversed ventriloquism": the other, past things the fragment had witnessed of which the present did not know.[34]

As a momentous break, the French Revolution forced upon the exiles of the revolution the feeling of complete abandonment in the present and reanimated the past as a historical site of confrontation, defeat, and resistance. Indeed, at the turn of the nineteenth century, the previously neglected ruins of the past seemed to pop into view all at once: the artifacts piled up at Petits-Augustins attracted considerable attention, as did medieval castles and Gothic cathedrals. In the span of a single lifetime, the ruin was transformed from a lifeless artifact of underdevelopment and superannuation into a haunting relic of historical possibility. The past became the site of anguished memory work and the location of alternative identities. This was in stark contrast to the eighteenth-century view in which the continuous stream of time inevitably left behind obsolescent forms and steadily realized the perfectibility of civilization, and, as it did, confidently took the measure of progress by mapping human forms in terms of comparative development in time and space.

It would be misleading to imagine that the fascination with the past at the beginning of the nineteenth century was simply the result of the physical destruction of artifacts and monuments or the carting away of national treasures to the central site of the Louvre, which occurred during the Napoleonic period; the Thirty Years' War had devastated many of urban and religious centers in central Europe without prompting much in the way of antiquarian activity. And although Napoleon's troops did in fact demolish hundreds of historic ensembles, it was the historical frame to the demolition work, the declared goal of republicans to establish a new political order, that gave the broken-down remnants their political and aesthetic expressiveness. Furthermore, contemporaries did not turn to the past simply as compensation for the difficulties of the present, because there was nothing simple or univocal about the past. In the light of the French Revolution, the past was full of conflict and violence and therefore hardly consoling. The revolution had the interesting effect of bringing the violence of the religious wars in the sixteenth and seventeenth centuries more prominently into view. It was precisely the post-revolutionary recognition of the unsettlement of the prerevolutionary past, and the gaps and interruptions it continuously revealed, that authorized the energetic antiquarianism of the nineteenth century. To understand the allure of the past in the European imagination, it is important to acknowledge that its potential to pose alternatives is at least as important as its ability to provide the illusion of durability and naturalness. Unfortunately, historians have mainly considered the latter, examining the ways the nation, in particular, forged its own antiquity and the properties of its own self-sameness. In so doing, they have overlooked the principle of difference in the constitution of new political subjects, including the nation. In the aftermath of the French Revolution, a generation of unlikely self-made cultural impresarios such as the art collector Sulpiz Boisserée and the folklorists Jacob and Wilhelm Grimm strenuously resisted neoclassical assumptions and quite self-consciously scrutinized the past for the different stories it might tell. They thereby reimagined social and political being in the present.

The campaign to complete the Gothic cathedral in Cologne indicates just how the ruins that evinced a conditional past (what might have been) also suggested a conditional future (what might yet be). Although the revisualization of ruins corresponded to broader European and even American trends, the German case is salient since Germany had long been regarded as underdeveloped in the Enlightenment schema, the unremarkable European periphery to a defining French center or a subordinate outpost in Napoleon's empire. For most of the eighteenth century, there was little interest in Cologne, which had been Germany's largest city in the Middle Ages. Visitors generally ignored its antiquity to comment on its dilapidation: "The streets and the inhabitants are as dirty as they are gloomy," reported one correspondent in 1784.[35] Of course, the great unfinished structure of the cathedral was difficult to overlook, but it was considered anachronistic: the result of over-ambitious patrons in the fourteenth and fifteenth centuries and of Cologne's hasty decline at the end of the Thirty Years' War. The cathedral, like Cologne and the rest of the Rhineland, for that matter, was analyzed in the universal terms of underdevelopment; the state-building process in France or in Prussia remained the normative model, while the dispersed, parochial situation on the Rhine denoted an earlier, superannuated time. After the French Revolution, however, the cathedral was seen afresh. Suddenly the ruin stood for (German) subjectivities which had been defeated again and again in recent centuries but might be rearticulated. That French occupation authorities prohibited religious services in 1796 and used the cathedral to house Austrian prisoners of war, to store grains, and, finally in 1802, to stable horses; this only heightened the sense of what the cathedral had been and was no longer. An impressive array of literary figures came to cherish it as a monument to a specifically German "prehistory," reconsidering its incompletion as premature foreclosure. In their view, the prospect of completing the cathedral made it possible to imagine following up the lost itinerary of German prehistory and thus introducing greatness and cohesion to German actions once the French had been defeated. With a wooden crane still perched on top of one of its stone towers, the cathedral stood out, according to Joseph Görres' famous 1814 pronouncement, as "a permanent rebuke" for what Germany could have been and as an admonishment for what its impoverished territories might yet become. For the journalist Heinrich Steffens, Cologne's cathedral was nothing less than an "inverted ruin." It beckoned an "indeterminate future," in which various possibilities of history remained alive. The subjunctive future corresponded to the conditional past, in which defeat and demolition were no longer regarded as foreordained.[36] The cathedral was no different in 1814 than it had been in 1714, but the manner in which contemporaries looked at the ruin, contemplated its lifelessness, and assigned it historical value changed dramatically. The difference is that by the 1810s the developmental logic of universal history, as Rivarol or Müller or Condorcet had once conceived it, no longer applied, so that the things that had been disqualified as outdated were now be mourned as lost and approached for what they might still yield.

Revisualizing the cathedral, or Cologne, or the Rhineland meant repossessing the landscape. The young Sulpiz Boisserée, the art collector who advanced the boldest claims for the historical and political value of German antiquities and who worked to create the networks and institutions to transform them into national heritage, took countless journeys up and down the Rhine River to inspect churches, catalogue artifacts, and visit art dealers. It is not clear how or why Boisserée concocted the idea of collecting medieval artifacts, but a clue can be found in the constant movement of people and things at the turn of the nineteenth century. Sulpiz himself, alone or with his brother Melchior, traveled constantly from Cologne to Rotterdam, Koblenz to Mainz, Cologne to Heidelberg, and along the Mosel to Trier and up the Main to Frankfurt—it was on a market boat from Frankfurt to Mainz that Sulpiz Boisserée left such a full report on the raucous political conversations in August 1815. These journeys were undertaken alongside the tides of soldiers and refugees and political agents who came with the French occupation of the Rhineland in 1794 and the Allied reconquest in 1813. Boisserée was keenly aware of the political forces of his day, and in his letters and memoirs he returned more than once to the fateful day in October 1794 when French troops entered the city of Cologne: "As they entered the city, the soldiers looked like *sans-culottes,* bread, meat, and coal hanging from their bayonets, wearing rugs and carpets instead of coats, and marching in wooden shoes."[37] The republicans appeared almost oriental, wrapped in "rugs and carpets," a contorted acknowledgment, perhaps, of the vast changes they introduced to a city in which inhabitants were not equal before the law, guilds still regulated commercial life, and Jews and Protestants were actually prohibited from staying overnight. At the same time, the stuff the French troops carried were plundered goods, and here Boisserée must have linked the plunder of the individual soldier to the wholesale plunder of the churches, convents, and abbeys in the years that followed, an action which both motivated and enabled his own collecting zeal.

There is no doubt about the terrible privations that came with French armies, but without the occupation Boisserée himself would never have been able to travel so far and so easily or to explore the conditions of his own subjectivity. In fact Sulpiz and Melchior first resolved to go to Paris in the fall of 1803, when French influence on the Continent was firmly established by the Peace of Amiens. "There was a huge movement," Boisserée later explained, "all the newspapers spoke about the advantages and comfort of examining altogether in Paris the most famous art works of the ancient and Christian era which one would otherwise have had to seek out in long journeys to various cities and countries; therefore countless artists, aficionados, and other hangers-on journeyed to the French capital." It was the revolutionary wars, of course, that made possible this fact of centralization, and the collections of the Musée Central des Arts in the Louvre, open to the public since 1800 and pointedly renamed the Musée Napoleon in 1804, continued to grow when war and thus imperial plundering resumed in 1805. And yet Boisserée ended up doing just what the collections at the Louvre had supposedly made unnecessary: "a wide-ranging journey in various countries." Here is a possible hint at Boisserée's motivations. On the one hand, for the young brothers—Sulpiz had just turned twenty—Paris was "the capital of the universe."[38] "This unbelievable city beckoned us from all sides," he remembered; "we couldn't possibly take in everything we saw. The big parades in honor of the First Consul in the courtyard of the Tuileries; the traces of the revolution with their black inscriptions: *Liberté, Egalité, ou la Mort!;* the public buildings and gardens, strolling along the boulevards, theater, libraries, art galleries, and even castles in the area—we wanted to see everything. The days sped by."[39] This was the city of empire, brimming with possibility and activity. On the other hand, the capital revealed a fundamental emptiness: the art came from Italy, or the Netherlands, or Cologne, places which no longer possessed the historical destiny that France had acquired. Thousands of visitors streamed into Paris during the Peace of Amiens (1802–03), and although they were attracted to the center of learning and culture, they also felt out of place, subordinate, emptied out. This was certainly the case with Friedrich Schlegel, who crossed Boisserée's path in Paris in the fall of 1803 and eventually joined him on the long journey back to Germany.

Schlegel had come to Paris to study eastern languages and philosophy, and along the way from Jena had been impressed by ruins along the Rhine. These aided him in outlining a historical vision for Germany, which he published in *Europa* that same fall. Schlegel declared that "Nowhere are the memories of what the Germans once were and what they could be so alive as along the Rhine." The fullness of the German-occupied past stood in contrast to the emptiness of the French-dominated present and therefore offered an alternative. According to Schlegel, the Rhineland offered a compact space in which the chain of "hills, cities, and villages along the wonderful stream" could be reconstituted as "a whole," were it not for "the deplorable fragmentation of the unity of countries and nation." The very force of destruction made reconstitution plausible. Schlegel undoubtedly had in mind the revolution and the wars, not simply a longer process of decay, when he wrote in categorical terms: "what was once great and beautiful is so totally destroyed, that I do not know in what way one can now argue that Europe as a whole is still with us." In the face of catastrophe, however, "there is a little room for something new, if only because everything is destroyed." From Jena to Paris, Schlegel read the historical landscape as a ruin, but by framing the movement from the castle to the village in parallel with the political supremacy of France over Germany in 1803, and by declaring Napoleon's "natural border" to be in fact "unnatural" *(unnatürlich natürlichen Grenze),* he devised a circumstantial explanation for historical loss and could therefore imagine other historical formations than Napoleon's Europe.[40] Schlegel brought this sense of unease with the present to Paris, and while he studied non-European languages in France, he became increasingly obsessed with European alternatives to France.

On almost every street corner in Paris, Friedrich Schlegel and Dorothea Veit, a young divorcée who was soon to become his wife, heard German and bumped into friends, but meeting the Boisserées was special.[41] Together the two families visited Notre Dame, which made a deep impression on Schlegel and prompted the Boisserées to tell him about Gothic treasures at home: "his attention became rapt as we promised him an even higher order of old monuments" in Cologne. Schlegel and Boisserée resolved then and there to work together and to return to the Rhine, to "landscapes that were quite overlooked because of their ancient folk customs."[42] Very likely it was at this point that Sulpiz Boisserée reconceived his fascination with medieval art—a passion which had, after all, first brought him to Paris—in more explicitly historical terms. This change prompted him to turn around, put the Musée Central behind him, and embark on "long journeys to various cities and countries."

The journey back to Cologne suggested a radically new understanding of history. Boisserée and Schlegel no longer regarded Paris as the center of a unified European culture, what Schlegel now mockingly referred to as "Europe as a whole," the place "all newspapers" celebrated for its convenience, and the Rhineland was no longer on the outskirts, inconvenient for the "long journeys" it demanded. Rather, the Rhineland offered evidence of former wholes and competing centers that were different from but comparable to Paris. The unified geography of center and periphery, and its one-way pilgrimages to the Louvre, gave way to a more fractured history of dispossession and repossession, of conquest, usurpation, and contrast, and to detective journeys up and down the Rhine, forth and back to Cologne. That the movements of Boisserée and of French soldiers, and later of the Allied liberators, so closely paralleled one another must have heightened the sense of loss and possibility; in any case, in his diaries and letters Boisserée kept close track both of his own travels and the itineraries of revolutionaries and soldiers.

At first, Boisserée rewrote the history of the Rhineland very much in terms of *dispossession.* An early trip up the Rhine in September 1808 revealed a sorry state of loss. "The whole Rhine valley!" he exclaimed, "a true picture of what we are and what we once were." "Rhense is very dilapidated"; "Boppard still has parts of its wall and towers." As he continued his journey, he commented not so much on what was wrecked or broken, but on what was lost, on the historical subject that was no longer: "The thought of how thoroughly over the centuries the evil enemy can devastate us to the core of our being, this thought, which had already haunted me in Worms and Heidelberg, seized me completely in the doubly ravaged city of Speyer—it is not just walls, gates, towers, churches, and cloisters that are wrecked and lie in pitiful ruins, but also, and what is worse, the people in all their comings and goings have completely lost the appearance of proud German city folk." The stress is not on the ruins *per se,* but on the cultural entity they conjured up, or rather on the disconnection between the collective past and the present inhabitants, who are strangers to their own history: in Worms, the entrance to the cathedral is hidden, in Strassburg's cathedral, the locals dry their tobacco. "O the slothful indifference of Germans—why have you let it come to pass and what you won't still let happen!" lamented Boisserée at the end of the journey.[43]

The first steps toward *repossession* were halting. After returning to Cologne in summer 1804, the Boisserées and the newly married Friedrich and Dorothea Schlegel wandered around the old walled city literally snatching medieval art from the carts of passing junkmen. They were frequent visitors to Cologne's "traders and junk-dealers," for the previous winter the republican regime had cleared the premises of the dissolved religious orders and carelessly sold off their furnishings and artwork. "The circumstances were extraordinary; everything that we knew and heard about the art pieces reminded us of a horrible shipwreck, in which a few works of art had been saved, but many other valuable things had been lost in the storm, though others might still be tossed up along the shoreline." In retrospect, the Boisserées cast this early activity in heroic terms, but at the time the two young brothers must have seemed hopelessly out of date. French-occupied Cologne calibrated itself closely to the new time of Napoleon's Empire. On the occasion of Napoleon and Josephine's visit to the city in September 1804, "honorary archways, allegorical pictures, trophies, garlands, and monuments" greeted "Napoleon the Great" and celebrated his victories: "Arcole, Mantua, Campo Formio, les Pyramides, Mont St. Bernard, Marengo." Cologne's leading citizen, the art historian Ferdinand Franz Wallraf, who also collected medieval art but did so without apparent political purpose, lavished praise on history's greatest emperor, whose task it had been to lift the city out of "darkness."[44] Dorothea Schlegel herself reported that "Cologne is enchanted by him"; "never before have I seen such folk festivals."[45] On this neoclassical stage, between the eighty-foot-high pyramid and the new obelisk on the Neumarkt, there was little room for Sulpiz Boisserée or his medieval relics.

Over time, Boisserée amassed an impressive private collection of early German masters, which he treasured for the vigor and directness of their depiction of Christian faith. They were unmistakable depictions of Germany's fifteenth- and sixteenth-centuries' "independence and freedom," Boisserée explained to Goethe some years later.[46] Dominated by the masters Hubert and Johann Eyck and Karl van Mander, the collection eventually numbered 250 pieces, arranged by style and chronology. Yet the sum of the individual pieces was not as important as the stylistic, historical, and thus national unity that Boisserée claimed for the collection as a whole. He worked strenuously to reconnect the German people to the heritage they neglected, enlisting the support of Germany's most authoritative critic, Johann Wolfgang von Goethe, and exhibiting the paintings first in Heidelberg and later in Stuttgart, where he anxiously retrieved statistics on the number of visitors: "looking through the window, I counted 86 people . . . yesterday it was 56, the day before yesterday at least 100 in front of the pictures," reported Bertram to his brother Sulpiz.[47] After negotiations with Prussian authorities fell through, Boisserée sold the collection in 1827 to the Kingdom of Bavaria, where it formed the basis of the Alte Pinakothek in Munich, where it can be seen today.

The claim that Boisserée made on behalf of his collection provided the justification for conceiving of such a thing as a distinct German heritage. Boisserée's intention was not to refurbish nineteenth-century Germany in medieval style, but to break the logic by which medieval art was regarded as a primitive or formative stage in the development of a rational and largely neo-classical aesthetic. He argued that the old masters represented an autonomous and highly expressive cultural formation that could be compared to and contrasted with the classical style, in opposition to a unified evolutionary scheme. This permitted him to conceive of a national or German style in political as well as artistic matters. Boisserée, like Germaine de Staël, who was following very similar thoughts through the "various countries and cities" of her exile, put forward an argument for the creativity and individuality of national genius. When he traveled to Frankfurt to try this interpretation out on Goethe, the critic was not convinced. "Sure, sure, um, that is all very well," he responded half-heartedly to Boisserée at their first meeting on 5 May 1811, "sure, sure, very interesting."[48] But over the next days, Goethe warmed to the young man, who was not even thirty, and gave him important backing. Over the years, Boisserée frequently visited "the old man" in Frankfurt, and they laughed at each others secrets. Of his own fascination with the order and measure of things Roman, Goethe quipped that he must have once led a life under Hadrian, and added to Sulpiz that surely he had once lived in the fifteenth century. This off-hand remark was already an important concession to Boisserée because it assumed the individuality of style rather than development over time.[49] Nonetheless, Goethe resisted Boisserée's conclusions, if not his charm: in his view, the collection was to be appreciated in universal terms. It was, as he put it in an early letter, "noteworthy, as a document of a stage in human culture." And the enthusiasm of "so many young people for the Middle Ages," the attraction to the period's "interiority, simplicity, detail, and workmanship," he wrote, was commendable, but nonetheless merely "a transition to higher stages of artistic development," comparable to his own youthful detour to Strassburg in 1772 before his more formative journey to Italy fourteen years later and the philhellenic philosophical idealism to which his important friendship with Friedrich Schiller inclined him in the 1790s.[50] For his part, Boisserée insisted on the vitality and endurance of national tradition, and he rejected "Hellenism as the only canon." "Every people and every age has to hold on to what the Gods and Fortune have given them." The Germans were distinct: "our conditions and our whole situation are completely different from the Greek way of life," he wrote in a priceless letter to Goethe; "when and where are we naked in public life?"[51]

The centerpiece of Boisserée's efforts to make visible the distinctive (national) quality of Germany was his campaign to restore and then to complete the cathedral ruin in Cologne. Already in 1810, in an early letter to Goethe, he praised the cathedral's stylistic unity; precisely because it was left unfinished, its Gothic form had not been compromised by later additions, as was the case in Heidelberg, Münster, and Strassburg. At the same time, the broken-off ruins seemed to aspire toward "further construction and completion."[52] In this case, the fragment form expressed national longing. To complete the cathedral would be to recognize the viability and vividness of the national and Christian faith that had conceived it so long ago. It would serve as both an acknowledgment of national identity and an exhortation to develop and remain true to national tradition. "Definitiveness," "struggle," "imagination," "self-confidence"—the vocabulary to which Boisserée returned again and again is muscular and formal: it is the example of achievement and confidence in the possibility of achievement that he recognized in the old masters and hoped to witness again in the modern era.[53] Having discovered old copper plates that depicted the original design for the cathedral's uncompleted twin towers, Boisserée could in fact realize his fantasies: construction work began in 1840 and was completed in 1880. But Boisserée's primary achievement was not so much technical as ideological. He redescribed the ruins of the Rhine in historical terms: they were evidence of other, fully completed life worlds, not early or primitive stages of development; they thus revealed a distinct national tradition which circumstances of long-term political and religious division had obscured in the early modern period; and they therefore established the principle of difference by which the Germans could conceive of themselves as a unique and independent cultural entity.

By 1814, Boisserée's vision was almost complete. The cathedral ruin had become the central architectural feature in a new national imagery held in common by an impressive roster of German writers and statesmen including Joseph Görres, Ernst

Moritz Arndt, and Baron vom Stein. What Boisserée believed he saw in his journeys up and down the Rhine was the public's recognition of the ruins as telling monuments and their possession of them as a nation. Traveling to Mainz and Heidelberg and back, Boisserée scripted his movements in tandem with the national uprising of the German people. Whereas in 1808 he had reported on loss and dispossession, in 1813 and 1814 he recognized the formation of a new historical subject, the German people. Along the Rhine, the world was in motion: "on November 3rd [1813], we first saw military men in Heidelberg, Bavarians who were escorting captured French soldiers, even some elite guards." "All along our journey" to Frankfurt, he continued, "we passed through Bavarian and Austrian troops under Wrede, departing we saw the night encampments, the assembly field, and the baggage trains. It was only when we got to Weinheim that we encountered large numbers of Bavarian troops marching in closed formation, followed by Austrian cavalry, hussars and dragoons. In Heppenheim there were engineers and the encampment of the commanders; around Bensheim lots of royal artillery, then Württemberg's foot soldiers and horsemen, everything quite contentedly mixed up, with lots of baggage trains in between. At the end, when it was already half dark, a large supply of pontoon bridges, and in Darmstadt, Russian generals." Boisserée does not just see Allied armies, however. Recalling "all the memories of the old days all the way back to my childhood," this "huge movement" was the counterpoint to the invasion of the French in 1794: "all our hopes for a final liberation and a better future awakened with double force." "Finally" German soldiers were serving the true and proper goal, the "liberation and security of the fatherland."[54] Slowly Boisserée made out the *Volk* among the sites and ruins of the river valley, although he was sober enough to realize that "in times of war and revolution, it is not just an affair of the people [*Volk-Sache*], but also of the rabble and the state [*Pöbel-* und *Staats-Sache*]."[55] Increasingly, Boisserée read into the landscape the familiarity he had missed on earlier voyages: on shore in Mainz in June 1814, he felt "freedom and the experience of home [*Heimatlichkeit*]" and commended Germany's "unity and harmony," a twinning of the general form and the particular content that he had seen previously only in the old masters or the cathedral ruin. A few days later, on the boat to Bingen, he noted repairs to a "ruined chapel": "I took it as a good sign of the new time to come," one founded on the recognition of old ruins.[56]

Two maps corresponded to one another, and each added detail and clarity to the other. One was the increasingly detailed sketch of the archeological and medieval sites that laid out Germany's national tradition: the cathedral in Cologne, the castles along the Rhine, the old towns of Worms and Speyer, the chapel outside Bingen. The other drew the itinerary of German national purpose: the battle site at Leipzig, the movement of Allied troops across the Rhine, the arrival on the scene, as Boisserée imagined, of "the farmer and the artisan" who had left "wife and children, house and garden" to fight for German freedom.[57] Over the course of the Wars of Liberation, the two maps had come together, and laid over each other they made an unmistakable case for the German nation. For Dorothea Schlegel, who had accompanied Boisserée to Cologne in 1808, and whose son Philipp had volunteered to fight with Lützow's free corps, the front was historical as well as geographical. "Don't you think he is across the Rhine, or still on this side?" she wondered in a letter to the patriotic writer, Friedrich Baron de la Motte Fouqué, about her son: "You can imagine how we stand in front of the maps, and look for all those well-known spots along the beloved banks; it seems impossible not to imagine Philipp right there—I wonder how he feels seeing the magnificent river, the familiar mountains and the shoreline."[58]

After the war, the two maps, one antique and local, the other imagined and national, continued to embellish each other. Boisserée made more and more trips up and down the Rhine, cataloguing sites, managing the exhibition of his art collection, drumming up support for the reconstruction of the Cologne cathedral, and growing increasingly enthusiastic over the new freedom of movement that the introduction first of steamships and later of the railroad allowed. Boisserée was a great supporter of steam travel, although it impoverished the rivermen who pulled boats up the Rhine. "The wonderful, thundering paddle steamer" was nothing less than a "triumphal passage," a triumphal strike," offering speed *(blitzschnell)* and flexibility and conveying many more passengers.[59] A few years later, the railroad facilitated even more sightseeing, "a simple flight" from here to there, he encouraged prospective visitors.[60] And of course it was not only Boisserée or Schlegel or Goethe who made these voyages. In the three decades after 1815, the Rhine valley became a vast "national museum," celebrated in the verse and song of Schenkendorf, Eichendorff, and Heine, described in annotated gazetteers, and the destination for German and international tourists: Victor Hugo, Alexandre Dumas, and Théophile Gautier all wrote extensively on the Rhine.[61] Seventeen years after the first steamboat, *De Zeeuw,* plied the river in 1824, more than 750,000 tourists annually made the trip from Cologne to Mainz; some two million did so in the last years before 1914.[62] Interestingly enough, Karl Baedeker, who first made his name publishing guidebooks on the Rhine and published his first guide to Koblenz in 1829, had joined up with German soldiers fighting Napoleon's armies in 1814, traveling the rivers between Bonn, Essen, Hagen, and Heidelberg.[63]

In the years after the French Revolution, local townspeople also took to visiting neighboring castles, fortresses, and churches, and supported the growing interest in the archeological remains of the early Germanic tribes, the "underground nation" that had resisted the Romans. Teachers and pastors excavated sites, reported on their work in local archeological associations, and published their findings in history periodicals.[64] In this sense, Germans gradually constituted a "nation of provincials," in Celia

Applegate's apt phrase. Their well-chosen circuits, and the footpaths, signs, monuments, excavations, museums, and taverns that marked the way, sketched out a new national picture.[65] It is not an accident that the painter Caspar David Friedrich frequently depicted wanderers contemplating historic sites. The signs of a journey, of an effort, are clear, since the destinations appear to be outlying. But these itineraries have little in common with the eighteenth-century meditation on the wilderness ruin; the scenes are carefully situated: the wanderers often appear in "old German dress," wearing the coats and berets favored by German patriots, and the sites are historically referenced.[66] "Father" Jahn himself recommended wandering, so that the German people would get to know each other.[67] This was hardly Biedermeier passivity, the diversions of hobbyists unwilling to take "history in their own hands," as Peter Märker uncharitably puts it, for that is precisely what contemporaries did.[68]

To be sure, the exploration of the local ruin was not a national activity in the sense that it involved a large proportion of a German population made up mostly of farmers and peasants. (However, it is interesting to consider the new knowledge of at least one farmer, who properly informed local authorities about the objects he found in the fields; this too was a recognition.)[69] But the argument for the revisualization and repossession of ruins does not rest on unanimity. The point is that new ways of looking at and handling ruins not only depended on a historical frame but enabled specific historical and national identities. These attracted the inclinations and interests of thousands of mostly middle-class Germans, who surveyed archeological ruins, took Sunday excursions, boarded a "paddle steamer" on the Rhine or the Mosel, and otherwise explored a landscape seen for its familiar "unity and harmony." The familiarity of the ruin also kindled a busy market in antiquities. From Cologne, Ernst Moritz Arndt reported that antique dealers had been "completely sold out in the last years."[70]

Goethe himself was amazed "at what ordinary people had quietly acquired in these difficult and sad times." About the fascination with medieval stuff, he added: "the spirits that I called upon have multiplied and I don't see how I will ever be able to shake them."[71]

The national project remained incomplete, to be sure, and patriots eagerly approached ruins such as the Cologne cathedral for the broader narrative unity they might provide to an unchurched public. The very materiality of the fragments was an unmistakable reminder of the "historyness" of history, both the destruction and peril and also the survival of cultural entities. Ruins were splendid sites to spur the national imagination. As one excited amateur archeologist put it: "How much more loudly the voice of prehistory speaks through these monuments than through the dead signs of books!"[72] Yet ruins did not speak for themselves; archeology required a voice that would represent and interpret the fragments as historical artifacts. It was the responsibility of patriotic intellectuals to school the people to see themselves as Germans. "There is an amazing amount to be done," acknowledged Ernst Moritz Arndt, "in particular all good men have to work to bring our history and our language to life again," for "only then will our people come to life again."[73] Despite the reluctance of the German princes to cultivate this potentially democratic sensibility, he was sure that "the flood can't be stopped."[74] Arndt's confidence rested in the intellectual apparatus of history, archeology, and poetry which would show local inhabitants how to recognize themselves as Germans.

That state authorities implemented a "politics of culture" and introduced regulations to protect local antiquities (passed in 1830 in Prussia) should be seen as both an initiative to strengthen the sense of national belonging and patriotism and a response to the expectations of a self-constituting national public. In an important 1815 recommendation provided to the Prussian Ministry of the Interior, the architect and state building inspector

Karl Friedrich Schinkel underscored the state's responsibility to preserve monuments and cultivate the past, "in order to engage the people and encourage national study and interest in the early fate of our fatherland." What is particularly noteworthy is that Schinkel argued against what he took to be the French model, the establishment of a national museum in the capital, presumably Berlin, to which local treasures and provincial visitors would come. Taken out of context, he claimed, artifacts would lose their eloquence. Moreover, the countryside would appear "unfamiliar, naked, and shorn, like a new colony in a previously uninhabited land," an argument as much for allowing local places to keep local antiquities as for cultivating specifically German history on a national scale.[75] To lose the past was to end up on the periphery, as had been in the case in the developmental schemas of the eighteenth century. In this early age of overseas empire, the fear was that Germany might be reduced to the status of a colony, which was also the fear of Dorothea Schlegel and Germaine de Staël as they considered their own national heritages. This then was an official restatement of Boisserée's principle of difference: national identity depended on local circuits to specific sites, even when it was upheld in a larger system of distinction between historical Europe and empty Africa or Asia.[76] Rebuilding a cathedral in Cologne or building a nation in Germany; each was a distinctly transnational operation. Ultimately, Schinkel added his support to the reconstruction of the Cologne cathedral, an undertaking which was always politically sensitive since it was imagined more as *Volk-Sache* than *Staats-Sache,* but proceeded only incrementally until in 1840 the Prussian crown prince committed the state to the cathedral's completion, which was finally accomplished in 1880, twenty-six years after the death of Sulpiz Boisserée.[77]

It is not surprising that ruins featured prominently on the new mental maps of the nation, because the historical ruin made the case for the particularity of the nation and also for the preeminence of the West. As a fragment, the ruin articulated the process of destruction, conquest, and renewal, and the fluidity of history in general; it invited a reconfiguration of the present because it conjured up counterfactual pasts. The field of difference distinguished separate pasts, which thereby enabled the "meaningfulness of separate territorial developments," in Karl Mannheim's words. All this rested in large part on a disjointed or ruptured archeological understanding of the past.[78] Given the importance of context, that is, the specific frame of time and place that surrounded the historical site and illustrated the specific case of "just as they were," as Staël put it, ruins made it easier to consider the different ways in which historical conditions shaped the actions of men and women and thus to imagine (Western) people as historically active subjects. The vanquished causes, unremitting violence, and sudden abandonments—in a word, the "loss," the melancholy with which ruins in the years after the French Revolution came to be associated—developed this notion of subjectivity. Ruins made plausible an investigation into historically interpretable world of events and contexts, and the historical record that resulted made it possible to visualize ruins and justify their preservation.

The emphasis here has been on Germany because it illustrates so well the creation of particularity and the rejection of schemes of underdevelopment, but a similar revisualization of the ruin took place as well in postrevolutionary France. In the 1820s, Charles Nodier, Alphonse de Cailleux, and Isidor Taylor embarked on a publishing venture to produce gigantic picture albums—the *Voyages pittoresques et romantiques dans l'ancienne France*—depicting the historical regions of France: Languedoc, Picardie, Dauphine, Normandie. Conceived on a massive scale—each of the volumes measured eighteen by thirty-six inches—the project was not completed until the 1870s. Rather than assemble historical events along a continuum, the authors traced indistinct origins, noted disruptive invasions, and described archaic religiosity, and thereby embellished France's rich and diverse past. Scattered across space, ruined castles and convents attracted the attention of antiquarians because these landmarks constituted evidence of political and religious struggles and brought into view a fabulous landscape of passion and belief.[79] Against what came to be seen as the ceaseless modernizing efforts of the state, particularly after the liberal July 1830 Revolution, Taylor and his collaborators pleaded the case for multiple French pasts. The melancholic cast to this violent history of the nation contrasted starkly with the work of Jules Michelet, for whom history moved lurchingly toward a free, secular, and republican France; the antiquarians proved much more sensitive to loss and thereby provided a sentimental place for a variety of political and religious constituencies. This field of difference was more internally differentiated than in Germany. It resembled the biography of the nation that Benedict Anderson analyzes: a family that is constituted through the evidence of fratricide, but is recognizably "our own."[80]

The *Voyages pittoresques et romantiques* were far too big and too expensive to have much public impact, but poets and novelists such as Victor Hugo broadcast the same message. Having grown up on 18 rue des Petits-Augustins, just a few steps from the defunct Petits Augustins convent where the tombstones of the French kings had been stored after being removed from Saint Denis, Hugo was especially alert to the ruins of the present. Throughout the revolutionary period, the wrecked statuary of the centuries accumulated "pell mell" in the convent. Michelet imagines a youthful Hugo, "intense, curious, apprehensive," moving from "room to room and epoch to epoch," exploring the roomy house that was France.[81] Hugo reworked the sights on rue des Petits-Augustins in *Notre-Dame de Paris,* his best-selling novel which in a few short years put "Victor Hugo's Cathedral" on every tourist's map of Paris.[82] Like the Rhineland, France too became a place for those who, as one English visitor put it, love "old churches, old books, and relics," who enjoyed tarrying "within this old fashioned place."[83] Guidebooks took care to point out the destruction that the Jacobins had wrought, and also lingered at the now vanished site of the execution of the king and queen. France had become more interesting because it juxtaposed the ruins of ardent faiths and true beliefs into a kind of national sublime, "our own" dust—*poussière,* the last word in Hugo's *Notre-Dame*—in other words, the debris-filled case of France.

One way to think about the importance of ruins in the postrevolutionary period is to consider the dread Europeans had of living without ruins. Insofar as ruins were not any longer part of a natural landscape of decay and regeneration, but the historical evidence of trauma, extinction, and difference, the act of obliterating the ruin was tantamount to annulling kinds of lives and varieties of belief. For Chateaubriand the French Revolution was horrific not so much for creating ruins—killing a king or washing up émigrés on foreign shores—but for destroying monuments to the past. He took his readers again and again to the abbey of Saint-Denis, outside Paris, where in August 1793 revolutionaries had plundered the royal tombs and smashed the bones of France's kings.[84] In what became a signature of conservative description, English and German visitors, too, condemned France as a country without memory. The empire was established in the stretched-out time of a forgetful and hence endless present. Upon arriving in France from Germany in 1803, Friedrich Schlegel purported to be immediately aware of dullness of the landscape. It was without remarkable features, lacking the wild residue of Germany's history.[85] Even in Paris, he reported, "luxury is the all-absorbing deity that governs the hasty revolutions of the fleeting day, amid an universal irregularity of existence, buildings, garments, and the ornamental refinements of life, interrupted only by the fantastic caprice of ever-varying fashion."[86] As a result of living without memory, the French lacked possibilities for recalling or retrieving alternate historical itineraries. Visitors who followed Schlegel pursued the same theme. For instance, Friedrich von Raumer heeded his political curiosity to travel to Paris in 1827 but was shocked at the degree to which the events and places of the revolution had been effaced. "Here," he was told, "where the new, beautiful Rue de Rivoli passes were once cloisters and gardens, here on this corner once stood the riding school, where the Constituent Assembly opened its deliberations in Paris, where the legislature sat, and where the Convention condemned the king of death." "How is it possible," he asked "that at the very place where the most fearful memories destroyed reason and faith there sits the most ordinary middle-class house, and neighbors quietly conduct their business, visit undisturbed the cafes, and speak and think and feel all sorts of things, just not those matters that should concern and move them most? Why isn't the old building preserved for all time as a general warning to humanity, or as a site of contrition and atonement, why just let people pass by, indifferent and forgetful?"[87]

What is interesting is not whether Schlegel and Raumer were right—there is no reason to think that France forgot whereas Germany remembered—but how forcefully contemporaries on both sides of the Rhine made judgments about places without memory, and about the value of ruins and the stories imputed to them. Nineteenth-century Europeans were increasingly conscious of the ways in which history enhanced the subject and enabled action. They fashioned their newly mobilized identities out of loss and displacement and constructed an unbearable (often French) alternative which supposedly did not. The culture of remembrance became a political force. In this view, then, it was the perpetual present, the ruin of the ruin, the permanence and preemption of empire, that constituted the real destructive potential of modernity. It was this melancholic rendition of history, with its stress on the prevalence of loss and the imperfection (but necessity) of remembrance, that invited Europeans to think of themselves as legatees of distinct, half-hidden pasts. Increasingly convinced that German or French or British identities were bounded by time and place, contemporaries after 1800 made the case for the particulars of their own historical specificity and, on that basis, for their own active, future-oriented subject positions. The age of nationalism opened beneath a proscenium of ruins.

To reconstruct the distinct cultural quality to the nation and to resist the claims of empire came at a price. If over the last two centuries nationalism has "enabled a population to transform its perception of difference from other groups into a political project,"[88] it has also smuggled in the difference of that difference by curtailing the historical subjectivity of non-Europeans. It is worth recalling Dorothea Schlegel's reference to the dumb expressiveness of the Danube, the impressions of which remained "raw" and "confusing." Schlegel's assumption was that history-making was an operation of refinement that could not be imagined under the primitive conditions of an Orientalized East. In much the same way, Staël contrasted a history-saturated France with a barren, African Corsica in order to disqualify Napoleon as French. Hegel did the same thing in his analysis of Africa, when he compared the continent's backwardness to Europe's movement. Although the elaboration of national difference had profound anti-imperial implications, as in the case of the opposition of the German nation to the Napoleonic Empire, it also served to obliterate non-Western differences and to justify Western imperialisms around the globe.

National identity was suffocating as well in the ways that it threw up boundaries against France and inhibited the intellectual exchange that had been characteristic of the Enlightenment. In Germany, the effort by Arndt, "Father" Jahn, and others to nationalize habits of speech and customs of dress went a long way to create an ethnic self-consciousness that merged Germans and Christians and usually excluded Jews. "What exquisite pieces for Boisserée's collection," wrote a bitter Konrad Engelbert Oelsner about German nationalists who were content to boil "Jews, witches, and free thinkers" in the same stew.[89] For Oelsner's close friend, Rahel Varnhagen, the national revival in the years after Jena and particularly after Leipzig represented a cultural narrowing. Although for a time the cosmopolitan literary world at the turn of the nineteenth century had given her, a Jewish woman, a place and identity, Napoleon's war against Prussia in 1806 destroyed this precarious security. Prejudice against French ideas, Jewish persons, and cosmopolitan sensibilities mounted, and Rahel was left alone. "Where is our time, when we were all together," she recalled ten years later: "Went down in '06, went down like a ship with the most beautiful of life's treasures, with the finest of life's pleasures . . . Adieu, adieu."[90] Forced to flee embattled Berlin in 1813, Varnhagen took on—she says so explicitly—"the title and the status: Stranger," *Fremde.*[91] Even after her marriage to a German diplomat, Ense von Varnhagen, after Napoleon's defeat and after her return to Berlin, the place of her birth, she still found herself in exile. "I don't have a real home, not a material one," Rahel confessed to her friend, the actress Auguste Beste. "What I see are lots of out-of-date characters; what I encounter are last year's opinions, worn out judgments, stuffy knowledge, and, on top of all this, unbearable pride!"[92] As for Cologne's cathedral: "well!—to think of remaking a dying, ill-considered old man into a fertile, growing adolescent!" "The old days," she hoped to know, "have *flowed on* down just *like* the Rhine."[93] What Rahel did not see so clearly was that new time did not always flow steadily into a progressive sea, but pooled and puddled around the wreckage of the past.

CHAPTER FOUR

Along the Hedges

In the postrevolutionary epoch, ruins corresponded to the national idea. The duration of the remnant over time produced, in the formulation of Judith Butler, "the effect of boundary, fixity, and surface" and attached to the nation a sense of permanence and naturalness.[1] The construction of the historical context for a particular epoch—Staël's lives "just as they were"—gave ruins the authority of representativeness and established boundaries to mark off the German from the French past. At the same time, the evocative quality of the ruin suggested the tenacious survival and indeed the unmistakable vigor of the cultural life of the nation. Once their presence was acknowledged, ruins could be animated with a half-life which testified to the durability of national forms. In this way ruins emerged as prominent features on a national landscape, and local circuits made these increasingly familiar and intimate. Growing numbers of villagers and townspeople found that the historical surface of "Germany" or "France" had become recognizable. It is telling that Ernst Moritz Arndt, who grew up in Rügen, a predominantly Protestant island set away in the North Sea, wanted nothing more than to live in the Catholic precincts of Strassburg or Cologne, "where all the stones express a great prehistory and inhabitants still adhere to old customs."[2]

The historical imagination collectivized memory by simulating the well-worn and familiar far beyond the ambit of family and home. The abstraction of the nation became more and more intimate over the course of the nineteenth century, no less important than family, village, and religion.

But it would be a mistake to push the point too far and argue that ruins naturalized a specific idea of the nation. This is the great mistake of many histories of the nation. It is important to keep in mind the open-endedness of the process by which the ruin was revisualized as a site of political rupture and historical discontinuity that justified national particularity. Although the archeology of the ruin made plausible the principle of national differentiation, it also contorted it, for it provided evidence for the intensity of local and regional traditions and for the juxtaposition of very different cultural formations in the same place. For example, Rudolf Virchow, the most prominent Prussian liberal in the years after 1848, pursued his interest in archeology in a characteristically local key. Stressing the need for careful observation, he argued against the "romantic fantasy" that linked archeological remnants to a postulated prehistoric unity of German culture and made the case for the messy, long-term interpenetration of Slavic and German peoples.[3] And the premise of Isidor Taylor's grand project of the *Voyages pittoresques* was to reintroduce France to its historical, religious, and political diversity. Moreover, the archeological method that rendered the idea of the nation in the first place also lent the achieved national union a tentative and fragile aspect; it recovered the nation in irrevocably broken, fragmentary pieces. The notions of history that emerged around 1800 presumed both the endurance and the frailty of social formations. "The flood . . . in stream," the mobilization at the end of the Wars of Liberation, which invigorated Arndt's faith in Germany's eventual national union, also troubled him for its promiscuous reach. "I consider the letting free of all things and relations to be almost as bad," he confessed, "as the previous bondage and serfdom. Dismantling all guilds, labor freedom, destruction of farms, arbitrary creation of a new, impoverished nobility, admittance of the Jews and equal rights for Jews—I'd like to see a people who can survive such horrible conditions."[4] Hopeful, exhortative, alarmist, suspicious all at once, the national idea expressed itself repeatedly in the conditional tense.

Put another way, the new home of the nation always had something unsettled about; it recalled the contingency of its claims, the strain of recovering its historical origins, the historicity of its premise. "There is no return to natality," points out Zygmunt Bauman; "the past has not been stored in a warehouse until such time as it may be taken out, dusted and restored to its former beauty."[5] Because the national home can only be imagined and postulated, the familiarity and safety it sought to establish were always experienced fleetingly and always needed to be refurbished. It is in this state of jeopardy that nationalism turns ugly.

The historical ruin expressed two things, then: continuity and rupture. The history that was retrospectively made at the gravesite was never completely finished off. On the one hand, continuity established the claim for the persistence of an entity against something else, Germany against France, for example, or Catholicism against Protestantism. On the other hand, rupture provided evidence for lapse and cessation. Virchow's studies show the temporal discontinuities in German or Slavic traditions; Arndt's nightmares portend annihilation of all customary social relations. The historical understanding of past lives "just as they were" always was unstable and potential, and the operational grounds for imagining a specific national narrative opened the way for the conception of counternarratives: renditions in local and regional history; and paths to degeneration, decay, and ruin, as well as those to unity and conquest.

In the case of Britain, the dominant sense of "Englishness" in the nineteenth century depended in large part on scrutinizing the seventeenth and eighteenth centuries in such a way as to blend

Scottish or Irish aspects into an agrarian prehistory that the United Kingdom's colonial might and industrial prosperity had left behind, and incorporate them in a progressive historical scheme. Potentially dangerous nationalisms on the periphery could thus be duly recognized and largely disarmed by a conception of history as an impersonal, inevitable process of economic development. The ivy that "climbs up and claims the stonework" at once made this process natural and claimed the eclectic relics of the dead cultures as signposts of national destiny.[6] Katie Trumpener calls this propitiatory version of events the "national tale," a happy ending exemplified by Walter Scott, who used the historical forces of modernity to reconcile the broken pieces of the heroic, but no longer valid organic societies of Scotland or Ireland into the new national community of empire. Yet the triumphant British story—the "United Kingdom"—was not the only history available at the graveside of the Scottish clans. According to Trumpener, "bardic performance" in both Ireland and Scotland repeatedly "reanimate[d] a national landscape made desolate first by conquest and then by modernization, infusing it with historical memory." The bards and other unlikely, quaint antiquaries challenged assumptions about the inevitability of the dynamic of British progress; for them, ruins in Ireland or Scotland were the unmistakable sites of the "violence of outside forces." "Their refusal to relinquish the memory of a preconquest society," Trumpener continues, "dooms them, personally and collectively, to a shadowy half-life, caught between past and present. Yet this refusal also keeps alive the hope of future autonomy and decisively blocks the conquerors' narratives of triumph and progress."[7] What established the credibility of either version, both the "national tale" and the bardic response, was a historical frame that made the particular case for the ruin, whether as a relic of a lapsed agrarian past or as a remnant of a culturally expressive collectivity. Each of these histories used ruins to construct what Anne Janowitz too hastily dismisses as a "reified, romanticized past."[8]

Yet a "reified, romanticized past" is precisely what history, whether in triumphant or resistant register, creates. After all, reification and romantization are operations that assign agency and facilitate judgment, and on this basis a collective, active subject is constituted out of evidence of continuity and rupture. It is worth examining the different ways in which the national landscape in Britain and Germany was scrutinized and its miscellany organized into alternative or vernacular narratives that resisted the imperatives of the present.

In Britain, in the years after Waterloo, the radical journalist William Cobbett rendered visible a historical landscape of beginnings and endings, breaks and discontinuities. His *Rural Rides*, sketched out in the 1820s, set a scene in constant motion and unending corruption. Landmarks were identified as tokens of "shocking decay"—houses that have been pulled down or fallen apart and churches too large for Salisbury's "little knots of people"; or else the "mock grandeur and "mock antiquity" belonging to a "new set of proprietors" such as Mr. Montague, a "gentleman" from "the 'Change" who had constructed "gothic arches" for his "park" in Berghclere to "denote the antiquity of his origin"; or the continual residency of the rector in Weston for "*twenty years!*" a record of duration that was "remarkable" because Cobbett did "not believe that there [was] an instance to match this in the whole kingdom"; or simply the town of Ross, described as "old fashioned" because its unblemished survival made it a rarity.[9] Cobbett has often been dismissed for his nostalgia, for letting the forcefulness of his criticism rely on a merry English past of "pristine innocence and uncorrupted virtue" that never existed.[10] But the point about accuracy is moot since Cobbett's gilding of the past simply amounted to "ahistorical extensions of his social and economic criticism."[11] The point is also misleading because Cobbett was quite unsentimental in his depiction of the historical transformation in the present. If his nostalgia recorded yesterday naively, it also indicted the present day uncompromisingly and, by virtue of the historical method, held out the possibility of the demise of what was now standing.

Cobbett's local circuits brought a larger national and more political picture into view. "People all along here complain most bitterly of the change of times," Cobbett wrote from Folkestone in Kent on 1 September 1823.[12] This scrupulous notation of place and date demarcated the desolate scenes of Cobbett's ride from the picaresque alternation of fortune and misfortune usually to be seen along the traveler's itinerary. For all of Cobbett's excisions, and his loud and angry voice, he was careful to place the reader in a historically specific geography and to dramatize the difference between then and now. The disorder along the rural rides is the work of history, not nature. In the words of Leonora Nattrass, Cobbett's rural rides across England in the 1820s evoked the sense of "an invasion from within." Cheltenham brimmed with "East India plunderers" and "West India floggers" and loitering laissez-faire "feelosofers." A national economic policy, more onerous taxation, and an increase in metropolitan power, all very much the result of the mobilization against Napoleon, left the impression that England was "in some sense an occupied country."[13] The penetration of "plunderers" and "floggers" into Sussex and Kent in the years 1821, 1822, and 1823 provided a structural frame to organize and interpret quotidian experience. "The vantage point," explains Jon Klancher, "shapes a discourse that brings rural and urban, northern and southern, handicraft and artisan laborers within a broader, national sense of being a public, since the kind of historical change Cobbett's language implies leaves no geographic or occupational realm untouched. Everything is connected, brought into a pattern, given a sense of historical movement . . . within which members of an audience find common ground."[14] In other words, history is a mass medium that uses a nostalgic key to give a general poignancy to otherwise isolated misfortunes. Cobbett wrote for a national public he hoped to animate, one that would recognize private losses in more comprehensive historical terms and, subsequently, redirect local customs and parochial resentments toward a "resistant national politics."[15] Cobbett's account renders the whole edifice of England, its degraded past and conspiratorial present, brittle and breakable. True, the commercialization of property, the enclosures, came late to Cobbett's birthplace in Farnham ("with its Farnham Common") and was already well advanced much earlier, in the eighteenth century. But this does not diminish Cobbett's contribution, which was to visualize social transformation in historical, indeed epochal terms, tracing as he did the scars across the landscape in mournful remembrance of what had been and holding particular social classes responsible for the violence done.[16]

What is notable about Cobbett's survey is not that he had discovered new ruination in the present whereas there had been none in the past, but rather that he and his readers believed this to be the case. The enclosure movement pulled down houses and upset stone walls long before Cobbett came along; Oliver Goldsmith's "The Deserted Village" from the year 1770 is clear enough evidence for that. Yet it was Cobbett and not Goldsmith who developed an emphatically national optics by which the fresh ruins and displaced people came prominently into view, and it was Cobbett who signposted a totally mobilized landscape that had to be understood historically. By systematizing the debris of the countryside within a comprehensive national and historical context, he created an image of the nation as broken. Cobbett's England was full of elisions (for being so rural) and highly suspicious (of vilified outsiders), but also radical for repossessing the nation in the name of an impoverished laboring class that vicariously followed along Cobbett's "rural rides" to see the historical case of the state of the nation.

The unity that Cobbett achieved anticipated the association of Englishness with rural countryside; it left out the city and the

North, not to speak of Wales, Scotland, and Ireland. Cobbett colluded with William Wordsworth, Mary Russell Mitford, and other Victorians in a pastoralism that celebrated "mute" and "inglorious" rustics for their rootedness to a particular place and reassembled the legends and tales that gathered there. Craggy localisms were "the necessary supports of national greatness," writes Elisabeth Helsinger, pastoral images to be mobilized against the "initially seductive" promise of revolutionary France, and later against the unfair play of striking urban workers or the peril of a resurgent Germany. Yet the national vernacular of the graveyard, the village church, and the tenant-holder's farm should not be regarded as a tightly organized system. The "customary culture" of the countryside did not speak for itself, and needed to reworked into "the histories, poems, and pictures of a disappearing rural life" before it could serve as "the ground for national consciousness."[17] This was the function of Cobbett's rural rides. At the same time these second-hand images also validated the experience of the crofter and artisan, in a literary representation that was politically enfranchising and, as was recognized at the time, potentially revolutionary.[18] Indeed, critics of Wordsworth such as Francis Jeffrey of the *Edinburgh Review* were well aware of how the poet's aesthetic created an unsettling political roominess. They attacked him for finding a "vein of poetry" to "accommodate" the "common people."[19] Local circuits of memory and mourning helped define the nation bounded in time and place, but they did not necessarily follow the highways of power. Rather, the national form was insistently vernacular, because it was local context that made it distinctive, giving it democratic potential from the outset. And finally, the organic unity of the rural view was always undermined by the acknowledgment of the violent interactions and occupations that have destroyed it, something many contemporary critics of the artful, nostalgic composition of rural England miss.[20] The idea of the whole is represented by way of fragments and debris that withhold any confidence in its rehabilitation. Cobbett conjured up the nation as a vanishing act; his England is mortally threatened, it is defined through the pieces that are broken. This incompleteness is the subversive aspect to Cobbett's melancholy.

John Clare, too, took poetic license in a burst of great writing in the years after the enclosure of his native Helpston between 1811 and 1816. He picked up the debris of local disaster and fashioned a sharpened awareness of the place of rural villagers in the newly emergent commercial society. Clare is interesting not simply because he was so angry at the enclosures or even because he quite precisely comprehended the historical transformation that tore away his liberties. He also reworked the fragments that remained of his past into richly textured artifacts of his own displacement and newly wrought identity. "One group of poems narrates quests for the hidden," writes Helsinger. "In patches of woods, heaths, or even the corners of fields, Clare finds remnants of unowned land in an enclosed landscape."[21] The displacement he felt enabled a reorientation to the hedges, the margins. The leftovers he collected there, "creeping on hands and knees through matted thorn"—"The Robin's Nest," "The Nightingale's Nest," "The Moorhen's Nest"—composed riches which though bounded by loss had not consciously been seen and therefore had not properly existed before. "How curious is the [nightingale's] nest!" As Clare points out,

> no other bird
> Uses such loose materials, or weaves
> Its dwelling in such spots: dead oaken leaves
> Are placed without and velvet moss within,
> And little scraps of grass, and—scant and spare,
> Of what seem scarce materials—down and hair;[22]

The poet too makes a structure out of scraps and debris.

Clare's first volume, *Poems Descriptive of Rural Life and Scenery,* published in 1821, met with surprising success, but his most unforgiving and socially pointed poems, "The Lamentations of Round-Oak Waters" or "To a Fallen Elm," for example, never appeared in print in his lifetime, and his cautious, though admiring publisher, John Taylor, tried to pass off the talented Clare as a political idiosyncrat: "A second thought tells me that I am a fool," Taylor speaks for Clare: "were people all to feel as I do, the world could not be carried on,—a green would not be ploughed."[23] A first reading of Clare's poems indicates that he owed a great deal to eighteenth-century forms in which the pleasure of landscape evoked the passing of childhood to produce a melancholy effect, and these are precisely the associations that John Taylor favored and believed would find a sympathetic readership. Yet Clare could not so easily find the old landscape, and its absence pushed his childhood even further away. The landscape is gone because it has been occupied: "Inclosure like a buonaparte let not a thing remain."[24] In "The Lamentations of Round-Oak Waters," Clare describes the aftermath of an attack of the fence builders which has stripped the place and disoriented its people:

Dire nakedness o'ver all prevails;
Yon fallows bare and brown
Are all beset with posts and rails
And turned upside down;
The gently curving, darksom balks,
That stript the cornfield o'ver
And prov'd the shepherd's daily walks,
Now prove his walks no more;
the plough has turned them under hand
And overturned them all,
And now along the elting-land
Poor swains are forced to maul.

These are not the common images of an adult looking back on childhood, although the losses of childhood are made more desolate by the historical context in which they are now understood. The reference to Napoleon underscores that this is no natural process, but a social, historically knowable catastrophe.

Against Taylor's advice, Clare wrote increasingly in dialect. "In 'Winter Fields,'" suggests John Barrell in his study of "the sense of place," "the phrase 'pudgy paths' means not simply paths full of puddles, but 'full of puddles in the way we know them to be in Helpston.'"[25] The local context reinforces the effect of particular, identifiable invasions such as "buonaparte" and keeps the damaged landscape from sinking back into a natural cycle of birth, death, and rebirth. Seeing Helpston in the context of history and not nature, Clare calls the locality into existence. Its "pudgy paths" are there mainly to display the scars of progress, but also to resist global processes by the very effort of distinguishing, marking, and narrating the local.[26] "Just as it had been" provided a context for thinking about people "just as they were" and worked against any naturalized or harmonized definition of national culture.

As it was, Clare, whether abridged by Taylor or not, never found a national audience. Still a young man, but a stymied writer, he returned to working the fields, and only with difficulty was able to support his family. His letters to friends and publishers reveal the anguish of "an intensely self-conscious literary talent taking on the established social and cultural power-structures of his day."[27] Clare, too, was in a kind of exile, "a straggler in this life" who was not only unable to return to old Helpston, but also unwilling to reconcile himself to the poetic conventions or the political authorities and economic premises of the day. He was also stranded in the present. Although a minor figure on the national stage, Clare nonetheless achieved local prominence; he reworked his poems into ballads and songs, constituting a sentimental material culture out of the ruins of the enclosures. His vision, which embraced rural laborers and their families, told a different, bitter story of English progress, the disquieting "triumphs of time" and the "fallen elms" these left behind.[28] Clare evoked the ruin to dramatize difference rather than continuity, alteration rather than alternation, loss rather than restoration. He created cultural attachments out of felt absences.

Conjuring the idea of the nation through the evidence of loss, Cobbett and Clare upheld a very particular kind of anthropology in which the fragments and pieces of everyday life evoked the national substance that has been wrecked. Their "rural rides" were national itineraries that went along neglected byways and hedges, the corners of the nation, out-of-the-way sanctuaries that preserved remnants of former lives. This is a melancholy rendition of the nation, but it is also more emphatic, more vernacular, more attuned to the everyday, more willing to allow a variety of subjects and artifacts to evoke the national idea, and more sensitive to the broken-downness of the imagined unity that spurred nostalgic memory work in the first place. The loving attention to the fragment, burnished, dusted, and preserved, was twinned with a sharp focus angrily, unreservedly directed onto the forces of dissolution, particularly the menace of real-estate speculation and market capitalism. Although the events of the French Revolution had passed, the melancholy effects they had produced continued to influence other places and generations well into the twentieth century. This was so because the revolution had dramatized change for particular histories and introduced new ways of thinking about the past as a felt absence that could mourned but not regained. The work of the brothers Grimm, who were painfully aware of how national custom was made visible by the threat of economic transformation, is perhaps the best illustration of the way the cultural production of the nation could be mediated through its own broken and incomplete form.

"Andacht zum Unbedeutendem" ("the fetish of the trivial") is how Sulpiz Boisserée dismissed the collection of old German sayings and nearly forgotten village habits that two young autodidacts, Jacob and Wilhelm Grimm, just a bit younger than he, had carefully gathered up and transcribed in their journal *Altdeutsche Waelder* (Old German Forests) in the early 1810s. Although Boisserée himself actively promoted the preservation of Germany's medieval heritage, he did so with the collector's discerning eye; a self-styled expert, he had little patience with the Grimms' lack of taste. His judgment was seconded by the prominent literary critic, August Wilhelm Schlegel, for whom the Grimms' "veneration of rubbish" *(Troedel)* revealed undiscriminating enthusiasm for anything old.[29] Boisserée and Schlegel mocked the two brothers as fumble-fingered antiquarians who could not distinguish German jewels from ordinary junk. That Jacob and Wilhelm were awestruck by even the most plain objects made them appear foolish as well as amateurish. The criticism stuck; for the rest of their lives, the Grimms never felt taken completely seriously by Germany's established academics, for whom they were always a little too gullible and a little too excitable.

Yet the Grimms stood by their materialist method and their ordinary collectibles. All around them, the brothers saw the demolition of a cultural world which had left only remnants, and these needed to be handled and pieced together carefully to reconstruct past lifeways. The fairy tales, which the Grimms collected and published in 1812 and 1815, are their best known literary production, but the brothers also obsessively tracked down the origins of words and their usages, laying the foundations for that great monument to German tradition, the national dictionary. The etymological pieces and story fragments that Schlegel dismissed as rubbish evoked veneration in the Grimms. Theirs was a distinctly archeological imagination, inclining them to see not only the ruinous force of historical change but also the fragmentary evidence of historical cultures that might be rescued.[30]

A childhood marked by "momentous change" undoubtedly made the two brothers especially sensitive to bits and pieces, to the evidence of rupture and discontinuity. The early death in 1796 of their father, an ambitious and successful lawyer, impoverished the large family and cut short a happy childhood in the small Hessian town of Steinau. A short while later Wilhelm and Jacob left Steinau for Kassel to complete their education at the Lyceum Fridericanum, and it was there, in the company of strangers, that the two boys felt most acutely their lack of social standing and economic security.[31]

From the vantage of Kassel and what followed, Steinau became a fabulous, ruined place. Many years later, Wilhelm recalled: "The most memorable moment when we left for Kassel for the first time is when we drove out of the town. We sat in the Kronen Tavern's coach, I was up front and I saw in the distance our bee garden with its white stone posts and red iron fence lying beneath a heavy fog. I thought of all the time I had spent there; it already seemed far, far away as if separated by a large ditch. I felt totally cut off from it and was starting something new."[32] The recollection is in very concrete terms. A "white stone post" in the ground and a "red iron fence" around the garden—these fragmentary images remained sharply drawn in memory and indicated a bold-colored security which the passage of time placed farther and farther at a distance, first by casting over the garden a veil of fog and then digging behind it a final ditch of separation.

Wilhelm regarded the passage of time as the movement of separation. I "am very attached to all the things that I have had for a long and with which I have lived," admitted Wilhelm Grimm many years later, but these possessions seemed to be far away. "It is as if centuries had passed," he echoed Chateaubriand.[33] What could be gathered up, however, were physical fragments: the white post, the red fence. "I wish I had written what I remembered, what the rooms and houses, the clothes etc. were like," elaborated an empty-handed Wilhelm to his brother some years later, in 1809.[34] An orderly inventory of material objects of the household would have enabled the recollection of the past. Memory and materiality reinforced each other.

Memories of the French revolutionary wars, too, were marked by the material debris they left behind. Ludwig Emil Grimm, a younger brother who illustrated many of Jacob and Wilhelm's fairy tales, recalled the military campaigns of the year 1796: columns of soldiers "passed repeatedly through, first French, then Austrian, Dutch, Prussian, Mainzer, and Hessian." As they marched through town, soldiers hawked the goods they had stolen along the way: "the finest tableware, silver, books, porcelain, cups, draperies, and a thousand other things." The French set up the camp right outside Steinau: they requisitioned hay for their horses and snatched household goods, "chairs, benches, and such," to feed their fires. At night, the younger Grimm remembered looking out the window: "we could see hundreds of camp fires burning in the enclosed meadow and in our bee garden."[35] The precise details of the political upheaval are rendered by the material disorder brought in its wake. Hundreds of households have been plundered and fires blaze on the meadows. Even the Grimms' cherished *Biengarten* is charred by burns.

Ten years later fires could once again be spotted along the rolling meadows of the Hessian highlands. "In the evenings last October, I watched the French camp fires with considerable alarm," remembered Wilhelm Grimm about the disastrous military campaigns in 1806. The very next morning the hometown that had been so familiar appeared to be a foreign place: "strange people, strange customs, strange, loudly spoken voices on the streets and sidewalks."[36] In this case, it is not familiar things ("books, porcelain, cups") put out of place but rather extraneous elements ("strange people, strange customs") thrown in that created the promiscuous jumble. Nonetheless the disconcerting effect is much the same. Either way, the movement of history could be identified by unwelcome admixtures.

Even during the last stages of the victorious campaign against Napoleon, which took place in 1813–14, after nearly another ten years had passed, there was no mistaking the physical disorder that the revolutionary wars had left behind. As a volunteer in the patriotic Landwehr regiments, Jacob Grimm crossed the Rhine and marched through the French countryside devastated by war: "In most villages, the windows and doors are smashed or latched and the farmers have run away," he reported. "The day before yesterday," Jacob recalled seeing a little girl amidst the ruins: She was "sitting and crying for her mother who had run away, who knows where." A disheveled company of abandoned souls offered the lonely child some measure of comfort; a Spanish priest, on his way back home, lovingly kissed the portrait of Ferdinand embossed on a lucky coin; and a Bohemian reservist, a tailor by trade, told the long story of how he come to be an unlucky soldier in a faraway country.[37] This sounds like the beginning of a Grimm fairy tale, but it is a true story of the aftermath of the revolution.

This odd scene reveals the work of memory in the context of overwhelming loss. The abandoned child, the refugee priest, the Bohemian soldier—each element in this French village is out of place because it is left behind or stranded or foreign. But Grimm also noticed occasional gestures which relieved the picture of homelessness. The priest's devotion and the tailor's tale are small-scale enactments of belonging. Again and again, in this quarter-century of war and revolution, when the Grimms looked out and saw stragglers and strangers, they also stumbled across bits and pieces of custom and devotion. Wilhelm too gathered up stories and incidents. One night in winter 1814 on guard duty at home in Kassel, he heard a folktale told by a fellow comrade who was killed the very next day. Once again, the cultural shell of an entire lifetime is torn away, and all that is left is a single fragment, a story. "It is one of the best, about the birds which a blind man hears talking and which disclose to him a healing potion."[38]

Around the same time, Russian soldiers bivouacked in Kassel, and celebrating the new year 1814 with traditional songs and dances, caught Wilhelm's eye: "It was really cold, and a snow storm had forced everyone else inside their homes: that is the power of national tradition."[39] That the Russians are not at home but still sing and dance indicated to Wilhelm the collective, redeeming power of everyday customs which made it possible to reconstruct a provisional home. Folk tales, dances, and songs endured even as political forces have dispersed the communities of which they originally formed a part. Stories about home and repatriation gave them added force.

Personal tribulations and political disorder left the Grimms unsettled. They were extraordinarily sensitive to how the great forces of war and revolution had dispersed so many people from their homes and had left so many places out of joint. Again and again, the brothers searched for a stable home, which corresponded not only to their private needs for order and security but also, as Jack Zipes argues, their anxious "concern for the welfare of Germany disturbed by war and French occupation."[40] "My wish for me and for us is a small city of 2,000, 3,000 people where we could remain," wrote Jacob to his brother Wilhelm in June 1809. "Oh, if only God could provide peace . . . If only the misfortune would stop just once."[41] Now and then Jacob saw such an undisturbed place. For a brief moment it was on the road to Paris, in March 1814: "This road to Burgundy makes me feel good again," Jacob assured Wilhelm; "it looked so peaceful, neither dead horses, nor burned out homes, nor Cossacks, but curious villagers, with weavers and spinners, a whole bunch of mothers and children, and farmers planting in the fields."[42] This village was precisely the revered place from which the Grimms and so many other refugees have been expelled and to which they hoped to return.

Whether there could be a proper return to Steinau or other restful places like the village in Burgundy was unlikely, either for the Grimms or for the other travelers, the Spanish priest or the Bohemian tailor or the orphaned girl whom they met on the road. One of the striking things about the tales that the Grimms anthologized is the sheer movement of people: soldiers, who have been scattered by the Napoleonic wars, but also tailors and other apprentices who must make their way in a free-market economy.[43] The upheaval of the French Revolution continues, and unsettlement is the primary register by which society is surveyed: this is the background against which the Grimms think about their own lives and cast their characters, and also against which poets such as Joseph von Eichendorff composed their melancholy verses or novelists such as Balzac set their traveling characters. Nonetheless, it was possible to pick up fragments that had once joined the former wholes; this had been the task to which John Clare appointed himself. For the Grimms, the "white stone post," the tailor's story, and the Russian songs were odds and ends that could be collected and preserved in compensation for the losses that had been incurred. Keenly aware of how people cultivated a link to their homes by singing songs and telling tales, the Grimms avidly collected the bits that war and revolution had scattered about. Like so many young Germans of their generation, the two brothers energetically visited "junkmen and antique dealers" and spent their last pennies "on books and copper etchings."[44] At the same time, they began to collect folk tales and folk customs. In the introduction to the first edition of their famous collection of fairy tales, *Kinder- und Hausmaerchen* (1812), the Grimms recounted the original act of violence that was the antecedent to their activity: "what belongs to children has always been torn out of their hands." The belongings could be partially restored to Germany's dispossessed children, the Grimms insisted, as long as the tales were written down "as purely as possible" and not refined by culture or fashion.[45] The nation was first recognized in the parts that were broken, torn, lost; specifically national activity, therefore, was first and foremost a matter of gathering up, preserving, cataloging, a busy production which gave definition and substance to the envisaged nation.

The Grimms compared the stories they transcribed to small shafts of grass that had been protected by hedges and bushes after storms had flattened a field of crops.[46] As they were tucked away in hidden places, the collector had to bend down and get close to the ground. With words similar to John Clare's, Jacob described the method: "quietly pick up the leaves and carefully bend back the twigs, so as not to disturb the *Volk* and to furtively glimpse this small, rare part of nature, smelling like fallen leaves, meadow grass, and fresh rain." The hedges recalled the wondrous explorations of childhood; Grimm himself compared the collector's method to the "innocent delight when children, playing in the moor and the heath, come across a little bird in its nest"[47] As children, both Wilhelm and Jacob had tramped the meadows and fields around Steinau, gathering up "insects, butterflies, and the like" to arrange and sketch them at home.[48] But collecting folktales was not simply a continuation of childhood habits. What had intervened was the storm that had flattened the meadows, destroying the self-evident nature of the rural place and making it instead something fragile and vulnerable, collectible and representable in the second-hand ways of anthologies, histories, and poetry. Likewise, Clare only rediscovered the collectibles of the rural margins after his native Helpston had been enclosed. The very consciousness of cultural remains under the hedges was thus another consequence of the storm.

Although careful work could bring a few artifacts to light, it was generally the case that national treasure was hard to find and easily trampled. The Grimms as collectors seemed to be back in their beloved bee garden in Steinau, retracing the explorations of their childhood, but, with the alertness of new knowledge about the breakability of the world gained since that time, also anxiously watching over the "red iron fence" for the marauding armies of 1796 and 1806 as they scurried about recording long lost tales. And it was not simply the wars of revolution; surveyors, who adjusted property lines throughout the eighteenth and nineteenth centuries, road builders, and other state-sponsored improvers flattened fields as surely as any summer's storm or soldiers' march, wiping away the lifeways that still prospered in the name of state-sponsored economic progress. Folksongs, a few books, and "these innocent fairy tales" were all that remained. And even these survived only in what might be considered the hedges of ordinary life: "around the fireplace, the kitchen stove, the cellar stairs." These out-of-the-way places were repositories of history, they contained scraps of local customs, sayings, songs, and recipes which gathered in the tangles of underbrush.

What kitchens and cellars were to the village, Hessen was to Germany. "It is in the hill country, and in isolated valleys, that an undecayed, authentic sensibility can still be found, in narrow little villages to which few paths lead, and no roads," the Grimms asserted. These coordinates put emphasis on "still" and thus on the menace of processes that would condemn things to be "no longer." What threatened the "old customs" were "roads" as opposed to "paths," newly built highways of economic progress and particularly of the "false Enlightenment," with its disdain for tradition.[49] In addition to Hessen, a few other places still preserved the past: "Swabia, Bavaria, Franconia, Saxony, Thüringen," the Grimms allowed, but not Prussia, which was associated with the standardizing projects of Enlightenment reformers and French revolutionaries.[50] The enthusiasm of lawmakers to improve and set norms and their impatience with local and ordinary customs mortally threatened Germany's heritage. "Here," concluded Wilhelm Grimm, "almost everything has been knocked down: the castles and ruins along the Rhine are also supposed to be torn down."[51] What is striking in the Grimms' view is not so much the rumors, but the prominence of elements past and present that produce the evidence of cultural loss and the drama of national repossession.

Although the Grimms were never explicit about the historical forces at work, the trend was clear. Casual indifference and particularly "empty splendor" combined to destroy the "secret places in house and garden." Contemporaries surely understood this "empty splendor" as a reference to the merely fashionable nature of the unfettered capitalist economy (in this period, "fashion" seems to function for the still unfamiliar word "capitalism"). Moreover, repeated references to hedges and to the modern things that threatened them, that is, railroads and highways, confirm that what the Grimms had in mind was a process of economic modernization which was as destructive as the deleterious effects of French occupation and the plunder of military campaigns. After all, it was the new commercial class that turned land into a common commodity that was to be refined and improved. Carrying out improvements, investors cut down hedges, tore down old houses, and built highways to connect nearby markets. Markets, newspapers, and railroads constituted the emerging public sphere, while village storytellers were "becoming ever more rare."[52] To be sure, bits and pieces of old customs could still be founded in the underbrush and in attics, and in isolated villages, but the work of collecting had to proceed quickly, the Grimms urged, before "total decomposition ensues."[53] This sense of the historical moment reveals how the Grimms, too, were wholly reliant on newly received ideas of periodicity that presupposed dramatic breaks between now and then. Thinking of the nation in terms of loss rather than rediscovery, they were rather different antiquarians than the Boisserées. It is difficult to imagine the Grimms happily steaming down the Rhine or railroading along its banks. By the same token, the national itinerary of the Boisserées was much better marked and less digressive than the local, haphazard circuits of the Grimms. Like the Boisserées, the brothers Grimm postulated an underlying unity to Germany, despite its political and religious fragmentation, but in their view this unity was much more tentative, more remote in time and space, and more imperiled by modern development. The Grimms were also more apt to celebrate ordinary people who, in the words of George Williamson, "suddenly seemed to be the repository of a noble religion rather than mindless superstition."[54]

The Grimms, like Cobbett and Clare, believed that they stood at the edge of a great divide, and that if attempts were not immediately carried out to "save what could be saved" the old customs and traditions would be completely destroyed.[55] The events of the French Revolution served to dramatize the violence of historical change. Not to embark on a program of preservation was to clear the way for the surveyors, the highways, and "empty splendor" of modern fashion. And for all the difficulties involved in gathering up and understanding "old customs," the relics offered enormous wealth. Protected underneath the hedges, "the individual shafts of grass" grew "ripe and full" and once harvested they provided sustenance throughout the long winter and valuable seeds for the future.[56]

The sustenance was, of course, cultural. "In these popular stories," the Grimms asserted, "is concealed the pure and primitive mythology of the old Germans, which has been considered as lost for ever." Straight from "the mouths of German peasants," the tales are "of the highest Northern antiquity," summed up the Grimms' English translator.[57] Passed on by oral tradition, the fairy tales were taken to be unchanged over the centuries. To illustrate the point, the Grimms introduced readers to one of their best informants, Frau Viehmann from the village of Niederzwehrn, near Kassel. Pointedly described as "still robust," Viehmann "preserves these old legends firmly in her memory." She narrates "totally lively and completely free," and "never changes anything materially."[58] Faithful iteration over the centuries rather than improvisation and adulteration had left the folk tales "innocent," that is, "purely German with nothing borrowed."[59] That modern scholarship has disproved the Grimms' claim for the rustic, Germanic origins of the folktales in no way challenges the observation that the brothers and their readers considered the stories to be recovered treasures.

The Grimms insisted on preserving the old folkways as they found them. They conceded that the stories and legends were no longer part of the larger society, even if they formed part of the living tradition of the villages where they had been found, and that efforts to translate them into more accessible, written forms could ruin them. On the one hand, the folktales formed a direct link to a much older past, which justified their collection, preservation, and dissemination. On the other hand, they had to be accepted as broken artifacts that could no longer be restored whole. They expressed both the richness of the past and its incommensurability with the present; ruins gave depth to national history, but withheld an immediate link to it. The "strange, noble creatures" that Jacob imagined his tales to be appeared as eloquent expressions both of the grandeur and of the alienation of the past.[60]

Any effort to rework the tales, the Grimms claimed, would destroy their "simplicity, innocence, and unadorned purity" and tear them from the places to which they belonged. They repudiated entirely the efforts of Romantic writers such as Achim von Arnim and Clemens Brentano to translate folktales into contemporary language, as if past and present were roughly commensurable, even as they honored the growing interest in collecting the tales in the first place. "They don't want to know anything about careful historical research," complained Jacob to Wilhelm already in 1809; "they don't let the old stand as the old, but want to graft it in our times, where it does not belong, to be cherished by an increasingly fatigued group of admirers." Literary adornment was basically an acquiescence to fashion. It only served the passing aesthetic sensibilities of editors but could never revive "the splendor of old poetry." "Only historically can it be appreciated undisturbed." Folk tales were like wild animals, Jacob added. If they were transported to the present they would lose their enchanted nature and simply walk around in a circle.[61] The wildness of customs was preserved only by keeping them at a distance, *in situ,* in the past. The past was the place where the wild animals roamed.

Just as bad as adorning or translating folk customs was trying to choose particularly worthy exemplars out of material culture and exhibiting them apart. The Grimms claimed that the fullness of the past could only be apprehended in its indiscriminate recovery. In this sense they would have accepted the gist if not the tone of Boisserée's haughty description of their method as "cult of the trivial." Stories had to transcribed exactly, not according to contemporary literary models.[62] Indeed, the Grimms freely admitted collecting just about everything that belonged to "the common man," "whether their content is happy or sad, instructive or frivolous . . . whether they are expressed in the meanest phrases or in rhyming prose, whether they conform to the history we know from books, or completely contradict it and therefore appear quite impure." The more unpretentious (because less exemplary) the prose the richer its meanings, they added parenthetically.[63] The Grimms set the customs of the "common man" and the unpretentious quality of his prose against "book learning," and raised the possibility of forms of vernacular knowledge that were really quite different from epistemological models current at the time. In so doing, they assumed an insistently historicist stance which admitted to the variety of fully developed folk cultures and resisted universal notions of progress. And it is precisely the ordinary pieces of the past which serve to deauthorize the normative judgments of the present. As Helmut Jendreiek concluded in his comparative study of Hegel and Jacob Grimm: "Hegel values the general and the idea as the absolute that reveals itself in the spirit of the people; Jacob Grimm the pure facticity of the spirit. The historical unity of humanity is represented by Hegel as a gradually staged, dialectically differentiated sequence," much like

Goethe's view of art history, whereas Grimm saw a "value-free plurality" and a "many-sided simultaneity."[64]

The Grimms' distinctive approach was that the past could not be translated into a contemporary vernacular by literary editorship; it could only be studied through material remnants. By insisting on the preservation and protection of the folktales from modern embellishments, the Grimms underscored the different, strange character of their artifacts. Of course, as modern scholarship has shown, both Jacob and Wilhelm did in fact edit the tales. By comparing the various published editions after 1812 with one another and with handwritten transcriptions taken in the field some years earlier (manuscripts recovered only in 1920), it is clear that the Grimms both edited and augmented—often at considerable length—the texts to make them more familiar, more rhythmic, and easier to read out loud. "They eliminated erotic and sexual elements that might be offensive to middle-class morality, added numerous Christian expressions and references, emphasized specific role models for male and female protagonists according to the dominant patriarchal code of that time, and endowed many of the tales with a 'homey' or *biedermeier* flavor by the use of diminutives, quaint expressions, and cute descriptions."[65]

By making the tales more accessible to a wide readership, the Grimms did exactly what they urged Romantic authors not to do. Yet the Grimms were careful to rewrite their fairy tales in a clean, economic prose and to stick to a straightforward story line. They thereby avoided the complexity and heavy symbolism which Romantics such as Brentano, Tieck, or Wackenroder had imposed on similar tales. Although the Grimms edited out many rough-speaking and social-critical aspects, the stories described a familiar world of commoners: soldiers, tailors, and other journeymen who struggled by their own industry to make their way in an increasingly unregulated bourgeois society. The Grimms also included in the texts a variety of household tips, village sayings, folk songs, and the like, giving them a vernacular quality at odds with "book-learning" or classical models. The stories therefore created a cultural space for a German national vernacular. Even before publication, the Grimms acknowledged the particulars of the readership they had in mind: "Step by step we have assembled quite a rich collection," wrote Wilhelm in 1812, "and we intend to simply publish it as an ordinary book of the people without any ribbons or gilt edges."[66]

With each new edition, the Grimms drew their nationally self-conscious, middle-class audience closer and closer, excising the academic apparatus, preparing more popular texts, and finally, just in time for Christmas, editing a collection suitable for children. Although neither the first volume, published in 1812 in an edition of 900 copies, nor the second volume, which came out three years later in an edition of 1,100, made much of an impact, a complete second edition followed in 1819 and an English translation appeared in 1823. Success came quickly after the Grimms prepared the unannotated *Kleine Ausgabe,* which contained a selection of fifty of the *Grosse Ausgabe*'s two hundred tales, a handy, canonizing volume that included best-known tales such as "Cinderella," "Snow White," "Sleeping Beauty," and "Little Red Riding Hood." Republished ten times between 1825 and 1858, the *Kleine Ausgabe* installed itself as fixture on the bookshelves of middle-class families; two million copies were in circulation in a German-speaking realm of some fifty million people. At the end of the nineteenth century, the tales were firmly established on the public school syllabus, almost universally praised by educators as the primary texts of national tradition.[67] "By the beginning of the twentieth century," concludes Jack Zipes, "the *Children's and Household Tales* was second only to the Bible as a best-seller in Germany."[68] In a few decades, the Grimms had literally fashioned a household inventory that included what was taken to be among the most ancient and enduring artifacts of the German nation.

The Grimms offered a distinctly German past to a particular German audience. By stressing the unadulterated essence and homegrown origin of the stories, they indicated that these artifacts were not commensurate with Europe's other national traditions or with its classical heritage. The local knowledge they championed formed the foundations of a specifically national tradition that resisted common cultural denominators. The audience, too, was defined in very particular terms: locals rather than cosmopolitans, commoners rather than aristocrats, readers in the nursery rather than in the schoolhouse, women and children as well as men. It is important to remember that the most popular tales introduced a cast of sympathetic lower- and middle-class characters; they were appealing precisely because they could be read as commentaries on the social and economic situation of the post-Napoleonic period. Despite the international success of the fairytales, they played a special role in nineteenth-century Germany, where they constituted the equivalent of national literature. The Grimms endowed their texts with magical and wild qualities which had the effect of enhancing the particularities of Germany's past and thus rescuing it from the stream of universal history. The tales attracted readers because they appealed to new forms of cultural identification based on exclusive difference rooted in the past. In this sense the Grimms were deeply indebted to the historicist tradition of Friedrich Karl von Savigny and Johann Gottfried Herder, and insisted on constructing identity around points of difference rather than correspondence.

The cultural specificity of texts quickly became more elaborate. By the end of the nineteenth century, the Grimms' native Hessen was transformed into "Wonderland Hessen." Readers and especially the Marburger painter Otto Ubbelohde, who illustrated one of the most famous editions of the tales at the beginning of the twentieth century, placed the stories firmly in the Hessian landscape.[69] To this day, thousands of tourists come to Marburg, Hameln, and other towns, quite consciously with the Grimms' fairy tales in mind, in order to see "authentic" Germany.

That the attic, the hedge, and the Hessian highlands suddenly came into view as repositories of the past at the beginning of the nineteenth century attested to a melancholic rendition of history. For the Grimms as for Cobbett and Clare, history was not a comprehensive process best approached from the highly developed center, but rather a differentiated process of movement, mixing, and destruction, which necessitated a new method of historical recovery. In the first place, history acquired unprecedented depth, not merely because contemporary scholars pushed back the origins of Christian and non-Christian settlements far into prehistory, but also because of a new appreciation for the variety of social formations. This mottledness provided a much more differentiated and in some ways recuperative conception of European developments. However, the more concrete operation of recovering past particularities was fraught with difficulty. With depth, history also became opaque: cultural artifacts were out of place, lost, mixed with impurities. They could be recovered as fragments, but not as wholes. Well aware of the intransparency of time, Thomas Carlyle laid out the challenge for the historiographer of his age in an 1833 essay: "Of the thing now gone silent, named Past, which was once Present, and loud enough, how much do we know? Our 'Letter of Instructions' comes to us in the saddest fate; falsified, blotted out, torn, lost and but a shred of it in existence; this too so difficult to read or spell."[70] This recognition demanded an empathetic hermeneutic method that was attuned to both the taciturnity and strangeness of material remains.[71] It was precisely this predicament that invited historians and poets to assume a creative, mediating role in assigning meanings to the past. Their retrieval of the past was primarily textual—*Rural Rides,* "To a Fallen Elm," *Kinder- und Hausmaerchen*—and cast readers off on time journeys in all directions.

The fragment expressed the imperfectibility of access to the past, but it also indicated the variety of lifeworlds that had once existed. Previously authoritative homologies between present and past, center and periphery, and harmonious wholes and fragmentary parts broke down as new nonlinear conceptions of time reconfigured space. The things that were out-of-the-way and out-of-place acquired value and potentiality. In this conception, history increasingly worked the disjoints as well as the joints of time, which made it at once melancholy in the appreciation of unknowable loss and unending transformation, and redemptive in its attention to broken parts, festering wounds, lost exiles, and the "moorhen's nest" in the hedge.

CHAPTER FIVE

Household Fairies

Over the course of the nineteenth century, domestic spaces came to define the character of the nation. The Grimms insisted that it was the tales and wares of the household that revealed historical and cultural differences. The folklorists who searched remote homes in rustic locations gave special status to village women, whose "inward looking sensibility" and household economy of scrimping, saving, and storing made them ideal informants. Their hearths, and the hearths around which these writers imagined their readers, made the home central to the transmission of national culture.[1] This was by no means a commonly accepted idea, as the contemptuous dismissal of the attic junk by the Boisserées indicates, but it was gaining authority. "To form a correct opinion of the English character," the American Irving Washington advised in the 1840s, the prospective traveler "must go forth into the country; he must sojourn in villages and hamlets; he must visit castles, farm houses, cottages; he must wander through parks and gardens; along hedges and green lanes; he must loiter about country churches, attend wakes and fairs and other rural festivals, and cope with the people in all their conditions, and all their habits and humours."[2] The demand to "cope with the people in all their conditions" in order to gain knowledge of national character invigorated vernacular literary genres: travelogues such those collected in Washington's *Sketch-Book;* folktales modeled on the Grimms'; an archeology of Pompeii's "private lives" "just as they were"; and also autobiographies, memoirs, and scrapbooks. The revalorization of domestic space also corresponded to the rearrangement of that space. The historical analysis of the household (like the collecting activity of the Grimms) unfolded alongside an increasingly historically-minded arrangement of the household (in which the Grimms' fairy tales were exchanged as gifts, read aloud, and treasured). The growing literary and historical value awarded to autobiographies (their publication, their citation) reflected the inclination to think about the individual self in historical and developmental terms (the impulse to reflect on and write about a lifetime). Increasingly, keeping house in the nineteenth century meant organizing family celebrations and cultivating family memories.

The sharpened consciousness of history over the course of the nineteenth century did not just bring into view the idea of revolution in public affairs but widened the scope of the study of historical subjects to include members of the household *and,* at the same time, encouraged people to think of themselves as historical subjects in the realm of the household. This amounted to a profound reorganization of cultural life. Henceforth families would not only recognize themselves as cultural agents and cultivate particular cultural identities, but value the stories and souvenirs of their lives. The historicization of private life went hand-in-hand with the celebration of home and the cultivation of domesticity that took place on both sides of the Atlantic. To appreciate the wide scope of this nineteenth-century transformation, I have set most of the domestic scenes for this chapter in the United States, which participated in the modern temporalities that I have described in ways that dispute American exceptionalism. Americans took up the work of memory as assiduously as did Europeans because the American Revolution came to correspond to the French Revolution, because dramatic mobility set unprecedented numbers of Americans on the road in the early 1800s, and because American republicanism and its westward conquests exposed a fundamental break with the colonial era and led to the nearly complete destruction of Native American cultures. Fallen Timbers, a decisive battle against the Indians in 1794 which marked out a historic divide between "back" East and "out" West, is an example of violent breaks in the American present around 1800. Dispossession is an American story too, and it justifies the placement of the United States in the trans-Atlantic realm under exploration here.

A telling example of the household context of historical consciousness in the early republic comes from Joan Hedrick's excellent biography of Harriet Beecher Stowe, the abolitionist and writer. She introduces a parlor scene in which the Beechers have just moved west from Hartford, Connecticut, to Cincinnati, Ohio, in the year 1832. The family members "had been waiting anxiously for the first news from the East," and it was twenty-one-year-old Harriet "who made sure that someone inquired daily at the post office." Once the long awaited letter arrived from her sister Mary Beecher Perkins, who had remained in Hartford, Harriet read the news aloud as the Ohio Beechers gathered together in "a kind of reunion with the family and friends left behind."[3]

The epistolary reunion in Cincinnati is remarkable for the penetration into the household of larger processes such as westward movement, which in turn creates entities such as "the East" and "the West." A number of events created a vast new (although not empty) space in which American destiny could be imagined: General Anthony Wayne's victory over the confederated Indian tribes at Fallen Timbers, near Lake Eire, in 1794; the Louisiana Purchase in 1803 and the first exploratory expeditions westwards up the Missouri River that followed; as well as the defeat of the British in the War of 1812 and the first 160-acre bounties established for veterans in its aftermath. It was at the turn of the nineteenth century that large-scale movement west first took place. Americans, even in colonial New England, had not been sedentary, but never before did so many young people strike out, so much so that the counterpart to the new boom towns on the frontier such as Cincinnati were neglected old places in Vermont, New Hampshire, and Massachusetts.[4] More Americans than ever before left home for the much richer agricultural territories of the western frontier, first to "the old Northwest" of Ohio, Indiana, and Illinois, then across the Mississippi to the western plains, and they moved with awareness of the broader historical movement in which they were participating.[5] History was recorded in terms of leaving old homes and building new ones. The letters back and forth from the East and the West reflected on this movement: on the advantages of migration; on the new, sometimes surprising mixtures of settlers, many from Europe; and on the familiar wear of regional cultures left behind. "Writing increasingly in western parlors," Hedrick points out, "Americans on the move recorded their growing awareness of a national culture." In fact, nineteenth-century novels were often "letters to the nation," quite deliberate attempts to encourage westward migration and promote a new amplitude to the idea of the republic; "the populace read them to see reflected back just who they were, in all their regional variety."[6] *Godey's Lady's Book,* with 150,000 subscribers the most popular magazine in the world on the eve of the Civil War, catered to this extraordinarily inquisitive constituency of mobile settlers. It advised on and made visible their collective efforts at national housekeeping, not least by celebrating Thanksgiving and urging that this household event become a national holiday. To be sure, many factors worked to promote the shared space of literary republicanism, including the national cohesion of the United States themselves and increasingly dense networks of communication and transportation. Nonetheless, a common designation of the historical process at work—westward movement and the making of the nation—pulled together a like-minded readership that differentiated between old houses and new homesteads. And just as literary production elaborated the idea of empire's new frontier along the Ohio or Missouri River, it also worked the theme of an increasingly old-fashioned New England, which was imagined more and more wistfully as a place of abandoned farms, weed-grown graveyards, and crumbling houses. To put it a bit simply, the people who wrote each other letters (and read novels as letters) knew where to find each other, not just with a knowable geographical address but also on a legible historical and national map. The settlers were not lost, even if they (unlike the wealthy Beechers in Cincinnati) would never see old friends and family again. In Europe, migration to the United States or the industrial cities proceeded in the same way: new experiences could be assimilated in a common historical frame (such as "Emigration to America" or the "Industrial Revolution"), which encouraged people to exchange news, read realist novels, and take greater interest in each other.[7] Households were places to look for the effects of these immense changes.

The second striking aspect about the Beechers' parlor in Cincinnati is the rich domestic setting of cultural activity. Letters such as the one written by Mary Beecher Perkins were anxiously awaited and read aloud, usually in the parlors among "family, friends, boarders, and servants." And the letters themselves opened with a description of a similar scene. Hedrick explains that correspondents "often peopled their first paragraph with those among whom they sat: 'I am seated upon one side of the table in our parlour Ann upon the other, Mary between us darning a pair of stockings with her little basket before her, Mother is the other side of Ann making piping for her frock,' begins an especially full catalogue" of Harriet Beecher's; "Sarah is sitting on one side of the fire place knitting Uncle is in the rocking chair the other side Sarah has gone to bed Paddy & Frederick are in bed little George is asleep in the cradle in one corner of the room." These introductions were often followed by detailed descriptions of the parlor itself and the "trifles" collected in it. Not only did this "'graphic sketch,' as Harriet put it in requesting a similar one from her brother," describe the activities and rituals of the household, and the family gatherings that accompanied their production and reception, but it enhanced those rituals.[8] Letters were thus not simple depictions of family circles; correspondence played a central role in strengthening their associations and memories. Letters themselves became part of family heritage: requested, anticipated, read aloud, and answered; they were also collected, tied with ribbons, and put away in boxes and drawers for safekeeping. The piping that "Mother" was making in the Cincinnati parlor also brings to mind "scrap bags," the pieces of old pattern cuttings that so many nineteenth-century women saved up, brought along on the journey west, exchanged with the sisters, daughters, or friends they had left behind, and eventually stitched together as the souvenir patches of a new commemorative quilt. The "trifles" in Harriet's letter refer to the small mementoes, portraits, and later photographs that accumulated on the "what nots," étagères, corner shelves, mantelpieces, and hanging cabinets of nineteenth-century parlors. These scraps of memory, whether in the form of a letter, a quilt patch, or a souvenir photograph, gained value as families separated. Things were accumulated on the journey west, perhaps not in sheer number, since the travel was long and arduous, but in sentimental weight. The rituals of correspondence indicate a new sensibility about things which turned family parlors into "memory palaces."[9]

In the Beecher household the exchange of news and impressions circulated knowledge about large-scale historical processes such as westward migration or the aging of New England places; indeed, these "letters to the nation" partly constituted those processes. And further, the correspondence reflected the household's deliberate effort to produce and remember its own history, and to think of its movement across space and through time in terms of separation, reunion, and loss. The vernacular histories under scrutiny in this chapter are personal versions of the commonly shared substance of public history, and they are also formal historical renditions of entirely private lives. These latter accounts are quite remarkable. The general course of history, which had severed the past from the present, had the additional and profound consequence of altering the continuity of private life. In this way it is possible to conceive of the enlargement of private space by means of the discontinuities of collective history. In modern times, private and public, household and nation, constituted each other.

The widespread recognition of historical change was a fundamental and novel experience, one which characterized the modern age. Given the ideological constitution of public life in the years after 1789, and the massive mobilization that came with the revolutionary wars, contemporaries increasingly came to cast their lives in historical scripts. For the first time, wrote Georg Lukacs about the French Revolution, "the masses no longer have the impression of a 'natural occurrence.'"[10] After the revolution, contemporaries continued to see historical, not natural forces at work, and thus subscribed to notions of "new time" which gained currency and definition in the early nineteenth-century decades of industrial development. The United States shared in this historical rendering of the world as much as Europe. It was a nineteenth-century American commonplace to reflect on the intrusion of the new. Here is what Francis Underwood wrote about the end of "good old colony times" in 1893.[11]

> The loss of Canada by the French; the attainment of independence by the United States; the French Revolution; the meteoric career of Bonaparte—Marengo, Jena, Austerlitz, Borodino, Waterloo, St. Helena; the birth of literature and philosophy in Germany; in Great Britain the appearance of Johnson, Burns, Coleridge, Scott, Byron, Keats, Wordsworth, Tennyson, and Browning; a dawning literature in America; the era of gas, railways, steamships, telegraphs, evolution, the spectroscope, bacteriology; the civil War in

> the United States, with all that followed; the sudden military prominence of Germany; so much, and more, past all enumeration, in the space of two lives!

This is quite a transnational inventory. What distinguished early republicans, agrees Joyce Appleby, was a "heightened awareness of 'firstness,'" which manifested itself not only in the steamboats, national elections, and public land sales, but in the particularly individual perspective from which these home-leavers, letter-writers, and occasional autobiographers recorded historical transformation.[12]

The broad and unmistakable public consciousness about the marauding movement of history after the turn of the nineteenth century had the effect of creating a common denomination to individual experiences so that people could recognize a general cause behind particular effects. This frames the moment when Wordsworth and the ferryman shared news about Robespierre at Rampside: they were both swept up in the same history and approached each other as contemporaries. But this "singularization of history" also had the effect of making socially meaningful very different experiences, which were no longer discounted as parochial happenings, but recounted as local renditions of understandable and pertinent historical transformations. Experiences and opinions differed even as they were absorbed in a common frame of meaning. The result was an extraordinary production and consumption of quite individual interpretations of general history. For this reason, the age of history was insistently autobiographical. "Since the interesting era of the French Revolution," commented one British observer in 1824, "the people of these Kingdoms have been an inquisitive, prying, doubting, and reading people . . . Their feelings received then an extraordinary impetus."[13] Writing at the same time, William Hazlitt agreed.

> The change in the belles-lettres was as complete, and to many persons as startling, as the change in politics, with which it went

> hand in hand . . . All the common-place figures of poetry, tropes, allegories, personifications, with the whole heathen mythology, were instantly discarded; a classical allusion was considered as a piece of antiquated foppery; capital letters were no more allowed in print, than letters-patent of nobility were permitted in real life; kings and queens were dethroned from their rank and station in legitimate tragedy or epic poetry, as they were decapitated elsewhere.[14]

As individual lives became socially poignant, and thus interesting, highly subjective genres such as memoirs, autobiographies, and biographies flourished. This autobiographical impulse no longer derived from the need to legitimize the name or to honor the reputation of the family, as had been predominantly the case in the early modern period.[15] By the beginning of the nineteenth century, historical ruptures interfered more and more violently with the continuities of family genealogy by which autobiographers had hitherto introduced themselves and established their presence via the past. Modern autobiographies typically began not with the family lineage but with personal experience. And they proceeded by recounting personal development and change.[16] It was with "extravagant self-consciousness" that nineteenth-century people began to write up the particulars of their own lives.[17] Chateaubriand's memoirs, for example, unfolded as a series of personal exilings. At least for the generation born into the revolutionary period, Thomas Nipperdey's magnificent opening line to his history of Germany applies: "in the beginning there was Napoleon." Again and again, reminiscences opened with the arrival of soldiers. "In my mind's eye I still see French troops gathered to march against Austria in 1805," remembered Franz Xaver Freiherrn von Andlaw-Birseck.[18] It is significant that the trope outlasted the wars themselves; countless autobiographers tracked their own lives against the accumulation of historical, economic, or technological developments. Indeed, they spoke up for themselves because of what they had seen. "Such new and unheard-of things! Such change!" wrote Ernst Wilhelm Martius near the end of his *Memories from a Ninety-Year Life:* "hard to imagine that earlier lifetimes had encompassed such extraordinary changes."[19] "Totally," "such," "hardly"—this is the new punctuation to nineteenth-century autobiography. And there is no doubt that the impulse to write a personal rendition of witnessed history was matched by the desire to read about it. After 1800, biographies and autobiographies were among the most popular items produced by publishing houses and lent by libraries.

One efficient way to grasp the sudden interest in autobiography is to consider the memoirs of ordinary soldiers. It was only at the end of the eighteenth century that soldiers and sailors began to emerge as empathetic figures with whom readers might identify. Before then, soldiers were regarded as mercenaries, unlucky at best, criminal at worst, and subjected to a harsh and brutal life that was as remote as it was horrible to the great majority of literate Europeans. After the turn of the nineteenth century, however, massive wartime mobilization extended the reach of the army into many more families. The burdens that both civilians and soldiers shared during the continental wars as well as new notions of citizenship made the soldier into a more sympathetic figure, a representative of "everyman," and even a civic model to emulate. It was only after the Napoleonic Wars that the nation claimed the sacrifice of the ordinary soldier for commemorative purposes: in a May 1813 decree, for example, the king of Prussia, Friedrich Wilhelm III, ordered that every church install commemorative tablets on which were written the names of the men of the parish who had fallen. Little of this sensibility to patriotic feeling could be seen in a multinational empire such as Austria-Hungary, but the European trend was clear. As Hew Strachan summarizes, "society came to reflect the army as much as the army reflected society. Fashion aped military uniform," for example, and "soldiers were present at festivals and marriages, their presence gave authority to the proceedings"—think of Carl Maria von Weber's *Der Freischütz.* "Thus was the soldier's calling validated: he was no longer engaged in a trade, but fighting for a cause."[20] At the same time, the soldier accepted the possibility of his own death as sacrifice for the national homeland. To fall for the fatherland brought history into ordinary life, not simply because the number of dead were so high, but also in the way these deaths were claimed and accepted as intimate renditions of national causes.

Yet it would be a mistake to think of the literary and political enfranchisement of the ordinary soldier in national terms only. One reason the soldier was congenial was because he mirrored the life and suffering of so many contemporaries during this period of war and revolution, whether or not they were French or German or British, whether or not they bore arms. In a remarkable letter, Dorothea Schlegel described an encounter in August 1808 with soldiers on a market boat from Cologne to Koblenz. Frightened at first, she began to recognize the sons of fathers, the friends of neighbors. "You can imagine my feeling," she wrote to Sulpiz Boisserée, "when you let go of my hand yesterday, and I had to climb down into that hole, where I was greeted with the tobacco smoke from a half-dozen soldiers' pipes." For several hours, she sat quite still: I "pulled my hat deep over my face and pressed myself into the corner," and feeling sorry for herself, "everything that was dear to me and pained me rose up through my body in the boldest colors." Ashamed of her tears, however, she then "pulled herself together" and looked around: "And there sat a whole bank of the most honest-looking, good-hearted faces in French uniform across from me and to my side. They were Germans from the Rhineland who had served in the previous war against Austria and Prussia, were slightly wounded, had taken their leave, and were now returning to their various homes." This was the first time she actually saw the soldiers or talked to them, and in her melancholy state, Schlegel recognized her own faraway home in thinking about theirs. "Lots of brave, nice people," she declared, "not at all so bad when you get to know them." Now it was the "soldiers' poetry" that attracted her: "very astonishing portrayal of the motives and characters of each and every hero." Since these were Rhenish and Westphalian soldiers in French uniform, Schlegel was not looking at German nationalism. Nonetheless she sketched her fellow passengers sympathetically, and in her mind's eye gave them homes. In the long, wayward motions of this nineteenth-century war, how many people did not come to see soldiers in this way?[21]

Schlegel did not completely identify with the common people; her literary enfranchisement remained incomplete. When the hungry traveler asked the ship's cook for some food, she received "a big piece of very black bread," peasant fare she would not touch. What Schlegel really wanted were the "the very cute sandwiches with ham" which two women in the opposite corner enjoyed. Obviously famished, she did accept "a piece of quite good white bread" from a nearby cavalryman, but declined the bottle of brandy the soldiers passed around, which, in turn, kept her from pulling out her own. That would have been an "impertinence," "so I ate my bread dry." Nonetheless, Schlegel dropped her reserve when she fell into conversation with "a friendly infantryman." He recounted "how they starved near Jena, and at Austerlitz had nothing to eat or drink for thirty-six hours except snow . . . I said to him that he surely had lots of adventures to tell when he got home. Indeed, he said. Good and bad, I continued—more bad than good, he answered." Schlegel also reported to Boisserée about the sites along the Rhine she saw up on deck. Andernach, Rheineck, "Hammerstein with the wrecked castle; I love this wonderful shoreline more and more"—"my whole soul recognizes the valley of the Rhine as my fatherland!" But the accounts of her conversations in the cabins below interrupted these travel reports. As if making a discovery on par with the ruins, she returned to soldiers' stories, "good and bad."[22]

For Schlegel's correspondents, who knew very well what Jena

and Austerlitz meant, the testimonies of the infantryman and his fellows had become compelling, parts in a larger story. And the parts would be told and retold again. Schlegel recounted her encounters in considerable detail; Boisserée did also (and included mouthfuls of dialect) after taking a market boat to Mainz seven years later, and a growing readership consumed the soldiers' stories which began to appear in print in the years after 1815. "The campaign in the Peninsula is the first in British history to be written up by a score or so literate men from the other ranks," writes Clive Emsley about Wellington's army in Spain in 1812–13; "the common man's participation in war was recognized as important by him and by his readers."[23] In the nineteenth century, then, it was not at all unusual for contemporaries to construct their own, quite idiosyncratic syllabi of readings, choosing from any number of different sources that now included John Green's *The Vicissitudes of a Soldier's Life* as well as the great Wellington's memoirs and the historian's fat book.[24]

The "good and bad" after which Schlegel inquired represented the irreducible personal evidence of a single soldier, which cannot be made to fit into a handy formulation about the meaning of the war. Although most of the soldiers' stories, like other autobiographical texts of this period, were formulaic, they still offered very personal testimony about departures from home, privation on the battle field, and the deaths of friends. They revealed the scars of historical displacement and validated those through the circle of readership. One of the reasons for the huge interest in biography and autobiography in this period is that these personal renditions encompassed private suffering; the life stories of writers inevitably reflected the life stories of readers in ways that more comprehensive accounts did not. "I show you the wrong side of events which history does not display," announced Chateaubriand about the third volume of his own memoirs: "history exhibits only the right side." "Memoirs have the advantage of presenting both surfaces of the texture: in this respect they depict the whole complexion of humanity better, by exposing, as in the tragedies of Shakespeare, low and exalted scenes."[25] For writers and readers alike, the ordinary self came to be interesting and spoke with eloquent authority as a result.

The German romantic writer, Adalbert Stifter, quite consciously counterposed the private work of memory with the public disruption of war. In "My Great-Grandfather's Briefcase," published in 1840, he introduced a soldier who after every battle wrote down his thoughts at night and then sealed each entry in an envelope as a kind of time capsule for the future. When opened many years later, these colloquial, first-hand accounts disputed official second-hand versions of the events that had transpired. Stifter's soldier had taken part in "heavy battles." "I distinguished myself" back then, he acknowledged, "but a little package later told me about my feelings at the time, that were much more telling than the decoration . . . By and by, I learned to distinguish virtue from praise, and intentions from consequences." With the figure of the old soldier, Stifter and his contemporaries came to recognize their own subject positions and their own alterity against the larger political frame. Although there is synchronization in Elizabeth Deed Ermarth's sense of "the connections between one character's present and another's, one person's experience and another's," all of which "reinforce the implication that all human activity in the scene takes place in the 'same' time and the 'same' world, and is part of the 'same' human nature," the general attentiveness that this definition implies enables other, deviant stories to be told and officially authorized accounts to be contested.[26] What Stifter labeled the "trivial" stories in his memory packets provided the evidence of experience that would otherwise have been overwhelmed by the "other, big history" written up and codified in "one thousand books."[27] They were the scraps of what Alf Lüdtke has called *Eigensinn,* the self-assertion of ordinary people, who render much more open-ended the meanings held out by historical events.[28] At the same time, the only reason Stifter's little stories existed is because they are upheld in a wider discursive field in which the bigger story of violence is written and circulated. There would have been no little stories without the self-aware recognition of the big story of historical change. Thus trivial stories, soldiers' stories, proliferated in dialogue with, and often enough in opposition to, the demands of patriotic duty or revolutionary politics.

In modernity, the self was intertwined with history and regarded itself as a historical formation, as Georg Lukacs famously clarified in his classic study, *The Historical Novel.* In contrast to "Swift, Voltaire and even Diderot," who "set their satirical novels in a 'never and nowhere' which nevertheless faithfully reflects the essential characteristics of contemporary England and France," Walter Scott and later Honoré de Balzac and the American James Fenimore Cooper, together with the characters introduced here, grasped "the specific qualities of their own age historically." Scott, in particular, made "great historical trends" tangible in "typically human terms" not only by introducing "middling" rather than heroic characters, but by moving them on the historical stage in a realistic manner. As the "great realist," Scott "recognizes that no civil war in history has been so violent as to turn the entire population without exception into fanatical partisans of one or other of the contending camps. Large sections of people have always stood between the camps with fluctuating sympathies now for this side, now for the other." This inner life of civil war is what makes Scott's characters such as Waverly so recognizable to readers, who themselves experienced revolution and war from the inside but not as heroes. What the European reader learned at the end of the revolutionary epoch was, Lukacs argued, that "similar upheavals are taking place all over the world." This, in turn, strengthened "the feeling first that there is such a thing as history, that it is an uninterrupted process of changes, and finally that it has a direct effect upon the life of every individual."[29] In other words, what Scott did was to interweave Stifter's "trivial stories" with "the other, big history." His novels are empathetic transcripts of social experience understood historically, which appeal through their verisimilitude: the close observation of type, epoch, and life and manners, and the attention to dialogue and individual motivation.[30] The little dramas of "the plight of individuals whose lives were caught up in an impersonal mechanism," as Marilyn Butler puts it, provided the key to Scott's success.[31] His stories most faithfully mirrored the extravagant self-absorption, the unchecked fears, and the persistent weakness of contemporaries in the postrevolutionary epoch. They offered illustrations in what James Chandler aptly terms "comparative contemporaneities," the fascinated interest in the disruption of lives "just as they were" amidst the disruption of one's own life in one's own time.[32] This viewpoint is what being a contemporary meant.

The animation of the ordinary through the historical was the premise for the astonishing success of the historical novel. Scott's popularity in Europe and America was enormous, and scores of writers considered themselves his followers. As James Smith Allen points out, French popular literature in the Romantic period was heavily historical, and complemented the historical themes that appeared in drama, verse, and painting. Popular culture became more historical and less folkloristic; it was more apt to strive for verisimilitude in a carefully crafted "here and now," and was proportionately less concerned with a parade of timeless, decontextualized heroes and saints.[33] The reach of this Romantic popular culture can, of course, be exaggerated, but its "pop cultural" quality, its appearance across various artistic genres, and its numerous imitators and flatterers in London, Paris, and Cooperstown, New York, indicated its unmistakable mass appeal. And as much as Walter Scott depicted the *vie privée* of his historical characters, thousands of private households of this historical age included among their possessions the works of Sir Walter Scott.[34]

It is the modern girl dressed in "the city fashion" who reads Scott, the fondly remembered Sylvie whom Gérard de Nerval's hero no longer recognizes when he wearies of stylish Paris and escapes to provincial Loisy, the place of his memories of an unchanging past. The former lovers meet and take a walk along the lakes.[35]

"It's a Walter Scott landscape," said Sylvie.

"And who has been telling you about Walter Scott?" I asked her.

The reunion has not got off to a good start; Sylvie no longer fits the hero's image of her, but he tries again:

> "Well then, sing me the song of the fair maiden carried off from her father's garden under the white rose-tree."
>
> "It's not sung any more."
>
> "Have you become a musician?"
>
> "A little."
>
> "Sylvie, Sylvie, I am certain you sing opera arias!"
>
> "And what's wrong with that?"
>
> "Because I like the old songs, and you won't know how to sing them any more."
>
> Sylvie warbled a few notes from a grand aria out of a modern opera . . . She *phrased!*

Gérard de Nerval's Sylvie is thoroughly modern, "phrasing" both opera and the second-hand landscape she sees around her. Scott had become kitsch, his history a household word.

Nerval's 1853 short story tells about a double displacement in which historical consciousness of the kind that makes it possible to see a "Walter Scott landscape" has ejected Sylvie from the (wholly imaginary) natural landscape of the father's garden, the white rose tree; and this, in turn, prevents the hero from inhabiting his own past, despite his attempts to do so. The desire to return to Loisy had been great. In Paris, where the story opens, the hero's eye "strayed vaguely through the newspaper in my hand and I read these two lines: '*Fete de Bouquet provincial.*—Tomorrow the archers of Senlis are to return the bouquet to the archers of Loisy.'" In a scene that Proust later compared to his own madeleine episode, "these extremely simple words" conjured up for Nerval quite unexpectedly "a whole new set of impressions, a memory of country life I had long ago forgotten, a distant echo of the simple festivals of my childhood. Horn and drum resounded far off in the woods and hamlets, the girls were weaving garlands and arranging, as they sang, bouquets tied in ribbons. A heavy cart, drawn by oxen, took their gifts as it passed, and we, the children of the district, formed the escort with our bows and arrows." The hero resolves to return to Loisy and to Sylvie, the girl whose love he squandered long ago. But the closer he gets to Loisy, the farther off it seems. It is finally the most ordinary items in Sylvie's household that indicate the wreckage of historical time and the poignancy of loss, and it is these items, and the songs that Sylvie no longer sings, that Nerval remembers and would like to recover. "She took me up to her room with all her old ingenuousness," but otherwise everything was different: "the room was simply decorated, though the furniture was modern; a gilt-edged mirror had replaced the old wall-glass where an idyllic shepherd offered a nest to a blue and pink shepherdess. The four-poster bed, chastely draped with old flowered chintz, had been succeeded by a walnut-wood bed hung with a net curtain; in the cage of the window there were canaries where there had once been finches. I was anxious to leave the room, for it contained nothing of the past." The disconnection to the past does not settle accounts with the past, however. Dream-like images and sadness at the irretrievability of the objects they represent remain. For Nerval, the modern self is displaced, in the form of either the always fashionable Sylvie or the hero's anguish at not being able to return home.[36]

In the "strange period, such as usually succeeds revolutions or the decline of great reigns," as Nerval put it, the displacement of the past by the fashions of the moment (the "Walter Scott landscape") serves to introduce a crisis of memory, which manifests itself in his repeated attempts and ultimate failure to retrieve the past. Sylvie's room registers the absence of the past and, in Nerval's imagination, contains its former presence. Thus the focus on the problem of the past moves from the public rhythm of revolutions to the private space of the household. Sylvie herself sets about arranging the household in a more fashionable interpretation of the past: canaries for finches. Nerval's private history of loss and remembrance was to be one of the enduring preoccupations of nineteenth-century writers, and one of the enduring preoccupations of nineteenth-century households.

Readers and writers became more self-conscious of breaks and disruptions in their own lives, parallel to the revolutionary discontinuities that dramatized public life. Autobiography as a genre was invigorated by the crisis of memory, which made the past an object of concern, while denying complete access to it. According to Jerome Buckley, "autobiography sets the self-portrait in time and motion, presenting, as it does, a changing personality, developing, declining, remembering, regretting, rather than a fixed and finite impression."[37]

The contrast with early modern autobiography is subtle but important, and rests on the role assigned to memory. Writing at a time of bitter religious struggles between Catholics and Protestants in the sixteenth century, Montaigne rescued the individual from the absolute claims of religious parties. He stressed the contradictory and provisional nature of individual actions, creating an almost Machiavellian economy of the self that corresponded to the political calculus of the absolutist state, which also endeavored to settle religious quarrels. For Montaigne, self-knowledge came through an understanding and management of interest, inclination, and illusion. The result was a kind of self-conscious stoicism that Enlightenment thinkers such as Locke believed led the way to the construction of an individual, knowable identity. Hume, by contrast, took up the notion of the radical contingency of the individual self: "The mind is a kind of theater, where several perceptions successively make their appearance; pass, re-pass, glide away, and mingle in an infinite variety of postures and situations." Yet for Montaigne and Hume alike the stress is on the mechanics of action in terms of immediate impressions and proximate circumstances.[38] In this conception, the present-day self, like the absolutist state, does not operate in a context that is fundamentally different from the one in which yesterday's self moved. In the nineteenth century, by contrast, the emphasis is on a self that resisted dispersion and became aware of particular loss, endeavoring to recover past impressions although anguished at the incompleteness of any reclamation, and showing more concern with interior meanings and less for exterior phenomena. The movement of the self away from its former habitations—childhood, youth, education, marriage—was experienced as a kind of accumulating violence of tears and departures. Yet it was precisely this awareness of injuries that laid the foundation for the new discovery of the self. The self fashioned in nineteenth-century autobiographies disavowed the transience that Montaigne had accepted, and, in its strain to recover what had been lost, established a stronger claim for itself than Montaigne would ever have granted. The romantic self was the broken self, just as the romantic nation was the broken nation.

Perhaps the most important expression of the layeredness of historical experience within individuals was the evocation of lost childhood. This longing relied on the very notions of discontinuity that the structures of modern temporality had brought into view. The sheer pace of change also became oppressive as people became increasingly aware of the technological and economic transformations that had taken place in their lifetimes. "The fact is," writes Richard Coe, "that the origins of the Childhood as a genre," with its sense of bitterness, frustration, and loss, "coincided from the outset with a major period of upheaval, with the French Revolution and the Industrial Revolution each in its own way hard at work destroying the past."[39] Childhood stood for a vast inventory of lost treasures, even as the child was regarded as an early version of the immanent self. Thus the exploration of the past was the means to define oneself, or as Carolyn Steedman puts it, "the dislocation is the loss that provides the aetiology of the self."[40] The figure of the lost child monitored the historicity of the self, something the unmistakable changes in material life and the increasingly historical forms of autobiographical narrative had clarified.

Nostalgia for lost childhood expressed the degree to which individuals constructed their own identities out of a sense of displacement. In this regard, the autobiographer was more "enamored of distance," to quote Susan Stewart, than concerned with the "referent itself." As she puts it, "nostalgia is the desire for desire."[41] The loss of childhood corresponded to a permanent itinerancy which, for better and worse, freed the self from the social bonds of home and enabled it to examine the particular journey the reflective individual has undertaken. Thus the melancholy of itinerancy is the substance of an irrevocable sense of individuality, just as loneliness can imply both aloneness and discreteness.

The link between itinerancy and autobiography is a strong one. As Julia Kristeva points out, it is precisely the wanderer, or the stranger, who thinks of life in biographical terms. Those at home are "perhaps owners of things, but the foreigner tends to think he is the only one to have a biography, that is, a life made up of ordeals—neither catastrophe nor adventure (although these might equally happen), but simply a life in which acts constitute events because they imply choice, surprises, breaks, adaptations, or cunning, but neither routine nor rest."[42] Who exactly are these foreigners? We know there was extraordinary movement of people as refugees and soldiers during the Napoleonic Wars, and certainly more mobility of labor (and incidence of pauperization) in the decades of industrialization that followed, as well as growing numbers of emigrants who crossed the Atlantic to make new lives in the United States and pioneers who left homes there to move on to the western territories. But it is misleading to think of Kristeva's foreigners primarily as a discrete demographic category. Foreignness derived from the ways people thought about the course of their lives and how their perceptions of home (and routine) changed even if they did not physically move. Once it was newly pictured in historical terms, the world moved through them.[43] The sense of itinerancy in the nineteenth century was strongly related to the historicization of the world. For an age that thought obsessively about the terms of its own unsettlement, autobiography was a characteristic literary genre to come to terms with emotional experiences not understandable in the frames of habit and custom. Kristeva's attention to the idea of the event is also noteworthy, for the narrative of lives came to be increasingly focused on exceptional moments, sudden upheavals, or dramatic revelations which broke through the security of expectation. The autobiographical texts as well as history books of this period belong to a hitherto undeveloped event-saturated genre of "momentarism."[44] This is why Chateaubriand could have several lives "laid end to end," while Joseph Görres believed he had had "six or seven."[45]

The nineteenth-century autobiography is narrated less from the perspective of the last person in a genealogy, as remained the case in aristocratic life-writings, than from the viewpoint of the first person who finds herself on the road.[46] For this reason there was a growing desire to document what Kristeva terms the ordeals—the departures and arrivals—of a lifetime. The invigoration of genres such as diaries and memoirs also manifested the autobiographical impulse. In recommending that his fiancée, Wilhelmine von Zenge, keep a diary, Heinrich von Kleist stressed the transience of experience: "Seldom are we able to take our bearings in this restless life—thoughts and perceptions die away like the notes of a flute in a hurricane—so many experiences are unusable because they are forgotten—a diary can prevent all that."[47] At the age of thirty-four, on 7 March 1812, Antoine

Métral, a solicitor in Grenoble, began keeping a diary for the same reason. Although the entries, which span the years 1812–1819, coincide fairly well with momentous historical events such as Napoleon's invasion of Russia, the fall of the French Empire, the Bourbon Restoration, the "One Hundred Days," and the Congress of Vienna, Métral commented very little on political events. Instead, he was obsessed with the decay of the present into past. Through the windows of his diary Métral looked out again and again at the movement of time. "With what rapidity time moves," he wrote in November 1812. "Every day I feel myself dragged into the abyss. In vain, I try to stop myself along the shores of time." And again in June 1814, he wrote with a pessimistic elegance worthy of Chateaubriand: "I feel that I will soon find myself in my grave. I see people getting all excited and instigating all sorts of torments without calculating the aim of their steps. Hélas! how everything goes, without returning: this fly will never fly again at the same time, in the same minute in eternity; every minute demolishes a part of itself." Métral's exercise in self-documentation was not for "rest or routine," but the agonized attempt to counter at every minute the ceaseless work of demolition.[48]

Most diarists and correspondents were not as poetically self-aware as Antoine Métral, but they still participated in the striking nineteenth-century phenomenon of "graphomania." In comparison to the past, more and more people of all social stations felt compelled to became cartographers of their own particular lives, even if the maps they left behind were fragmentary and incomplete.[49] "The age . . . was swamped with unremarkable self-revelations," concludes Peter Gay. "Literally thousands wrote [these up], men and women with no claim to fame of any kind. They left their memoirs moldering in attics or buried in local archives, or asked a job printer to make an unpretentious book." What they reported on was "their childhood, their schooling, their army service, their business dealings, their dazzling moments with the great," "unremarkable" at first glance, perhaps, but remarkable surely for the degree to which they plotted their lives according to the dramatic "right angles" of postrevolutionary temporality.[50]

The most telling evidence for the historicization of private life, however, is not the existence of a handwritten manuscript in a trunk but the wholesale rearrangement of the household and its rituals and "trifles." "What sets our age apart," explains John Gillis, "is that each family is now the creator and custodian of its own myths, rituals, and images."[51] In her analysis of bourgeois family rituals in the nineteenth century, Anne Martin-Fugier refers to the "thirst for memory," the manic energy with which families ritualized birthdays, reunions, and summer vacations and cultivated the memories of these celebrations in letters, scrapbooks, and photographs. This effort revealed a deeply suspicious view of the work of time. Memories were "hoarded like capital" in order to string together "fleeting happy moments" into a "fruitful duration." A sense of contentment over time was secured by the retrospective management of history. Martin-Fugier points out that holidays, for example, often began with the recollection of previous, joyful summers. Children, in particular, had to be given a stock of "joyous souvenirs" that would last them a lifetime. In this way, the family operated on the double assumption that even its own private existence was imperiled by the rapid passage of empty time, and that rituals established the family's own "time scheme, independent of the vicissitudes of history and of public competition."[52] It is not surprising that in nineteenth-century North America, with new roads of economic opportunity traveled over vast distances, families hoarded memories with special care.

The United States has always been thought of as a new country, with an undeveloped sense of history. Throughout the nineteenth century, "the millennial investment of the American republic," writes Dorothy Ross, "turned the past into prologue and the future into fulfillment of America's republican destiny."[53] Yet it is striking to see how the distant past came into view after the establishment of the new republic and the opening of the western frontiers. New England in particular, the place from which so many settlers emigrated in the 1820s, 1830s, and the 1840s, suddenly, in the perspective of contemporaries, turned into an old-fashioned place. The idea of "old-fashioned" and views of New England constituted themselves together. The place aged remarkably quickly; observers believed that the signs of degeneration had set in just before their own births, some thirty or forty years earlier. In 1869, Harriet Beecher Stowe referred to the "ante-railroad times—the period when our own hard, rocky, sterile New England was a sort of half Hebrew theocracy, half ultra-democratic republic of little villages, separated by a pathless ocean from all the civilization and refinement of the Old World, forgotten and unnoticed, and yet burning like live coals under this obscurity with all the fervid activity of an intense, newly kindled, peculiar, and individual life." Other texts dated the recollectable past to the 1810s and 1820s. It was at this point that the last Native Americans had left the area, or had died as outcasts on the edges of town, "last moments" about which white settlers were quite conscious.[54] Especially on the frontier, the disappearance of the Indians and battles such as that at Fallen Timbers in 1794 cleaved time into two parts, "'Indian times' and those that came after."[55] Not surprisingly, departures westward and breaks in time coincided with the founding of historical societies, a trend which occurred in Europe at the beginning of the nineteenth century as well. What emerges is both the coherence of the new nation and the more muted acknowledgment that it was founded upon the ruin of the Native American peoples. After the defeat of the French by the British in the 1760s and, in turn, the defeat of the British by the American colonists twenty years later, there was no longer any geopolitical ambiguity or "middle ground" which might have enabled white American subjecthood or abridged American empire. Native Americans now stood in the way of the destiny of the American nation, and literary testimony in the early 1800s quite literally buried them, creating a distinctively American ruin in the "short remnants of their days" and the "final resting places" into which Native Americans disappeared. This is certainly one way to think of the literary monument that is James Fenimore Cooper's *Leatherstocking Tales.* Thus the figure of the "last Indian" testified not simply to the violence of national independence, but also to the uncontested "friend/foe" imagery that accompanied it. The dispossession of the Indians confirmed the possession of American settlers, although the confirmation had a melancholy aspect and admitted the possibility that Americans too might vanish or ruin themselves.[56] It is not surprising, then, that the moment in which the historical itinerary of the American settler nation was finally clarified also brought forth the first evidence of ruins, which represented the other existences and the lives left behind. And from the perspective of European visitors to the United States it was precisely the wreckage of Native Americans, made a "beggar at the door of a factory," in the words of Chateaubriand, that turned America into a historical rather than natural landscape.[57] Thus folded in among the millennial epics of American history are these more melancholy texts in which "time" was perceived as disconnecting Americans from the remembered past in an unmistakable way.

It is New England and particularly New England households that were visualized as the sites of historical transformation. Although the "westward progress" of the nation is told and retold in triumphalist fashion, the counterpoint to this movement, which was northeastern stagnation, is rarely related. Since the landing at Plymouth Rock, New England had been the founding place for newcomers, but by the end of the Civil War, at the very latest, it was a place from which people departed. New-growth forests won back the stonewalled pastures, and wildlife returned as small towns lost one-half or more of their inhabitants. New Hampshire won back its 1840 population only in the 1980s. Appearing at the endpoint of this process of depopulation, the novelist Sarah Orne Jewett's simple-wrought stories of nineteenth-century New England surveyed a landscape in ruin. The rounds in *The Country Doctor* revealed New England to be a place of forgotten houses, abandoned grandparents, and old sailors. Jewett explored the "decaying, shipless harbors of Maine," and old secretaries stuffed with paled yellow letters and forgotten childhood treasures, "a lock of brown hair" and "some dry twigs and bits of leaf which had long ago been bright wild roses."[58] The broken pieces of New England also composed a new geography of shock and surprise. "That afternoon," Jewett relates in "An Autumn Holiday," "I found something I had never seen before—a little grave alone in a wide pasture which had once been a field. The nearest house was at least two miles away, but by hunting for it I found a very old cellar, where the child's home used to be, not very far off, along the slope. It must have been a great many years ago that the house had stood there; and the small slate head-stone was worn away by the rain and wind, so there was nothing to be read, if indeed there had ever been any letters on it."[59] Jewett's American voice acknowledged irretrievable loss. She knows that the little grave will not yield up a name, the cellar will not tell the story it contains.

The village graveyard and the haunted house are perhaps the most prominent features among the ruins of the New England landscape. "The grass was long and tangled, and most of the stones leaned one way or the other, and some had fallen flat"—Jewett writes about Deephaven's burying ground in the 1870s in ways that were already current in the 1830s.[60] No description of mid nineteenth-century New England was complete without a visit to or at least a look at a haunted house. "The house itself tells a sad tale of decay," wrote one F. A. Durivage in "The Old Mansion: A Sketch from Domestic History." "The roof is green and rank with an unhealthy antiquity and the damp moss clings to the very weather-beaten shingle." "Every village has its haunted house," the author concluded in 1842, "and why should Brookline be without one?" What is particularly interesting about these places is not so much their chronological age, which was not so very old, but their abandonment; they are stranded in new time. In the case of the Brookline "Witherhells," they have been ruined by their Tory loyalties during the Revolution; the older son was killed fighting alongside the British, and the younger son subsequently bankrupted the family.[61] The same sort of house stood in Harriet Beecher Stowe's "old town." There, children stumbled onto an abandoned big house and dared themselves to peek into the still partially furnished rooms. "To this modern time," Stowe explains, every New England town preserved "one or two of these monuments"; "The histories of these old houses, if searched into, present many romantic incidents, in which truth may seem wilder than fiction." After the American Revolution, which compelled Tories to abandon their estates, "the moss of legend and tradition grew upon these deserted houses . . . simple villagers by their firesides delighted to plunge into the fathomless abyss of incident that came from the histories of grand, unknown people across the water . . . they exaggerated the records of the pomp and wealth that had environed them. They had thrilling legends of romantic and . . . tragic incidents . . . More than one of them had its well-attested ghosts."[62] Without the Revolution, and the passions dividing Tories and republicans, and the final expulsion of Native Americans, these New England ghosts would not have been nearly as lively. Ghosts were the exiles of particular historical conflicts and thus the distinctive creatures of a historical age. Again and again, New England visitors recounted the ghost stories they had been told, the most famous one of which was Irving Washington's "The Ghost of Sleepy Hollow," which is about a headless corpse of a Hessian trooper killed in some "nameless battle" of the revolutionary war, but there were many other tales of former slaves, conquered Indians, and repatriated Tories.[63]

Less scary but more numerous were the old houses which suddenly came into view as relics. Like the haunted houses, they stand as ruins of past futures, abandoned by the sons and brothers who left to start new families in the west, and now inhabited by a final generation of spinsters and widows, "Aunt Tabitha," "Aunt March," and "Aunt Esther," New England figures who recounted stories about the "olden times" and often enough their ties to Tories and other royalists. New England's ruin was thus the consequence of history, not nature; of new, datable developments, not simply the passage of time. In one story, "'Moving' in the Country," which appeared in *Godey's Lady's Book* in 1852, the three Barton sisters finally take leave of the "old homestead," "a rambling, tumble-down house, full of great echoing rooms and dark passages" that had not seen any real life since "sister Sarah's wedding—nearly twenty years before." One brother lived in Wisconsin, another in a big city, their departures recalled by the locomotives that "thundered by a dozen times each day, just back of the old dwelling." As the sisters move from the old house to a small cottage, the past, here dated as something "nearly twenty years" ago, is on display as curious-looking stuff. Antique dealers do not yet exist, so "the indescribable and heterogeneous mass which lumbers the garret" will be either kept or sent off with "one of those miscellaneous dealers whose cart contains a little of everything." The cast-off items that emerged from the Bartons' attic in this story are precisely the ones that historians identify as "the quintessential symbols of the New England home": the warming pan, brass kettle, and spinning wheel, all of which were soon enough to be "highly sought after by early antique collectors" who began marketing at the end of the nineteenth century, and would find "a new usefulness when they were enshrined as relics in the parlor."[64] As it was, the sisters, under the understanding eye of their Wisconsin brother, decided to safeguard the "relics of our forefathers." The warming pans and kettles, set apart from the "two or three crates full of 'old iron,'" and the "'Alps on Alps' of rubbish" that was carted away, remained as prized possessions in the newly furnished cottage that blended "old and new."[65]

Once it was seen as the old house, the domestic place prompted a string of associations and intimacies. The "indescribable mass" in the lumber room was gradually reconceived as a messy attic filled with mysterious treasures. In colonial New England, the garret had traditionally been a lumber room, or a storage place for "meal, flour, and dried food stuffs." Until the hard freezes of winter, the dry air of the attic was well suited to preserving apples, squashes, and onions. William Pyncheon of Salem, Massachusetts, for example, noted in his diary at the end of October 1788 that the weather had turned "excessively cold," and "people's roots were frozen in the garret."[66] Otherwise the attic was an unfinished loft where boys and girls were bedded down. One hundred years later, however, the scenery in the attic and the things people did there were very different. In *The Story of a Bad Boy,* a novel published in 1870, Thomas Bailey Aldrich reported:

> What a museum of curiosities is the garret of a well-regulated New England house. Here meet together, as if by some preconcerted arrangement, all the broken down chairs of the household, all the spavined tables, all the seedy hats, all the intoxicated-looking books, all the split walking sticks that have retired from business (weary with the march of life). The pots, the pans, the trunks, the bottles—who may hope to make inventory of the numberless odds and ends collected in this bewildering lumber-room? But what a place it is to sit of an afternoon with the rain pattering on the roof! What a place in which to read *Gullivers' Travels!*

The attic is also Jo March's favorite reading place in Louisa May Alcott's *Little Women.* Of course, attics were still used as spaces for storage, and rooms for lumber, but they were also turned into places of memory and imagination.[67] With its "odds and ends," "numberless" and "bewildering," the attic provided a place where the past could be encountered, though in unmistakably fragmentary and incomplete fashion. This meant a dramatic change of scene and emotion in nineteenth-century homes.

In popular letters, old things acquired new liveliness. In *Godey's Lady's Book,* for example, readers perused the "autobiography of an old sofa," which narrated its life in the first person ("I first saw light . . . about the year 1780"), or "the old arm chair," rediscovered in the "old lumber loft," and refinished "as old chairs are all the fashion now." The old armchair also tells the story of its life from birth in France to a happy youth in England and finally to storage and rediscovery in the United States.[68]

What exactly are talking sofas and chairs saying? For Harriet Beecher Stowe the things that furniture might communicate were vitally important for making a home. In the concept called "associationism," things stood for qualities in a way that compelled Americans to collect their pasts and display their achievements. Against the merely fashionable, men and women endeavored to cultivate unique associations which told about their past and their interests, creating as they did the private lifetime of the family. A typical household scene in the country's domestic stories opened with the sons and daughters urging their parents—"gracious, mamma!"—to redecorate the parlor and throw out the old sofa: "an exact model of the one Noah took into the ark!"[69] The fashionable was expedient, but also cold and disposable, which is the lesson about collecting and displaying that the parents have to teach the young. "Do they love plants?" Stowe inquired about up-to-date families in her 1864 book, *House and Home Papers:* "Do they write letters, sew, embroider, crochet? Do they ever romp and frolic? What books do they read? Do they sketch or paint?" Rooms adorned with old and new things served to answer questions about individual feelings, habits, and histories. Done up in this commemorative way, houses were enchanted spaces inhabited by what Stowe approvingly identified as "household fairies."[70] "Associationism" rested on the assumption that sofas and chairs were cherished for their evocations, for their ability to say things about their owners.

These nineteenth-century interiors were in contrast to their eighteenth-century counterparts. Whereas a gentleman such as Delaware's Nicolas Ridgley, who died a wealthy man in 1755, lacked rugs on his floors, curtains in his windows, and cushions on his chairs, estate inventories from the early nineteenth century indicate that the "hard and bare" of Ridgley's house had given way a culture of adornment and sentiment. Even log cabins on the western frontier contained a notable piece of walnut furniture or two, held a shelf for ceramics, covered the floor with rag rugs, and were hung with pictures and mirrors.[71] Americans developed a new way of keeping house at a time when, as the philosopher Agnes Heller suggests, feeling not quite at home became a "typical home experience."[72]

Not to have domestic memories was to lose the ability to tell a story about oneself. It would leave families as unknowable as if they lived in Kamchatka, a reference of Stowe's which sounds remarkably similar to Karl Friedrich Schinkel's unmemorialized landscape, "unfamiliar, naked, and shorn, like a new colony."[73] Without memories and the ability to name and designate, people as much as nations stood to lose their subjectivity and hence their power. They would not be able to talk about their tragedies and ordeals, or make judgments and seek restitution. An "unrememberable past" or an "unimaginable future," writes Avery Gordon, consigned individuals to one and the same place; remembering was to take the first steps to abandon Kamchatka.[74]

Housekeeping meant saving collectibles and cultivating memories, and *Godey's Lady's Book* offered no end of suggestions to properly domesticate the rooms of the "model cottages" it advertised to America's builders. In the first place, the generation of the grandparents had a secure place in the nineteenth-century home. "Americans," writes Celia Betsky, "were in less and less danger of having to be warned, as Jennie June Croly had done in 1864: 'Don't Be Ashamed of Grandmother.' Quite the opposite."[75] It was female figures such as aunts, great-aunts, and grandmothers who served as links to the past. In the stories of Louisa May Alcott, which in the 1860s and 1870s worked themes already quite familiar to readers a generation earlier, a stay at "Grandma's" was a time for stories from long ago; and visits to Aunt March opportunities to ransack "big wardrobes and ancient chests": "the girls each opened a drawer and turned over the contents till they found something they wanted to know about." The debris of one previous life, the "oddly shaped linen bag" and the "long white kid glove," tickled the imaginations of Maud, Tom, and Polly in Alcott's story, "An Old-Fashioned Girl."[76] But even larger objects in the household were valued: "how memory links the heart to dull material things," wrote Mary Nealy in praise of "The Old Bureau" (1868), which calls up "in a moment the loves, and hopes, and enjoyments of years that have passed away." It held a private history of the family, one that in its references to war and emigration was interlinked with national history: "When my grandmother was young," the drawers contained "clothing, trimmed and embroidered for a bride"; "after a time . . . tiny little garments of white, of the softest cambrics, and linens, and muslins, and flannels were carefully laid away." "The years passed on," and, in what must have been the first years of the republic, "other little wardrobes were locked up in that drawer . . . sometimes kissed and fondled, sometimes watered with tears shed for the fallen husband and father." The bureau moved overland to Ohio, "what was then called the 'far west,'" and stored the clothes of the next generation and eventually "my first clothes!"[77] In Europe as in North America, the old wardrobe, often filled with bridal dresses, stitched sheets, and quilts, was a familiar feature in the front room.[78]

Over the course of the nineteenth century, things regarded as antique moved into the American home, just as the itinerant junkmen established themselves as recognizable antique dealers. Giving warmth, identity, and duration to the nineteenth-century family, old collectibles evoked "household fairies"—"fairies," not ghosts that drift through the "old town's" haunted houses (only abandoned houses are haunted, not "kept" homes). Parlors and attics were turned into "mini-museums, filled with heirlooms, mementos, and souvenirs of family."[79] Family portraits and later photographs dominated domestic interiors; antiques, whether inherited, found, or bought, and also engravings of an idealized New England past, such as those successfully sold by Currier and Ives, were typical commemorative objects. By the end of the nineteenth century, the New England colonial period had become the idealized version of the American past, and New England places had become the attic of the nation, a destination for summer visitors, pensive souls, and avid antiquers. Charity functions, carnivals, and the big end-of-the-century expositions in Philadelphia and Chicago exhibited reconstructions of New England kitchens complete with public servings of Boston brown bread, pork and beans, and pitchers of cider, as well as pumpkin, mince, and apple pies.[80] To this day, it is New England husbandry that provides the model for that most American festival, Thanksgiving, which *Godey's* editor Sarah Josepha Hale championed as a national holiday beginning in the 1850s, and it is the New England Cape that provides the basic building model for the American home.

What is striking about the attention to antiques is the plainness of the objects. Warming pans, spinning wheels, cooking pots, and other American antiques indexed historical change on an unmistakably domestic scale. Antiquing did not celebrate the great events of important men—people did not generally collect the belongings of George Washington or Abraham Lincoln—but rather cherished the antiques that symbolized the "small occurrences, frail mementoes, and trifles of everyday life."[81] Collections in the attic thereby privileged the ordinary or typical over the exemplary, "the private over the public sphere." "Hearth and home, rather than scepter and sword," writes Raphael Samuel, became "the symbols of national existence; samplers and patchwork quilts the tradition-bearers."[82] Both for the nation and the family, the historical case was thoroughly domestic.

The guardianship of "household fairies" was all the more important given that so many American families cultivated their private histories across great distances. For most early emigrants to the western frontier, those in "ante-railroad times," there was little prospect of ever seeing again the friends and family left behind, and those who departed saw themselves overtaken as millions of American and European settlers moved the demographic center of the United States further and further west. Practices of remembering such as writing a letter or sitting for a photographic portrait came to be intertwined with the physical leave-takings that punctuated nineteenth-century domestic life. This was especially the case in New England, where agricultural decline, the rise of river mill towns, and the growth of a sentimental tourist industry left hundreds of colonial communities with only the barest threads of demographic continuity. To repair some of the loss, New Hampshire towns such as Center Sandwich and Mount Vernon organized Old Home Days for late August, beginning in the 1890s, in order to invite those "oldtime" folks who had left their birthplaces for the cities and western lands to return for a visit and to attract summer visitors. Old Home Days ritualized both the abandonment of New England places and the aestheticization of the remnants left behind through tourism.[83] They were the regional equivalent of family reunions such as Thanksgiving.

Although photography made keeping a record of family history infinitely easier after the 1860s, technology in itself did not prompt archival activity. "Never burn kindly written letters," *Godey's Lady's Book* advised Americans; "no photograph can so vividly recall" memories. The advice was evidently heeded, for the discovery of old letters by boys and girls rummaging through an antique chest or playing in the attic was a staple narrational device to turn the plot in nineteenth-century stories.[84] To make a scrapbook also reflected the value that trivial miscellany held out for private history. Although commonbooks had been popular since the eighteenth century, their function changed as the emphasis on religious reflection and literary self cultivation gave way to the collection of the bits and pieces of everyday life and the recollection of lives left behind. Scrapbooks became souvenir albums. The carefully signed and dated notations, and the effort to collect the autographs and recommendations of friends, teachers, and schoolmates, reflected a strong desire to compile one's own life and to leave a record of social circles which were apt to scatter in a few years time (or were seen to be so). Collectors often interspersed documents, pictures, and clippings of events of national importance, but they attached the greatest value to personal artifacts. What distinguished the aesthetics of ephemera, argues Todd Steven Gernes, was "its appreciation of the common rhymes, phrases, and occurrences of everyday life, in its transfiguration of the commonplace." "Trifles in themselves are to the feeling heart / Of greater wealth than India's richest gems," wrote Anstic Chace of Providence, Rhode Island, in her commonplace book around 1801; "great events give scope for great virtues," agreed Maria Brockway in 1835, "but the main tenor of human life is composed of small occurrences."[85]

Perhaps the most poignant connection to the family past for nineteenth-century Americans was the quilt. As Laurel Thatcher Ulrich reminds us, "household textiles became the paper on which poets, novelists, centennial orators, and family chroniclers all over America wrote their stories."[86] This was never more true than in the middle and end of the nineteenth century. While many quilts were produced out of necessity and economy, out of scraps saved up by pioneers, they were also integral parts of a culture of sentiment and were thus endowed with rich historical meanings. The remarkable fact is that far more quilts were produced than were actually needed. According to one estimate, "three-quarters of the bed coverings in the United States were quilts," and thousands were kept out of harm's way as family treasures. This is extraordinary evidence of domestic production; according to Elaine Hedges, "quilts became a vehicle through which women could express themselves; utilitarian objects" that were "elevated through enterprise, imagination, and love to the status of an original art form." At the same time, it is important to realize that quilting flourished precisely because of the abundance—not the shortage—of printed and manufactured textiles, which invited imaginative experimentation with pattern and design. Beginning in the 1820s and 1830s, account books and newspaper advertisements indicated the wide range of imported textiles: "broadcloth, shalloon, tammy, harreteen, kersey, and other woolen yard goods, as well as blankets, silks, velvets, and corduroy; damask, woven, plain, and checked linens; and block- and plate-printed, striped, checked, or plain cottons of all kinds were readily available in city and country. With independence, French prints and Italian silks, Russian linens, Indian cottons, and Chinese silks and coarse cottons called nankeen were added to the offerings."[87] This abundance had two consequences. First, it encouraged the free use of color and ever more extravagant creativity with pattern. "Quiltmakers everywhere seemed to vie with each other in the creation of one geometric pattern more dazzling than another."[88] Secondly, it invited the association of particular individuals or memories with distinctive printed clothes—a dress, a bonnet, a wedding gown—which gave the scrap pieces incorporated into quilts their historical poignancy and stimulated their production. As late as the 1970s, in west Texas, "quilters still worked out of piece bags containing scraps their mothers and grandmothers had placed there." "The quilts were a compendium of family history, each person symbolized by a bit of textile."[89] Already in the 1860s, *Godey's Lady's Book* referred to quilt patches as "'storied' fragments."[90] Rather than being merely the invention of necessity, quilts flourished as a way to remember, and scrapbags were nothing less than attics in a bag. Quiltmaking, like homemaking, revealed new ways of thinking about time, history, and identity.

American quilts collaborated with American mobility. Quilts always marked important comings and goings: births, marriage, the entry into adulthood. But at the height of their popularity in the middle of the nineteenth century, quilts expressed more than the traditional life cycle in a stable community. Popular signature quilts, in which each block was stitched by a friend or relative and signed and then assembled into the whole, typically accompanied women who were leaving their communities to move west. "It is hardly coincidental," concludes Ricky Clark, "that signature quilts were most popular during the period of America's westward expansion."[91] And since most migrants took scrap bags along with them, they repeatedly restitched memory pieces into new designs. Quilts thereby became lifelines connecting broken families and severed friendships. In one family, the parents and all but one of nine children moved from New York to Wisconsin and on to Nebraska. Only a single daughter remained in Poughkeepsie, and the separated family members probably never saw each other again. Over the course of the 1850s and 1860s, the sisters and mother sent scraps of fabric to one another. "I have been looking for something to send you, but I could not find anything that I could send in a letter [but] a piece of my new dress," wrote the mother. "Mother to daughter" and "sister to sister" the correspondence continued. "Here is a piece of my gingham Lydie made me"; "a piece of my dress of delanés"; "a piece of my bonnet, trimmed with green plaid ribbon."[92] "There is a heap of comfort in making quilts," remembered "Aunt Jane" of Kentucky, "just to sit and sort over the pieces and call to mind that this is of the dress of a loved one."[93]

Westward movement and its losses and new opportunities were apparent in the design of quilts as well. New patterns bore the names Star of the West or Rocky Road to Kansas or Ohio Rose or Arizona Cactus. Quilts reproduced the novelty of the western prairiescape, often in striking abstract geometries: Straight-Furrow Stripe, the Log Cabin, or the Flower Garden.

But these domestic memorializations were also ruins. Indeed, for all the recognition of the fine workmanship, and the companionship of the quilting party, the stories behind the fragments disintegrated faster than the patches themselves. In quilting, there is no restitution of the losses, and no direct connection to the past, just a melancholy "calling to mind." Quilts memorialized the menace of time. They acknowledged the growing sense that Americans had of not being at home anymore. Spaces like attics and tapestries like quilts, and personal evocations of lost childhood or the national insistence on lost innocence, all indicated the degree to which modern times represents itself by what it has lost, as debris, scraps, and ruins, rather than in terms of continuity and solidity.

The memorialization of domestic space granted women the distinctive role of guardians of memory. It was mostly women who oversaw the family celebrations, maintained scrapbooks, and collected quilt patches.[94] This gendered responsibility was certainly clear to the commercial promoters of photography, who not only recognized that cameras would be utilized mostly to record the private history of births, marriages, and holidays, but quite early on identified the woman as the person behind the camera and targeted women in advertisement campaigns at the turn of the twentieth century. "The historians, the guardians of memory, selecting and preserving the family archive" were mostly wives and mothers, agrees Patricia Holland in her study of family photography and family memory.[95] The centrality of the household in the recording of historical time and place not only put women in charge of family memory practices, but made it increasingly important that wives and mothers rather than nurses or servants transmit aspects of national culture and family history.[96] The memorialization of domestic space differed, then, from the nationalization of regional space, a process in which it was men and intellectuals who gathered, collected, interpreted, and repositioned local artifacts into newly imagined national frames. The domestic vernacular of memory also helps account for the theme of lost childhood, as the child was the most avid, indeed was the designated consumer of family history and lore. And the child's supposedly unselfconscious consumption is subsequently mourned by his or her adult self, grown more self-aware and introspective.

As guardians of memory, women were assigned characteristically domestic roles, but their histories were not simply disinterested reports on the family. Alphonse Daudet used the term "feminine chronologies" to describe an alternative history of children, marriage, and households that was both tragic and encouraging.[97] Moreover, scrapbooks, photo albums, and quilts invited compilers to organize and arrange according to personal interest and inclination. The work of memory created new parameters for self-expression and self-discovery, as recent analyses of early American photographs have suggested.[98] This subjective dimension adds to the plurality of narratives that flourish in historical time.

The memorialization of domestic space corresponded to the domestication of national space in the sense that both nineteenth-century trends have to be understood in the context of the growing authority of a historical point of view that lifted the cyclical, repetitive, and incidental events of empty flowing time into bounded (family or national) narratives of lost intimacies and recovered collective feeling. By imagining the passage of time in the conditional tense, and by recognizing what was absent and what was present, history gave poignancy to otherwise parochial, unremarkable occurrences. When taken up by historical time, these evoked a common feeling of what had been, or what was potential and might be. Historical transformation was expressed in a nostalgic as well as in a hopeful mode. The melancholy of history carries both these meanings: the visibility that history as a mass medium gives to the melancholic event and the melancholic cast to the narrative of beginnings and endings which composes the event-saturated idea of modern history.

Conclusion: The Historical Age

In the last two centuries, more and more people have come to see history in terms of relentless, often painful movement away from the past and toward an uncertain future. Already by 1800, their points of orientation refashioned by the French Revolution, contemporaries across Europe relied less on a view of history in which customary cycles returned a past condition to the present day just as new years restored old seasons, or one in which long-term continuities made it seem as though things happened but nothing much changed, or as inevitable progress toward enlightenment. Instead, they saw dramatic discontinuities which broke up the *longue durée* of history and thereby disconnected past, present, and future from one another. There is no reason to think that this way of seeing history, which to us is quite familiar, is superior to or more advanced than a cyclical conception or the denial of historicity altogether, although nineteenth-century scholars certainly believed so. Rather than back any one view, my argument has emphasized the passionate and intimate kinds of cultural activity that this particular conception of history made possible. In the decades after the French Revolution, a way of thinking about time that dramatized radical transformations and inserted fundamental differences into history became widely accepted. Within this historical world view, Europeans became more aware of the frailty of cultural and social formations. The world appeared to them more restless than it had in the past, which was as much due to thinking about events in terms of revolution as it was due to the revolutionary nature of events themselves. This rather drastic dimension to social description is perhaps the most fundamental outcome of the French Revolution. Thus the Industrial Revolution of the early nineteenth century was as much a category of analysis distinctive to the period as it was an unmistakable material process shaping the period. It was the opponents of the French Revolution who more quickly deployed concepts of fundamental difference in historical analysis, something Novalis noted when he pointed out that "many anti-revolutionary books have been written for the Revolution, but Burke has written a revolutionary book against the Revolution." This observation indicated that those most invested in the authority of the past were also quickest to acknowledge the challenge to its "common maxims" and to begin a process of remapping the social world in terms of the newly acknowledged conditions of displacement, with the more dubious aim of containing the unexpected admixtures that resulted.[1] It is this new apprehension of eventfulness that this book has explored.

Novalis singled out Edmund Burke, but I have attempted to argue that the new historical mindedness had far-reaching European and trans-Atlantic consequences and extended to shape social discourse and cultural practices in general. In the first place, this sightfulness focused on dramatic movement through time, away from the past. History was choreographed as an endless number of departures, which is why I describe its contents as melancholic and much of the activity that concerned itself with the past as nostalgic. To be sure, contemporaries often considered these passages through time progressive and a necessary part of realizing the individual self or national culture or the advance of civilization. They modeled the relationship between past and future in terms of development, maturation, and evolution. But even this Whiggish conception of history did not ignore the vast scenes of destruction which history had now formed, so that notions such as the end of community, the spoliation of the landscape, the innocence of childhood, or the "last Indian," or even a concept like "tradition" could become part of a common cultural lexicon that distinguished the nineteenth and twentieth centuries from the seventeenth or eighteenth. It was not only public activity that was historicized, but the private lives of family and individuals; the organization of life in terms of loss was not an abstract or bookish matter at all, but deeply, personally felt.

By challenging the invoked authority of the past in fashioning the future, this drastic vision of history expanded the applicability of the subjunctive tense, which is my second point. In the distinction between the past, the present, and the future, the historical mind imagined the very changeable nature of social habits, political entities, and cultural meanings. In this way, the durable things that made up the present appeared to be much more fragile, and the flimsy items that seemed completely notional or merely preliminary seemed more potential, and might well come to pass. Thanks to the subjunctive tense, a new balance of power was established between the "here and now" and the possible, between the present and the future. As soon as time was considered in terms of things cast aside and others brought forth, contemporaries became more aware of their own historical stature and their own subjectivity. History thereby acquired the characteristics of provisionality and malleability.

Third, the discontinuities between the past and the present suggested looking for discontinuities in the past. This is to say, not only was the past different from the present; the past itself was no single authoritative entity but instead a record of untimely deaths, abrupt endings, and foreshortened possibilities, all of which created whole new categories of discord, disparity, and incommensurability applicable to the past. The past gained new potential, contained in the phrase "what could have been." This explains the evocative nature of the many pasts that nineteenth-century Europeans explored. Conceived in this way, the past offered itself as the dimension in which various national cultural itineraries could develop and take root without any one taking logical precedence over another. Rather than furnish a common heritage to European civilization, it provided separate identities and violent separations. Distinct cultural trajectories such as Staël's Italy or Boisserée's Germany were no longer tied together by a hierarchic scheme of diachronic development, as had been the case during the Enlightenment, or through the imperial unity of center and periphery in the Napoleonic period. The recognition of lost itineraries in the past had the effect of liberating contemporaries from a view that regarded history as a single coherent, exemplary narrative. Introducing difference into the flow of time, it suggested the possibility of counterlives in the present. This apprehension exploded Machiavelli's *magazin d'expériences.*

A conception of history in which, to cite the testimony of an unhappy conservative, "everything has begun to move, or has been set in motion,"[2] was so comprehensive and so perceptible that people of all social ranks began to see the particulars of their lives in terms of great historical transformations. History became a way to describe and connect far-flung situations. In many ways, history should be regarded as a globalizing mass medium in the nineteenth century. It enabled contemporaries to recognize themselves as contemporaries, that is, as very differently situated subjects who nonetheless shared the same time and place; who, moreover, could be regarded as products of historical forces; and who were seen to have investments in how those forces resolved themselves. It was in the very casualness of references to recognizable markers such as "1789" or "'06" that the new temporal order revealed itself. Longer-term processes such as the expansion of state control, the regularization of schooling and military service, and technologies of communication and transportation further enabled the synchronization of time over space. But the particular idea of history is what provided nineteenth-century contemporaries with a common sense of experience, thereby fashioning the discursive space that civil society would occupy. Mutually recognizable experience is what created contemporaries. That history was a mass medium does not mean that people thought alike. On the contrary: political and economic revolutions created very adverse ideas. However, people did recognize each other as inhabitants of the same historical space, which made them take interest in one another. As a mass medium, history had the effect of creating the common recognition of its own comprehensive forcefulness.

The condition of contemporaneity had unmistakable borders. It made contemporaries out of Europeans and Americans in the first decades of the nineteenth century, but it also excluded most of the rest of the world, which was regarded as unconscious of precisely these newly visualized historical forces, at least until more sustained colonial contact with the West pulled the so-called primitive into history.[3] The German philosopher Georg Wilhelm Friedrich Hegel believed that Europeans were not just burdened by history but also privileged by being self-conscious of that burden, which made it possible for them to take the lead in realizing their own subjectivity. For that reason Hegel dismissed Africa, just as Dorothea Schlegel could not comprehend the "tartaric wild" of the Danube: both places stood outside history. If most of the world was uninteresting to Europeans because it supposedly remained unselfconscious, the synchronization of history so conceived worked to create new intimacies among Europeans (and white Americans). Contemporaries with very different backgrounds came together in the great social fictions pioneered in this period by historical novelists such as Walter Scott, and their characters and stories were consumed by newly formed literary publics across the continent. Scott, Balzac, Dickens, Dumas, Sue, Hugo—"it is a regular, even monotonous pattern: all of Europe reading the same books, with the same enthusiasm, and roughly in the same years (when not months)," notes Franco Moretti.[4] This pattern was possible because readers recognized their own lives in the lives of others, and thus took a keen interest in hugely popular nineteenth-century forms such as memoirs, biographies, and historical novels. History lifted individual misfortunes out of obscurity and gave them social poignancy by connecting them to comprehensive afflictions and general processes and thus made them arresting to others who also contended with those same afflictions and processes. This production of the poignant out of the parochial allowed people to see themselves as contemporaries, to recognize each other as fellow victims, and to empathize with one another's sentimental narratives. With anecdotal evidence taken from market boats and ferries, and through a more sustained analysis of the genres of autobiography and recollection, the idea of the contemporary reorganized society at large, not just a literate elite. It is in this historical age that real value is placed on the ordinary and the vernacular.

A great moment of enfranchisement around 1800 provided wide social recognition to diverse vernacular voices. Recent scholarship has placed too much emphasis on unified national narratives in the nineteenth century, and too little on the variegated syllabus of letters, memoirs, and diaries. In my view, the proliferation of, and general interest in, individual testimony in the nineteenth and twentieth centuries meant that historical narratives were constantly confronted by (less authoritative) counternarratives, which traced scars, accounted losses, and contradicted official versions. Subjective texts such as memoirs not only gave "the wrong side of events," as Chateaubriand put it, but the conditions of the production and consumption of historical narratives brought forth the many-sidedness of events.[5] Embedded in relations of economic power and national sovereignty, historical narratives generally sought to cast a good light on events and favored the side of the nation—historical, if vernacular genres made it possible to write in a minor or nostalgic key and to insist on answering the "big yes" with a "small no," to paraphrase George Grosz. Narrative and power—sufficiently different forms—did not work together with utter consistency.[6] Modern history legitimated vernacular voices not only because they were often the most evocative expressions of the cultural or national particularity, but also because they were powerful expressions of how extensively historical ideas had saturated the population and created common interest in the processes and events of history. The richly detailed customs, carefully wrought dialect, and political testimony of the country cottager stood for both things: history's legitimating capacity *and* its critical capacity. My argument thus makes a claim for the shared nature of historical space and for the differences of perspective that that space enabled. The synchronization of time did not prohibit the articulation of difference.

At its root, history is an account of difference. It must account for the flow of events and tell why and in what way today is no longer like yesterday. It is not about the reiteration of the same, but introduces the startling presence of the new and different. Herodotus' histories begin with encounters, often sea voyages, trading expeditions, or naval raids; Thucydides' *History of the Peloponnesian War,* too, is about what happens when Athenians leave Athens; countless other histories begin with arrivals and departures, conquests and reclamations, exilings and discoveries. For Thucydides, in particular, a historical account is premised on the knowledge that "the quiet life" can never be preserved; self-sufficiency is not attainable.[7] History as a narrative thrives when new things are added or old things lost, and a historical age such as the nineteenth century thus sought out evidence of both innovation and displacement. History, therefore, is constituted in large part by testimonies of loss. Losses do not disappear into obscurity, precisely because they are restored to history in the form of testimony that contemporaries find interesting and pertinent. They serve collective ends. Historical narratives serve to identify losses, to recognize them as the result of social forces and not simply as individual misfortunes or natural calamities. Modern history redeems individual losses in social narratives just as it advances by virtue of the accumulation of those losses. The melancholy of history contains the testimony of tragedy, the sympathetic ear of the listener, *and* the organization of events into sequences of dispossession and partial redemption.

History is written on the open road, along which fugitives and refugees travel and take note of their displacement as they survey scenes of terrible destruction and imagine the homes they once possessed. The witnesses to history are, in the end, exiles and émigrés and strangers. They will not return to their homes or to their former lives. So it is not surprising that travelers feel out of place or portray themselves as stranded in the present. This sense of anachronism is one of the results of the differences between past and present that are embedded in the logic of modern history. However, feelings of bewilderment and isolation are not necessarily permanent and they can be alleviated. After all, Chateaubriand *writes* about his exile. The travelers on the road are always *fellow* travelers and they are making sense of their dislodgings together and doing so by means of a common vocabulary. Otherwise we wouldn't know about them. The historical texts they produce are not only shared by readers but, by providing events with explanation, motive, and judgment, place individual catastrophes into an embracing collective narrative. Given the power they have to offer recognition and to provide meaning to loss, these postwar or post-catastrophe explanations are under enormous pressure to maintain a coherent, redemptive story in which the individual is comforted in the name of the collective. While the story of the nation, for example, is unmistakably selective and exclusionary, the degree to which it is bounded is also what keeps the travelers together and enables the mutual accounting of their losses. National feeling congealed in the nineteenth century to the extent that it made poignant and pertinent the suffering of individuals. What history produces, then, are the collective meanings to commemorate individual losses. The familiar setting for history is at the graveside.

The knowledge of dispossession facilitates the production of historical narratives and these, in turn, supply hitherto undeveloped but emotionally binding possessions in the form of collective identities.[8] The idea of the nation establishes new intimacies whereby dispersed strangers can recognize each other as contemporaries and treat each other as compatriots and eventually kill others as foes. The nation is undoubtedly the most durable collective established in the nineteenth and twentieth centuries, and it provides basic legitimacy for social solidarity and social services, and for war. I do not see its obsolescence. Yet national histories do not hide the displacements from which the national form originated or the dangers nations face. In my view, historical subjects, whether the nation, ethnic group, or other collectives, persist very much through the references to their (reconstructed) collective ordeals. It is misleading to think of national discourse only as something complete, unchanging, and naturalized; it expresses itself strongly in a subjunctive tense, a "longing for form," as Timothy Brennan puts it.[9] After all, the nation is much talked about as dangerously imperiled from within and without. Its monuments are in jeopardy through neglect; its people haphazardly subjected to dispersion. National assimilation seems always incomplete. Historical connections do not appear self-evident, so it is in this tentative state that they are considered carefully for the first time. War and economic disaster thus play an especially crucial role in nation-making, because each intensifies the moment of danger and the effort at reconstitution and reintegration. Of course, historical narratives authorize other collective imaginaries that intersect and even contradict national allegiances. And national feeling may express itself in more or less populist, reconciliationist, or xenophobic tones.[10] Nonetheless, the national form has been particularly powerful because of the ways the nation's history appropriates and thus recognizes as exemplary the ordeals of its people in the struggle to constitute itself as a nation. History is deeply complicit in the construction of the modern nation and in its inclusions and exclusions.

New ways of seeing and thinking about the displacements of history gave emotional substance to the work of memory, the rituals of commemoration, and the retrospective inventorying of so-called tradition. The powerful apprehension of loss was the premise for a whole range of cultural activities with the debris of the past. The retrieval of national cultures, in particular, occupied intellectuals, writers, and artists over the course of the nineteenth century, but loss was also the premise for the embellishment of individual histories and family traditions which commemorated quite ordinary lives. It was in the nineteenth century that the domestic interior of the family came to be organized around memory and commemoration. This richly embellished world of holidays, souvenirs, and quilts was built upon the recognition of loss, whether in the form of untimely deaths or simply the passages of time which snatched people from their childhood and pulled them away from their parents and then their children. Joseph von Eichendorff wrote of the melancholy of history that permeated spaces of public and private life. "The autumnal farewell song of migratory birds, the falling leaves which seem to bury our lives," and "the unease, the yearning into the distance, and at the same time the homely comforts of well-heated rooms, when it is snowing and storming outside—that is what occupies the heart of the true poet."[11] Eichendorff attested to the unsettlement of the post-revolutionary era, which had torn people away from the places they had once belonged to, but he also allowed them to look back at what has been lost. Eichendorff endeavored to create the moment of the "rupture in time" and thereby to open up "the ungraspable, the strange, that leads you at once into the distance and into the dark depths."[12] The presence of absence takes the form of new knowledge.

It is precisely the forms of the "ungraspable" and the "strange" that the past has taken on in modern time. The past could not be reliably or readily known. It was opaque; for the first time, around 1800, contemporaries approached the emotional and mental structures of their forbearers with a great sense of mystery and incomprehension. (Of course, the previous sense of familiarity with the past was equally artificial and equally, if differently evocative.) Given this newly considered state in which things were not self-evident, nineteenth-century scholars and scientists fashioned a vast array of historiographical techniques to try to make sense of the past, paying special attention to context, to time and place, as Staël and Chateaubriand recommended at Pompeii. The fragment, in particular, became the telling symbol of the past, recalling the break with the present and indicating the unknowability of the former whole. Broken pieces were cherished for their ability to reflect the twilight of other worlds.

The genres of popular culture became increasingly historically minded and respectful of the difference of the past, carefully producing the effects of "period," fashion, and dialect, and tidying the ordinary household so that it was expressive of time and place. Historical scenes were no longer dressed up in the classical garb of ancient Greece or imperial Rome but regarded quite specifically and painstakingly as particular creatures of a past moment. As a result, the historical age was more liberal in its use of specific names and dates, which signified the chronologies of periodicity. The recognition of the particularity of the "spirit of the age" did not make the past completely unapproachable, however. The great achievement of Walter Scott was not simply to have produced the effects of historicity in his fictions, but to have drawn attention to the "just passed" quality of a still half-remembered age; not a "tale of other days," but rather one "sixty years hence," just short of what scholars consider to be the eighty-year life-span of memories handed down from generation to generation. Scott's formula to recreate what had "just passed" proved popular. Both Theodor Fontane, in his first novel, *Before the Storm,* and Theodor Storm in his last, *The Dykemaster,* explicitly refer to Scott's diachronics of "sixty year's hence," and Storm also relies on Stifter's evocation of the generation of the great-grandfathers.[13] The accent thus fell both on an actual, datable historical moment and on its passing. And the fact that this moment had *just* passed made the movements of history in general seem all the more unrelenting and close-at-hand.

The broken relationship of the past to the present promoted a dramatization of history as a series of abrupt endings and new beginnings. What had seemed the evidence of nature or necessity was taken more and more to be the result of conquest or revolution, about which some specific knowledge could be recovered. This discovery of what might be called the conditional but datable past, in which defeat and demolition were no longer regarded as foreordained, had the effect of making available a greater variety of historical subjects in the vicissitudes of history. A new array of cultural traditions could be retrieved and embellished in some provisional way: the self-appointed task of Boisserée and the brothers Grimm. More and more aware of their dispossessions, nineteenth-century contemporaries endeavored to reestablish some sort of connection to the past, one that was tenuous but also enriching and suggestive of the possibilities available in historical time, past and future. The past was endowed retrospectively with the formal contingencies of the future. The work of recollecting the past thus raised the specter of alternative modernities: the stories of nations challenged the standard of empire, as was the case in the construction of German nationhood vis-à-vis French hegemony; the exile crossed the border to tell a story very different from that of the victorious revolutionary in Paris; religious believers or ethnic minorities questioned the assimilationist history of the nation, as in Nodier's voyages or Scott's romances; individual diaries and letters disputed official accounts, as Stifter showed; and childhood memories interrupted developmental schemes with the lamentations of nostalgia.[14] The debris of very different pasts provided the raw material for the operations of history, which aim to create active subjects in acknowledged conditions of displacement.

The new past of the nineteenth century I have tried to describe with the term "half-life."[15] Whereas eighteenth-century observers placed ruins in nature and in a process of decay and degeneration, a kind of "half-death" that was their common fate, by 1800 the fragments of the past were used to evoke other, distinct lifeways, and they told a plethora of different stories. There was an insistence on the retrieval of the partial evidence of particular cultures and a change to history writing that not only recorded vanquished entities but held out the possibility of their reemergence.

The evidence of the past is present in fragmented form because of the violent discontinuities between present and past. These fragments are particularly poignant because they are all that remains of former, irrecoverable wholes. But they are also evocative because they contain evidence of other lives and other meanings, enable some sort of connection to another life, and thereby propose the partial resurrection of that life in the stream of history. Broken forms also deny the commensurability of the past to the present. Since the whole scheme of modern history is based on periodization, in which the most ordinary things are the best measure of cultural specificity in time and place, and since the evidence that history invades even the most ordinary households serves as the sign of historical mindedness, the exemplary fragments of the past have often become mundane domestic objects such as the inventory of the "old houses" of New England: the warming pan, the brass kettle, and the spinning wheel.

In the historical age, the material traces of the past appeared to be everywhere; they turned landscape into a rendition of archeology. Fragments of past lives became highly regarded, and they were collected and recovered and revered by museums, historical societies, and amateur connoisseurs such as Boisserée or Goethe.

The very materiality of the signs of history—the colors and textures and patterns of the patches in a nineteenth-century quilt, for example—invited contemporaries to explore their own historical natures and facilitated their engagement with very particular versions of historical experience. This new past is broken; although opaque, it is evocative; and for these reasons, it is also valuable for political or imaginative refashioning. It is also unmistakably vernacular, even democratic, and potentially defiant. Given its counternarratives and alternative itineraries, the past does not necessarily authorize or legitimate the present. For these reasons, I would argue that the past in the nineteenth century is profoundly different from the past as it had been conceived before then, and that the knowledge it provides has become at once more complicated, more provisional, and more open-ended.

The broken things of the past themselves did not change, and despite Napoleon's anti-ecclesiastical destructiveness, they were not fundamentally more imperiled as physical objects in 1810 than they had been one hundred years earlier. What had fundamentally changed were the ways in which ruins were apprehended and the uses to which they put. Although the strenuous efforts to preserve historical ensembles such as Notre Dame, to collect paintings and other artifacts as did the Boisserées along the Rhine, and to otherwise repair where possible the broken vessels of the past certainly contributed to material restoration, their importance lies in the reconstitution of the meanings of the past that they facilitated. "Historical consciousness," writes Susan Crane, "incorporates the aspect of caring about the past, of finding it personally meaningful."[16] Suddenly the debris of the past, which had lain about and indeed had survived for hundreds of years without attracting much interest, spoke to contemporaries in a wide range of voices. The ruins of the past did not immediately create unmistakable connections to a recognizable national past, but they did evoke strange and mysterious lives that invited an imaginative response from viewers. Seen through a historical gaze, remains there and here signaled entities beyond the horizon of the known and the present-day.

The physical ruin quickly came to be highly valued. Contemporaries worried over its durability: the debris which had not attracted the particular attention of previous generations was all at once regarded as quite talkative but also extremely frail. And what imperiled the antique loquaciousness of the ruin most were the fashions and opinions of the moment. As Victor Hugo suggested, it was not so much the wear of nature or even the attack of revolutionaries that endangered the monuments of the past, but rather the fickle dictates of the present. Thus the fear that the present situation would be the norm accompanied the recognition of the historical nature of the past. Chateaubriand, in particular, anguished over the imperatives of today that threatened to destroy the traces of other lifeways. Whether it took the form of the French Revolution, in which republicans ransacked the tombs of the Bourbons, or of mercantile expansion, as American settlers dispersed Native Americans along the Ohio River, the empire of modernity annihilated the "bones of their fathers" and thus "the proofs of their existence."[17] Dorothea von Schlegel and Germaine de Staël also recognized that empire seeks to make the present permanent. In their view, only history as method and practice could undermine this claim and break up the single-mindedness of empire. What is powerful about the historical gaze is its ability to confront the "eternal present." It makes visible the half-lives and untimely deaths in the past and thereby provides partial restitution and enacts provisional restorations, both of which serve to unsettle the present day.

The fear of an unchanging present is another reason for modern people to focus on the past. The past provides a record of difference which introduces characters, storylines, and situations that challenge the self-evident qualities of the present-day moment.

Although the past itself cannot be changed, its ruins enable contemporaries to think in subjunctive and conditional tenses that may lead them to transform their lives and their situations. As a practice, history sets seemingly immovable things into motion, applies scare quotes to unsteady the "natural," and revises timeless duration with contingency's sharp edges. Even the saccharine effects of nostalgia rest on a fundamental distinction between the past and the present. Nostalgia, the keyword with which I initially began this project, calls for a return to home, but it does so in conditions of homelessness and with the knowledge that home is lost and loss is what remains. It is the sentiment of the dispossessed, and it does not defer easily to the standards and satisfactions of the moment.

In this book, I have tried to historicize the historical age and its preoccupation with the past. Strange places at the beginning of the nineteenth century such as Chateaubriand's graveyard or Frenchman's Island, and also attics, haunted houses, and the remote villages the Grimms idealized, all indicated the extent to which everyday material life bore the marks of newly imagined ruptures of history. They contained a past increasingly regarded in terms of its incongruencies with the present and approached as a separate place in time, bounded, distant, and opaque. It would be silly to argue that suddenly the vast majority of Europeans and Americans consciously upheld this new historical consciousness or identified with the experience of exile or consorted with ghosts. What is striking, however, is the degree to which the past was represented in terms of public and private loss and the degree to which memory work became an obsession both for nations and families. An awareness of the breaks of the past made nostalgia for a different lifetime a familiar emotion: the reconfiguration of time necessarily impinged on the emotions of men and women and parents and children. To an increasing degree, the sense of nineteenth-century selfhood depended on the recognition and exploration of loss, which should be considered one of the "sources of the self" and a constituent part of "modern identity."[18]

In some ways the historical imagination is deeply complicit in the violence of the modern era. History confronts empires with nations, but also challenges localisms with nationalism. It creates solidarities but also imposes identities, and advances onto the world stage belligerents of all kinds. It has also created problematic divisions between modern and premodern and between historical and ahistorical. Indeed, the idea of history depends on a transnational geography in which some societies were invested with historical self-consciousness and other, non-Western societies were described as primitive and passive. Since the nineteenth century, this border has shifted, but it remains in place. Anthropologists such as Johannes Fabian have indicted the West for not recognizing the contemporaneity and ultimately the subjecthood of non-Western people. Although Fabian is perhaps too quick to overlook past evidence of emphatic exchange (between displaced European nobles and dispossessed Native Americans, for example), his main point is also the argument of this book: the extension of the concept of contemporaneity across the entire globe is the first and necessary step in providing all people with political power. I have tried to show how the historical imagination created new political possibilities in Europe, and I believe that history can continue to serve this function. Still, it needs to be recognized that although historical consciousness may well be politically liberating, it also destroys very different ways of thinking about time, organizing continuity, and creating intimacies with people, spirits, and nature. Insofar as history is ultimately a story of departures, it is predicated upon a self-consciousness of insufficiency and impermanence and it establishes a kind of globalizing synchronicity. This is not easy to accept. Historical mindedness disenchants before it re-enchants; it presumes that whole forms have been irretrievably broken. But I believe these losses have to be accepted because the only way to resist the asymmetries of political and economic might and to reconsider the proportions and potentials of social solidarity is to imagine history. This imperative is the final meaning of the melancholy of history. And it is the only way forward.

Notes / Acknowledgments / Index

Notes

Introduction

1. Joseph Eichendorff, "Troest-Einsamkeit," *Werke in sechs Bänden*, Wolfgang Frühwald et al., eds. (Frankfurt, 1993), vol. 5, pp. 381–390.
2. Cited in Lothar Pikulik, *Romantik als Ungenügen an der Normalität. Am Beispiel Tiecks, Hoffmanns, Eichendorffs* (Frankfurt, 1979), p. 511.
3. Eichendorff and Novalis quoted in ibid., pp. 295–96.

1. The French Revolution

1. Entry for 17 August 1815 in Sulpiz Boisserée, *Tagebücher,* I, *1808–1823,* Hans-J. Weitz, ed. (Darmstadt, 1978), pp. 249–54.
2. George Steiner, *In Bluebeard's Castle: Some Notes Towards the Redefinition of Culture* (New Haven, 1971), pp. 12–13.
3. Lynn Hunt, *Politics, Culture, and Class in the French Revolution* (Berkeley, 1984), pp. 2, 12; François Furet, "The Ancien Régime and the Revolution," in Pierre Nora, ed., *Realms of Memory: The Construction of the French Past: Conflicts and Divisions,* Arthur Goldhammer, trans. (New York, 1996), p. 91. On the bells, see Alain Corbin, *Village Bells: Sound and Meaning in the 19th-Century French Countryside* (New York, 1998).
4. Niklas Luhmann, "The Future Cannot Begin: Temporal Structures in Modern Society," *Social Research* (1976), pp. 131–32.

5. Hunt, *Politics,* p. 27.
6. On the revolutionary self, Gerald N. Izenberg, *Impossible Individuality: Romanticism, Revolution, and the Origins of Modern Selfhood, 1787–1802* (Princeton, 1992).
7. Ernst Schulin, "'Historiker, seid der Epoche würdig!' Zur Geschichtsschreibung im Zeitalter der Französischen Revolution—zwischen Aufklärung Historismus," *Tel Aviver Jahrbuch für deutsche Geschichte* 18 (1989), p. 15.
8. Ernst Wolfgang Becker, *Zeit der Revolution!—Revolution der Zeit? Zeiterfahrungen in Deutschland in der Ära der Revolutionen 1789–1848/49* (Göttingen, 1999), pp. 38–48.
9. Friedrich Gentz to Christian Garve, 5 Dec. 1790, in *Briefe von und an Friedrich von Gentz,* F. C. Wittichen and Ernst Salzer, eds., 3 vols. (Munich, 1909–13), 1: 178–79.
10. Quoted in Hunt, *Politics,* p. 54.
11. Hunt, *Politics,* p. 19.
12. Mary A. Favret, *Romantic Correspondence: Women, Politics, and the Fiction of Letters* (Cambridge, 1993); and Nicola Watson, *Revolution and the Form of the British Novel, 1790–1825: Intercepted Letters, Interrupted Seductions* (New York, 1994).
13. Frederick C. Beiser, *Enlightenment, Revolution, and Romanticism: The Genesis of Modern German Political Thought, 1790–1800* (Cambridge, Mass., 1992), pp. 223–24. See also Hans Wolfgang Kuhn, *Der Apokalyptiker und die Politik: Studien zur Staatsphilosophie des Novalis* (Freiburg, 1961), pp. 127–28.
14. Edmund Burke, *Letters on a Regicide Peace* (1796), quoted in Conor Cruise O'Brien, "Introduction," to Burke, *Reflections on the Revolution in France,* O'Brien, ed. (Middlesex, Eng., 1969), p. 9; and Burke, *Reflections,* pp. 92, 181–82.
15. Burke to A. J. F. Dupont, 29 Mar. 1790, cited in O'Brien, "Introduction," to Burke, *Reflections,* p. 23.
16. Burke, *Reflections,* p. 92.
17. François-René de Chateaubriand, *The Memoirs of François René Vicomte de Chateaubriand,* Alexander Teixeira de Mattos, trans., 6 vols. (London, 1902), 2: 155–56; entries for 5 and 11 September 1802 in Sir Samuel Romilly, "Diary of a Journey to Paris in 1802," in *Memoirs of the Life of*

Sir Samuel Romilly, Written by Himself; with a Selection from His Correspondence, Edited by His Sons (London, 1840), pp. 78–79, 84–85; and Adélaide de Kerjean de Falaiseau, *Dix ans de la vie d'une femme pendant l'émigration,* Broc, ed. (Paris, 1893), pp. 289–91, 297–98. On words, Marilyn Bulter, "Revolving in Deep Time: The French Revolution as Narrative," in Keith Hanley and Raman Selden, eds., *Revolution and English Romanticism: Politics of Rhetoric* (New York, 1990), pp. 1–23.

18. Biancamaria Fontana, *Benjamin Constant and the Post-Revolutionary Mind* (New Haven, 1991), pp. xv, 132–33.
19. Johannes von Müller to his brother, 20 May 1797, in Johannes von Müller, *Briefe in Auswahl,* Edgar Bonjour, ed. (Basel, 1954), p. 212. See also letter of 2 July 1796, p. 208.
20. On Hegel, see Perry Anderson, *A Zone of Engagement* (New York, 1992), p. 293; Marx, David Harvey, *The Condition of Postmodernity* (Oxford, 1990), p. 261; Walter Benjamin, "The Storyteller," in *Illuminations,* Harry Zohn, trans. (New York, 1969), p. 159; Herbert Fischer Modris Eksteins, *The Rites of Spring: The Great War and the Birth of the Modern Age* (Boston, 1989), p. 291; and Eric Hobsbawm, *The Age of Extremes* (New York, 1995). See also Thomas Carlyle, *The French Revolution* (Oxford, 1989), pt. I, bk. I, ch. II: "The world is all so changed; so much that seemed vigorous has sunk decrepit, so much that was not is beginning to be!"
21. Joseph de Maistre to M. le Chevalier de Rossi, 26 Apr. 1804, in Joseph de Maistre, *Oeuvres Complètes* (Paris, 1884), 10: 106. See also Mohamed-Ali Drissa, "La Représentation de la Révolution dans *Les Considérations sur la France* de Joseph de Maistre," in Simone Bernard-Griffiths, ed., *Un Lieu de Mémoire Romantique: La Revolution de 1789* (Naples, 1993), pp. 289–309; and Steiner, "Aspects of Counter-Revolution," in Geoffrey Best, ed., *The Permanent Revolution: The French Revolution and Its Legacy, 1789–1989* (London, 1988).
22. "Schilderung des Robespierre," *Politisches Journal,* August 1794, p. 856; "Historisch-politische Uebersicht des Jahrs 1796," ibid., January 1797, p. 3.
23. *Politisches Journal* (1799), quoted in Becker, *Zeit der Revolution,* p. 90–91.
24. Dorothea Schlegel to August Wilhelm Schlegel, end of Oct. 1810, in

Josef Körner, ed., *Krisenjahre der Frühromantik: Briefe aus dem Schlegelkreis,* 3 vols. (Brünn, 1936), 2: 168; and Ernst Moritz Arndt, *Geist der Zeit* in *Sämtliche Werke* (Magdeburg, 1908), 1: 53.

25. Gentz quoted in Becker, *Zeit der Revolution,* p. 59; Wordsworth in James Chandler, *England in 1819: The Politics of Literary Culture and the Case of Romantic Historicism* (Chicago, 1998), pp. 249–50.

26. *Politisches Journal,* December 1794, pp. 1266–67.

27. *Politisches Journal,* November 1800, pp. 1095–96. See also Klaus Behrens, *Friedrich Schlegels Geschichtsphilosophie (1794–1808): Ein Beitrag zur politischen Romantik* (Tübingen, 1984), pp. 16–20.

28. Ronald Paulson, *Representations of Revolution (1789–1820)* (New Haven, 1983), p. 1.

29. *Politisches Journal,* November 1800, p. 1097.

30. Reinhart Koselleck, *Futures Past: On the Semantics of Historical Time* (Cambridge, 1985), pp. 13, 15. See also Mack Walker, *German Home Towns: Community, State, and General Estate, 1648–1871* (Ithaca, 1971).

31. Clemens Menze, "Der Humanismus in Johannes von Müllers Donstetten-Briefen am Beispiel des Zusammenhanges von Geschichte und Bildung," in Christoph Jamme and Otto Pöggeler, *Johannes von Müller—Geschichtsschreiber der Goethezeit* (Schaffhausen, 1986), pp. 22–23.

32. Fernand Baldensperger, *Le Mouvement des Idées dans l'Emigration Française, 1789–1815,* 2 vols (Paris, 1924), 2: 76–77.

33. Gentz to Müller, 13 Nov. 1805, in Friedrich Gentz, *Briefwechsel zwischen Friedrich Gentz und Adam Heinrich Müller, 1800–1829* (Stuttgart, 1857). On Gentz' writing, see Golo Mann, *Secretary of Europe: The Life of Friedrich Gentz, Enemy of Napoleon,* William H. Woglom, trans. (New Haven, 1946), p. 36.

34. *Historisches Journal* (1799), quoted in Becker, *Zeit der Revolution,* p. 60.

35. Gentz to Adam Müller, 23 Oct. 1802, in *Briefe von und an Friedrich von Gentz,* F. C. Wittichen and Ernst Salzer, eds., 3 vols. (Munich, 1909–13), 2: 383.

36. Mann, *Secretary of Europe,* p. 141.

37. Metternich to Gentz, 21 Jan. 1806, in Gentz, *Briefe,* 3: 44–45.

38. Quoted in Mann, p. 154.

39. Marwitz to Rahel Varnhagen, 31 Dec. 1812, in Rahel Varnhagen, *Rahel Varnhagens Briefwechsel,* F. Kemp, ed., 4 vols (Munich, 1979), 1: 225.
40. Entry for 18 Mar. 1815, quoted in Clive Emsley, *British Society and the French Wars, 1793–1815* (London, 1979), p. 168. *The Gentleman's Magazine* had very similar words: "There is nothing parallel to it in history, scarcely in romance." See issue of March 1815, p. 266.
41. Germaine de Staël, *Considerations on the Principal Events of the French Revolution,* 3 vols. (London, 1818), 3: 136.
42. Rahel to Markus Levin, 29 Mar. 1815 in Varnhagen, *Briefwechsel,* 4: 80.
43. Rahel to Markus Levin, 2 April 1815, ibid., 4: 83.
44. Rahel to Varnhagen in Paris, 11 Oct. 1815, ibid., 2:355.
45. François-René de Chateaubriand, *An Historical, Political, and Moral Essay on Revolutions, Ancient and Modern* (London, 1815), pp. 4–5.
46. Hunt, *Politics,* pp. 172–73, 181.
47. Hew Strachan, "The Nation in Arms," in Best, *Permanent Revolution,* pp. 57, 63; Linda Colley, *Britons: Forging the Nation 1707–1837* (New Haven, 1992), p. 287; and Jacques Houdaille, "Pertes de l'armée de terre sous le premier empire, d'après les registres matricules," *Population* 27 (1972), pp. 27–50. On the comparison with World War I, Karen Hagemann, *Mannlicher Muth und Teusche Ehre: Nation, Militär, und Geschlecht zur Zeit der Antinapoleonischen Kriege Preussens* (Paderborn, 2001), p. 23.
48. Wilhelm to Jacob Grimm, 18 Jan. 1814, in Hermann Grimm, Gustav Hinrichs, and Wilhelm School, eds., *Briefwechsel zwischen Jacob und Wilhelm Grimm aus der Jugendzeit* (Weimar, 1881 [Weimar, 1963]), p. 238.
49. See, for example, Sulpiz Boisserée, "Fragmente einer Selbstbiographie," and diary entry for 9 Jan. 1814, in *Tagebücher,* 1: 9, 108–09; and J. Bröcker to Melchoir Boisserée, 5 Sept. 1830, in *Sulpiz Boisserée,* Mathilde Boisserée, ed. (Stuttgart, 1862), 1: 555; or Franz Xaver Freiherrn von Andlaw-Birseck, *Mein Tagebuch: Auszüge aus Aufschreibungen der Jahre 1811 bis 1861* (Frankfurt, 1862), pp. 1–2, 32–33. In general, see Werner K. Blessing, "Umbruchkrise und 'Verstörung:'

Die 'Napoleonische' Erschütterung und ihre sozialpsychologische Bedeutung (Bayern als Beispiel)," *Zeitschrift für Bayerische Landesgeschichte* 42 (1979), pp. 78–79.

50. Charlotte von Stein, in Weimar, to Fritz von Stein, 26 Dec. 1805, quoted in Günter Jäckel, ed. *Das Volk braucht Licht: Frauen zur Zeit des Aufbruchs 1790–1848 in ihren Briefen* (Darmstadt, 1970), p. 93; entries for 18 July 1793, 1 Jan. 1794; 1 Jan. 1795, 4 Oct. 1794, in Johann Peter Delhoven, *Die Rheinische Dorfchronik,* Hermann Cardauns and Reiner Müller, eds. (Neuss, 1926), pp. 82, 88, 107, 98. See also Sulpiz Boisserée, *Tagebücher,* p. 1: 8, describing Austrian troops in Cologne in 1792 and 1793.

51. Kleist to Wilhelmine von Zenge, 11/12 Sept. 1800, in *An Abyss Deep Enough. Letters of Heinrich von Kleist,* ed. and trans. Philip B. Miller (New York, 1982), p. 58.

52. Caroline Böhmer-Schlegel-Schelling to Meta Liebeskind, 28 Aug. 1809, cited in Jäckel, ed., *Das Volk braucht Licht,* pp. 241–42.

53. "Fürsten- und Völker-Wanderung," *Politisches Journal,* December 1806, pp. 1246–51.

54. Katharina Goethe in Frankfurt to her son in Weimar, 10 Oct. 1805, in Eckart Klessmann, ed., *Deutschland unter Napoleon in Augenzeugenberichten* (Düsseldorf, 1965), p. 42.

55. James J. Sheehan, *German History, 1770–1866* (New York, 1989), p. 251. See also Blessing, "Umbruchkrise und 'Verstörung,'" p. 91; and Walker, *German Home Towns,* pp. 234–43, on what eventually became Bavarian Weissenburg.

56. Cited in Colley, *Britons,* pp. 307–08.

57. Ibid., p. 369.

58. Emile Erckmann and Alexandre Chatrian, *The Conscript: A Story of the French War of 1813* (New York, 1912), p. 7.

59. Quoted in Chandler, *England in 1819,* p. 42. See also Blessing, "Umbruchkrise und 'Verstörung,'" p. 84.

60. Boisserée, *Tagebücher,* pp. 1:9–10; and Lynn Hunt, "The Unstable Boundaries of the French Revolution," in Michelle Perrot, ed., *A History of Private Life: From the Fires of Revolution to the Great War* (Cambridge, Mass., 1990), p. 21.

61. Charlotte von Stein to Charlotte Schiller, 6 Mar. 1790, in Jäckel,

ed., *Das Volk braucht Licht,* p. 82; Anne-Charlotte Trepp, *Sanfte Männlichkeit und selbständige Weiblichkeit: Frauen und Männer in Hamburger Bürgertum zwischen 1770 und 1840* (Göttingen, 1996), pp. 271–72.

62. Chateaubriand, *Memoirs,* 1: 174–75; George D. Painter, *Chateaubriand: Volume I (1768–93), The Longed-for Tempests* (New York, 1978), pp. 138–39.

63. Diary entry for 9 Feb. 1794, in William Roberts, ed., *Memoirs of the Life and Correspondence of Mrs. Hannah More* (London, 1834), 2: 415.

64. Cited in James K. Chandler, *Wordsworth's Second Nature: A Study of the Poetry and Politics* (Chicago, 1984), p. 17.

65. See James M. Brophy, "The Common Reader in the Rhineland: Calendars as Political Primer in the Early Nineteenth Century," unpubl. ms.

66. *Godey's Lady's Book* 4 (1832), p. 16. Other articles include "French Revolution," 2 (1831), p. 230; "The Monk: A Tale, Descriptive of the Political State of France in 1793," 5 (1832), pp. 306–14. It was much the same in New York's *The Family Magazine,* "a general abstract of useful knowledge," which published "Death of Napoleon" (1833), p. 87, and "Napoleon at Rest" (1834), p. 56; and in Cincinnati's *The Family Magazine,* "Napoleon's Advice to a Young American," 1 (1836), p. 280; "Sketches of the Life of Talleyrand," 3 (1838), p. 521; "Napoleon and the British Sailor," 4 (1839), p. 428; "Waterloo at Noon," 5 (1840), p. 287. See also the reference to "the late news from France" in "Miss Denby," Harriet Beecher Stowe, *Oldtown Folks* (Boston, 1869), pp. 513–14.

67. Rahel to Caroline von Schlabrendorf, 9 May 1809, in Jäckel, ed., *Das Volk braucht Licht,* p. 470. See also Joseph von Görres to his bride, 27 Mar. 1800, in *Gesammelte Schriften* (Munich, 1854), 7: 49.

68. Marilyn Butler, *Romantics, Rebels, and Reactionaries: English Literature and Its Background, 1760–1830* (Oxford, 1981), pp. 99–100; and Watson, *Revolution.*

69. Chandler, *Wordworth's Second Nature,* p. 270n10.

70. Favret, *Romantic Correspondence,* p. 9.

71. Letter dated end of December, 1809, Dorothea von Schlegel, *Dorothea von Schlegel und deren Söhne Johannes und Philipp Veit. Briefwechsel,* 2 vols. (Mainz, 1881), 1: 396.

72. Rahel to Varnhagen, 10 Dec. 1808, in Rahel Varnhagen, *Briefwechsel,* 2: 77.
73. Varnhagen to Rahel, 21 May 1813, in ibid., 2: 214.
74. This formulation is drawn from Favret, *Romantic Correspondence,* p. 9.
75. On letter writing, see Cecile Dauphin, Pierrette Lebrun-Pezerat, Daniele Poublan, *Ces bonnes lettres: une correspondance familiale au XIXe siècle* (Paris, 1995); as well as Roger Chartier, ed., *La Correspondance. Les usages de la lettre au XIXe siècle* (Paris, 1991). See also Benedict Anderson, *Imagined Communities,* rev. ed. (London, 1991).
76. Quoted in Mann, *Secretary of Europe,* p. 154.
77. Ulrich Raulff, *Der unsichtbare Augenblick: Zeitkonzepte in der Geschichte* (Göttingen, 1999), pp. 64–66.
78. Kenneth R. Johnston, *The Hidden Wordsworth: Poet, Lover, Rebel, Spy* (New York, 1998), pp. 72, 419.
79. Johnston, *Hidden Wordsworth,* p. 162.
80. Rahel to Markus Levin, 29 Mar. 1815, in Rahel Varnhagen, *Briefwechsel,* 4: 79. The English essayist, Thomas de Quincey, left suggestive remarks on the emergence of both a national and a historical sensibility during the Napoleonic Wars. "The grandest chapter of our experience, within the whole mail-coach service," he wrote in retrospect, "was on those occasions when we went down from London with the news of victory." At every stop just a few words about "the heart-shaking news of Trafalgar, of Salamanca, of Vittoria, of Waterloo" prompted "peals of brotherly congratulations . . . like fire racing along a train of gunpowder," "multiplying the victory itself." As de Quincey first described it, and as Linda Colley has more closely analyzed it, the victory was not simply that of Great Britain at Waterloo but of a kind of Britishness at "Lincoln, Winchester, Portsmouth," a national fellowship that was distinguished by the common recognition of the historical moment. See Thomas de Quincey, "The English Mail Coach," in *Confessions of an English Opium Eater and Other Writings* (New York, 1985), pp. 184, 201, 204–05; as well as Colley, *Britons.* For a similar description for France, see Alphone de Lamartine quoted in Martyn Lyons, *Napoleon Bonaparte and the Legacy of the French Revolution* (New York, 1994), pp. 153–54.

81. Koselleck, *Futures Past,* p. 31; see also Georg Lukacs, *The Historical Novel* (Lincoln, 1983), p. 23.
82. Walker, *German Home Towns,* p. 248.
83. Klaus Behrens, *Friedrich Schlegels Geschichtsphilosophie (1794–1808): Ein Beitrag zur politischen Romantik* (Tübingen, 1984), p. 11.
84. Alfred de Musset, *A Modern Man's Confession,* G. F. Monkshood, trans. (London, 1908), pp. 6, 10.
85. Quoted in Sheehan, *German History,* p. 392.
86. Gentz to Brinkmann, 8 Nov. 1824, in Gentz, *Briefe,* 2: 341.
87. Chateaubriand to de Caraman, Paris, 3 Aug. 1823, in *Correspondance générale de Chateaubriand,* Louis Thomas, ed. (Paris, 1911), 4: 353.
88. Quoted in M. H. Abrams, *Natural Supernaturalism: Tradition and Revolution in Romantic Literature* (New York, 1971), p. 328.
89. Seamus Deane, *The French Revolution and Enlightenment in England, 1789–1832* (Cambridge, 1988), p. 41. See also Hedva Ben-Israel, *English Historians and the French Revolution* (Cambridge, 1968); and Stanley Mellon, *The Political Uses of History: A Study of Historians in the French Revolution* (Stanford, 1958).
90. Linda Orr, *Headless History: Nineteenth-Century French Historiography of the Revolution* (Ithaca, 1990), p. 21.
91. Thomas Carlyle, *The French Revolution* (Oxford, 1989), pt. I, bk. VI, ch. I; pt. III, bk. VII, ch. VI.
92. John Rosenberg, *Carlyle and the Burden of History* (Cambridge, 1985), p. 30. In fact, Carlyle anticipates this charge in *The French Revolution,* pt. III, bk. V, ch. I.
93. Barton R. Friedman, *Fabricating History: English Writers on the French Revolution* (Princeton, 1988), p. 112; Carlyle, *The French Revolution,* pt. II, bk. III, ch. V.
94. Cited in Albert Cook, *History/Writing: The Theory and Practice of History in Antiquity and in Modern Times* (Cambridge, 1988), p. 124.
95. Carlyle, *The French Revolution,* pt. I; bk. I, ch. I; Karl Kroeber, "Romantic Historicism: The Temporal Sublime," in Kroeber and William Walling, eds,. *Images of Romanticism: Verbal and Visual Affinities* (New Haven, 1978), p. 159. See also Hugh Honour, *Romanticism* (New York, 1979), pp. 192–93.

96. Rahel Varnhagen to Ludwig Robert, 5 Feb. 1816 in Varnhagen, *Briefwechsel* (Munich, 1979), 4: 101.
97. Cited in Chandler, *England in 1819,* p. 87.
98. Joyce Appleby, *Inheriting the Revolution: The First Generation of Americans* (Cambridge, Mass., 2000), p. 23.
99. Koselleck, *Futures Past,* p. 251.
100. Rondo Cameron, "A New View of European Industrialization," *Economic History* 38 (1985), pp. 1–23; Jordan Goodman and Katrina Honeyman, *Gainful Pursuits: The Making of Industrial Europe, 1600–1914* (London, 1988).
101. Elisabeth Helsinger, *Rural Scenes and National Representation: Britain, 1815–1850* (Princeton, 1997), pp. 6, 146–47.
102. Ibid., p. 142.
103. Chateaubriand, *Memoirs,* p. 6: 223; and Arndt to sister Dorothea, 24 June 1834, in Ernst Moritz Arndt, *Briefe,* A. Dühr, ed., 3 vols. (Darmstadt, 1972–75), 2: 484. See also Johanna Schopenhauer, *Ihr glücklichen Augen: Jugenderinnerungen, Tagebücher, Briefe* (Berlin, 1979), pp. 29–32.
104. Ernst Wilhelm Martius, *Erinnerungen aus meinem neunzigjährigen Leben* (Leipzig, 1847), p. 11.
105. Todd Steven Gernes, "Recasting the Culture of Ephemera: Young Women's Literary Culture in Nineteenth-Century America," Ph.D diss. (Brown University, 1992), p. 39.
106. Raphael Samuel, *Theatres of Memory: Past and Present in Contemporary Culture* (London, 1994), p. 161.
107. Chandler, *England in 1819,* p. 150.
108. Ibid., pp. 78, 91. See also A. Dwight Culler, *The Victorian Mirror of History* (New Haven, 1985), pp. 40–41.
109. Inge Rippmann, "'Die Zeit läuft wie ein Reh vor uns her.' Der Zeitschriftsteller als Geschichtsscreiber," in Rippmann and Wolfgang Labuhn, eds., *"Die Kunst—eine Tochter der Zeit." Neue Studien zu Ludwig Börne* (Bielefeld, 1988), pp. 139–40. See also William Hazlitt, *Spirit of the Age* (London, 1971 [1825]).
110. According to Martin Heidegger, "the world picture does not change from an earlier medieval one into a modern one, but rather the fact

that the world becomes a picture at all is what distinguishes the essence of the modern age." See *The Question Concerning Technology and Other Essays* (New York, 1977), p. 130.

111. Cited in Peter Osborne, *The Politics of Time: Modernity and the Avant-Garde* (London, 1995), p. 11.

112. On popular culture, see Stephen Bann, *Romanticism and the Rise of History* (New York, 1995); and Petra ten-Doesschate Chu, "Pop Culture in the Making: The Romantic Craze for History," in Chu and Gabriel P. Weisberg, eds., *The Popularization of Images: Visual Culture under the July Monarchy* (Princeton, 1994), pp. 166–88.

113. Frederika Bremer, *The Home; or Family Cares and Family Joys,* E. A. Friedländer, trans. (London, 1845), pp. 28, 31.

114. Theodor Fontane, *Vor dem Sturm* (Munich, 1990 [1878]), p. 283.

115. Elizabeth Deeds Ermarth, *Sequel to History: Postmodernism and the Crisis of Representational Time* (Princeton, 1992), p. 28. See also Ermarth, *Realism and Consensus in the English Novel* (Princeton, 1983); and Franco Moretti, *Atlas of the European Novel 1800–1900* (London, 1998).

116. Ingrid Oesterle, "Der Führungswechsel der Zeithorizonte in der deutschen Literatur. Korrespondenzen aus Paris, der Hauptstadt der Menschheitsgeschichte," in Dirk Grathoff, ed., *Studien zur Ästhetik und Literaturgeschichte der Kunstperiode* (Frankfurt, 1985), p. 20. See also Burkhart Steinwachs, *Epochenbewusstsein und Kunsterfahrung—Studien zur geschichtsphilosophischen Ästhetik an der Wende vom 18. zum 19. Jahrhundert in Frankreich und Deutschland* (Munich, 1986).

117. Koselleck, *Futures Past,* pp. 275–76; Rudy Koshar, *Germany's Transient Pasts: Preservation and National Memory in the Twentieth Century* (Chapel Hill, 1998), p. 18.

118. Bruce James Smith, *Politics and Remembrance: Republican Themes in Machiavelli, Burke, and Tocqueville* (Princeton, 1985), p. 243.

2. Strangers

1. François-René de Chateaubriand, *The Memoirs of Chateaubriand,* selected and translated by Robert Baldick (New York, 1961), p. 174.

In the complete edition, François-René de Chateaubriand, *The Memoirs of François René Vicomte de Chateaubriand,* Alexander Teixeira de Mattos, trans., 6 vols. (London, 1902), the quote appears at 2: 38–39.

2. Chateaubriand, *Memoirs,* 2: 179.
3. Chateaubriand, *A Letter from Rome,* W. Joseph Walter, trans. (London, 1815), pp. 20–23, originally a letter to Jean Pierre Louis Marquis Fontanes, 10 Jan. 1804, and thereupon published in *Mercure de France,* 3 Mar. 1804. The line appears also in Chateaubriand, *The Genius of Christianity,* Charles I. White, trans. (Philadelphia, 1856), p. 468.
4. Baldick, ed., *Memoirs,* p. 73.
5. Chateaubriand, *An Historical, Political, and Moral Essay on Revolutions, Ancient and Modern* (London, 1815), pp. 4–5.
6. Baldick, ed., *Memoirs,* p. 12.
7. Quoted in Pierre Barbéris, *Chateaubriand: Une réaction au monde moderne* (Paris, 1976), pp. 189, 219.
8. Chateaubriand, *Memoirs,* 6: 255.
9. Ibid., 2: 95.
10. Quoted in Barbéris, *Chateaubriand,* pp. 107–08.
11. Tom Conner, *Chateaubriand's* Mémoires d'outre-tombe: *A Portrait of the Artist as Exile* (New York, 1995), p. 167.
12. George D. Painter, *Chateaubriand: Volume I (1768–93), The Longed-for Tempests* (New York, 1978), p. 4.
13. Chateaubriand, *Memoirs,* 1: 17, 76.
14. Ibid., 1: 93.
15. Cited in Jean-Pierre Richard, *Paysage de Chateaubriand* (Paris, 1967), p. 110.
16. Chateaubriand, *Memoirs,* 1: 186–87. Consider also the episode with Charlotte Ives, 2: 86–94.
17. Chateaubriand, *A Letter from Rome,* pp. 20–23.
18. Chateaubriand, *Memoirs,* 1: 108–09. See also Chateaubriand, *Genius,* p. 518n1.
19. Chateaubriand, *Memoirs,* 1: 231.
20. Chateaubriand, *Genius,* pp. 136–37, 151.
21. Chateaubriand, *Memoirs,* 1: 23.
22. Quoted in Conner, *Chateaubriand's* Mémoires d'outre-tombe, p. 24.
23. Barbéris, *Chateaubriand,* pp. 126–27, 129.

24. Cited in Ghislain de Diesbach, *Chateaubriand* (Paris, 1995), p. 510.
25. Joan Scott, "The Evidence of Experience," *Critical Inquiry* 17 (1991).
26. Maurice Halbwachs, *On Collective Memory* (Chicago, 1992), p. 39. See also Halbwachs, *The Collective Memory* (New York, 1980), p. 19.
27. Reinhart Koselleck, *Futures Past: On the Semantics of Historical Time* (Cambridge, Mass., 1985), p. 282.
28. Vladimir Jankélévitch, *L'Irréversible et la nostalgie* (Paris, 1974).
29. Fernand Baldensperger, *Le Mouvement des idées dans l'émigration française, 1789–1815,* 2 vols (Paris, 1924), 1: 113.
30. Lloyd Kramer, *Threshold of a New World: Intellectuals and the Exile Experience in Paris, 1830–1848* (Ithaca, 1988), p. 2.
31. See, for example, James Clifford, *Routes: Travel and Translation in the Late Twentieth Century* (Cambridge, Mass., 1997); Hamid Naficy, ed., *Home, Exile, Homeland: Film, Media, and the Politics of Place* (New York, 1999); Liisa H. Malkki, *Purity and Exile: Violence, Memory, and National Cosmology among Hutu Refugees in Tanzania* (Chicago, 1995).
32. M. de Bacquencourt to Mme de Falaiseau, 15 Oct. 1791, quoted in Adélaide de Kerjean de Falaiseau, *Dix ans de la vie d'une femme pendant l'émigration,* Vicomte de Broc, ed. (Paris, 1893), p. 53.
33. James Roberts, *The Counter-Revolution in France* (London, 1990), p. 5.
34. Quoted in Painter, *Chateaubriand,* p. 249.
35. Entries for 19–29 Aug. and 21 Sept. 1792 in Joseph Thomas d'Espinchal, *Journal of the Comte d'Espinchal during the Emigration,* Ernest d'Hauterive, ed., Mrs. Rodolph Stawell, trans. (London, 1912), pp. 327, 341.
36. Goethe, "Campaign in France," *Miscellaneous Travels of J. W. Goethe,* L. Dora Schmitz, ed. (London, 1882), p. 118.
37. Ibid.; and Nicolas Boyle, *Goethe: The Poet and the Age, Volume II* (New York, 2000).
38. Charles de Cezac, *Dix ans d'émigration: souvenirs de Cézac, Hussard de Berchény, volontaire à l'armée de Condé,* Baron André de Maricourt, ed. (Paris, 1909), p. 36. See also Chateaubriand, *Memoirs,* 2: 54.
39. Marie-Charles-Isidore de Mercy to Gabriel-Laurent Paillou, 16 Nov. 1792, in Mercy, *Lettres d'émigration 1790–1802* (La Roche-sur-Yon, 1993), p. 97.
40. Comments dated January 1793, d'Espinchal, *Journal,* p. 411.

41. Baldensperger, *Mouvement des idées,* 1: 63–64.

42. Arnulf Moser, *Die französische Emigrantenkolonie in Konstanz während der Revolution (1792–1799)* (Sigmaringen, 1975), pp. 20–25, 53; and Klaus Epstein, *The Genesis of German Conservatism* (Princeton, 1966), p. 369. See also Donald Greer, *The Incidence of the Emigration in the French Revolution* (Cambridge, Mass., 1951); Georges Andrey, *Les émigrés français dans le canton de Fribourg 1789–1815* (Neuchatel, 1972); and Frances Sergeant Childs, *French Refugee Life in the United States, 1790–1800: An American Chapter of the French Revolution* (Philadelphia, 1978 [Baltimore, 1940]).

43. Chateaubriand, *Genius,* pp. 152–53.

44. G. J. Martinant de Préneuf, *Huit années d'émigration: Souvenirs de l'abbé G. J. Martinant de Préneuf 1792–1801,* G. Vanel, ed. (Paris, 1908), pp. 175–76, 215.

45. Michael Call, *Back to the Garden: Chateaubriand, Senancour and Constant* (Stanford, 1981), p. 41.

46. Auguste de la Ferronays, *En émigration: Souvenirs tirés des Papiers du Comte A. de la Ferronnays,* Costa de Beauregard, ed. (Paris, 1900), p. 315.

47. Mme. de Falaiseau to Paul du Camper, 29 Sept. 1798, in *Dix ans de la vie,* de Broc, ed., p. 276. See also Mme. de Ménerville, *Souvenirs d'émigration* (Paris, 1934), p. 127.

48. Letter to de Jouville, 3 Oct. 1792, in *Correspondance originale des émigrés peints par eux-mêmes,* 2 vols. (Paris, 1793), 1: 104–05.

49. Pauline de Noinville and Changy, both cited in Adélaide de Kerjean de Falaiseau, *Dix ans de la vie,* Broc, ed., pp. 289–90, 297–98. See also Chateaubriand, *Memoirs,* 2: 155–56.

50. Honoré de Balzac, *Lily of the Valley,* Katherine Prescott Wormeley, trans. (Boston, 1901), pp. 49–50. See also Balzac, *The Gallery of Antiquities,* Katherine Prescott Wormeley, trans. (Boston, 1901). On the indemnification debate, see André Gain, *La Restauration et les biens des émigrés* (Nancy, 1929).

51. See also Hugh Honour, *Romanticism* (New York, 1979), p. 196.

52. Klaus Behrens, *Friedrich Schlegels Geschichtsphilosophie (1794–1808): Ein Beitrag zur politischen Romantik* (Tübingen, 1984), p. 148.

53. Chateaubriand, *Memoirs,* p. 22; Barbéris, *Chateaubriand,* p. 255; Louis-

Joseph-Amour de Bouille, *Souvenirs et fragments,* P.-L. de Kermaingant, ed. (Paris, 1906), p. 2; La Ferronays, *En émigration,* p. 1. See also Hauteville quoted in Wilhelm Wühr, *Die Emigranten der Französischen Revolution im bayerischen und fränkischen Kreis* (Munich, 1974 [1938]), p. 56; and George Armstrong Kelly, *The Humane Comedy: Constant, Tocqueville, and French Liberalism* (Cambridge, 1992), pp. 27, 38.

54. Baldensperger, *Mouvement des idées,* 1: 44, 111.
55. Ibid., 1: 111.
56. Ibid., 1: 81. See also Chateaubriand, *Memoirs,* 2: 141–42.
57. Charlotte Hogsett, *The Literary Existence of Germaine de Staël* (Carbondale, 1987), p. 95.
58. Germaine de Staël, *Considerations on the Principal Events of the French Revolution,* 3 vols. (London, 1818), 2: 299–300.
59. Germaine de Staël, *Corinne, or Italy* (Oxford, 1998 [1807]), pp. 137 [8.I], 111 [7.I], 291 [15.IX].
60. Germaine de Staël, *Ten Years in Exile,* Doris Beik, ed. (New York, 1972), p. 189.
61. Staël to Gaudot, 20 Dec. 1808, quoted in Sylvia Raphael, "Introduction," to *Corinne,* p. x.
62. Staël, *Corinne,* p. 8 [1.II].
63. Staël, *Considerations,* 2: 300.
64. Staël, *Ten Years,* p. 138.
65. Baldensperger, *Mouvement des idées,* 1: 11, 305–06.
66. Alphonse to Germaine, 8 June 1793 in Charrière's fictional *Lettres dans des port-feuilles d'émigrés* (Lausanne, 1793), p. 460.
67. La Ferronays, *En émigration,* p. 289.
68. *Mercure de France,* 30 Nov. 1800, quoted in Baldensperger, *Mouvement des idées,* p. 1: 308. See also Abbé Canat, *Romance d'un exilé,* cited in Georges Andrey, *Les émigrés français dans le canton de Fribourg 1789–1815* (Neuchatel, 1972), p. 137.
69. Baldensperger, *Mouvement des idées,* p. 1: 309.
70. Broc, ed., *Dix ans,* p. 147.
71. Abbe Huet to Modème, 4 Aug. 1795, in E. Droz., ed., *Le Comte de Modène et ses correspondants: Documents inédits sur l'émigration 1791–1803,* 2 vols. (Paris, 1942), 1: 107.
72. Chateaubriand, *Genius,* pp. 182–83.

73. See, for example, Broc, ed., *Dix ans,* pp. iii, vii, ix; Louis-Joseph-Amour de Bouille, *Souvenirs et fragments,* p. 2; *Memoiren der Marquise von Nadaillac, Herzogin von Escars,* Oberst Marques von Nadaillac, ed., E. v. Kraatz, trans. (Braunschweig, 1913), pp. 29–33; Comte de Neuilly, *Dix années d'émigration. Souvenirs et correspondance,* Maurice de Barbery, ed. (Paris, 1865), pp. v–vii; and, more generally, Ernest Renan, *Recollections of My Youth,* C. B. Pitman, trans. (London, 1883); and Philippe Ariès, "Ein Kind entdeckt die Geschichte" (1946), in *Zeit und Geschichte,* Perdita Duttke, trans. (Frankfurt, 1988).
74. Unpublished letter of 4 May 1858, cited in André Jardin, *Tocqueville. A Biography,* Lydia Davis, trans. (New York, 1988), p. 377.
75. Jardin, *Tocqueville,* p. 8.
76. Jon Vanden Heuvel, "A German Life in the Age of Revolution: Joseph Görres," Ph.D diss. (Columbia, 1996), p. 288, citing the writer Friedrich Hebbel.
77. Moser, *Die französische Emigrantenkolonie,* p. 25; Staël quoted in M. Charles Nicoullaud, ed., *Memoirs of the Comtesse de Boigne,* 3 vols. (New York, 1908), 1: 231.
78. Stephanie de Genlis, *Les petits émigrés, ou correspondance de quelques enfants; ouvrage fait pour servir à l'éducation de la jeunesse,* 2 vols. (Paris, 1812), 1: 95. See also Todd Steven Gernes, "Recasting the Culture of Ephemera: Young Women's Literary Culture in Nineteenth-Century America," Ph.D diss. (Brown University, 1992). On fragments: de Bouille, *Souvenirs et Fragments.*
79. Michael Seidel, *Exile and the Narrative Imagination* (New Haven, 1986), pp. x, 107.
80. Hogsett, *The Literary Existence of Germaine de Staël,* pp. 95–96.
81. Mme. de Ménerville, *Souvenirs d'émigration,* pp. 168–69.
82. Baldensperger, *Mouvement des idées,* 1: 208.
83. Madame de La Tour du Pin, *Memoirs,* F. Harcourt, ed. and trans. (London, 1969).
84. Agnes von Gerlach to Marie von Raumer, 23 Dec. 1808, in Hans Joachim Schoeps, ed., *Aus den Jahren Preussicher Not und Erneuerung. Tagebücher und Briefe der Gebrüder Gerlach und ihres Kreises, 1805–1820* (Berlin, 1963), pp. 368–69. In an earlier letter, dated 30 Oct. 1806 (p. 359), Gerlach wrote of the whereabouts of family members after

the fateful Battle of Jena: "My son is being held prisoner and he reappeared here the day before yesterday safe and sound . . . Henri, the son of my brother, is also apparently prisoner. My brother Eugen was slightly wounded and returned to Brieg. My brother Henri has probably been taken prisoner, but we don't know for sure." For examples of the genre, see Adélaide Sousa Botelho Mouraoe Vasconelles, *Emilie et Alphonse* (Paris, 1799), *Eugénie et Mathilde* (Paris, 1811), and *Adèle de Selange* (Paris, 1821); as well as August Heinrich Julius Lafontaine, *Clara du Plessis und Clairant. Eine Familiengeschichte französischer Emigranten* (Berlin, 1795).

85. Ariès, "Ein Kind entdeckt die Geschichte," p. 12.

86. Marilyn Yalom, *Blood Sisters: The French Revolution in Women's Memory* (New York, 1995), pp. 1, 10–11. See also Ariès, *Zeit und Geschichte,* pp. 51, 54–55, 70; Pierre Nora, "Die Staatsmemoiren von Commynes bis de Gaulle," *Zwischen Geschichte und Gedächtnis* (Berlin, 1990), pp. 98–111; Gustav René Hocke, *Das europäische Tagebuch* (Wiesbaden, 1963), pp. 201–02; and more generally, Shoshana Felman and Dori Laub, *Testimony: Crises of Witnessing in Literature, Psychoanalysis, and History* (New York, 1992). Bibliographic aids include Jean Toulard, ed., *Nouvelle bibliographie critique des mémoires sur le Consulat et l'Empire écrits ou traduits en français* (Paris, 1988); and Guillaume de Bertier de Sauvigny, et al., eds., *Bibliographie critique des mémoires sur la Restauration* (Paris, 1988).

87. On the significance of the appropriations of Des Watines' story, see Irena Gross, *The Scar of Revolution: Custine, Tocqueville, and the Romantic Imagination* (Berkeley, 1991), pp. 103–20. She relies on the splendid study by Victor Lange, "Visitors to Lake Oneida: An Account of the Background of Sophie von La Roche's Novel *Erscheinungen am See Oneida,*" *Symposium* 2 (1948), pp. 48–78. See also Sophie von La Roche, *Erscheinungen am See Oneida* (Eschborn, 1995 [Leipzig, 1798]).

88. Gross, *Scar of Revolution,* p. 103.

89. Harry Liebersohn, *Aristocratic Encounters: European Travelers and North American Indians* (Cambridge, 1998), pp. 2–3, 6, 43. See also Barbéris, *Chateaubriand,* p. 46.

90. Chateaubriand, *Travels in America and Italy,* 2 vols. (London, 1828), 1: 98, 112, 123–34, 167; 2: 101.

91. Liebersohn, *Aristocratic Encounters,* pp. 39–47, 59. See also Johannes Fabian, *Time and the Other: How Anthropology Makes Its Object* (New York, 1983).
92. Lewis Perry, *Boats Against the Current: American Culture Between Revolution and Modernity, 1820–1860* (New York, 1993), pp. 100–01.
93. Liebersohn, *Aristocratic Encounters,* p. 142.
94. Donald Ringe. *The Pictatorial Mode: Space and Time in the Art of Bryant, Irving and Cooper* (Lexington, 1971), pp. 138–39.
95. Perry, *Boats Against the Current,* p. 215.
96. Suzanne Nash, "Introduction," to Nash, ed., *Home and Its Discontents in Nineteenth-Century France* (Albany, 1993), p. 5. See also Harvie Ferguson, *Melancholy and the Critique of Modernity: Søren Kierkegaard's Religious Psychology* (London, 1995).
97. Gerald N. Izenberg, *Impossible Individuality: Romanticism, Revolution, and the Origins of Modern Selfhood, 1787–1802* (Princeton, 1992), pp. 236–37. See also F. M. Todd, *Politics and the Poet: A Study of Wordsworth* (London, 1957).
98. Letters of 20 Apr. and 26 Apr. 1800, Joseph von Görres, *Gesammelte Schriften* (Munich, 1854), p. 7: 67, 69.
99. Barbéris, *Chateaubriand,* pp. 128–29. See also Nash, ed., *Home and Its Discontents.*
100. Renan, *Recollections of My Youth,* pp. 25, 82–83, 97, 100. See also the letters and revolutionary mementoes in Adolf von Knigge, *Aus einer alten Kiste. Orginalbriefe, Handschrften und Dokumente aus dem Nachlasse eines bekannten Mannes* (Leipzig, 1853), p. 21; and Knigge's letter to his daughter, 15 July 1790, in Claus Träger, ed., *Die französische Revolution im Spiegel der deutschen Literatur* (Leipzig, 1975), as well as Gustave Flaubert, "A Simple Heart," *Three Tales* (London, 1961), p. 43.
101. Zygmunt Bauman, *Modernity and Ambivalence* (Ithaca, 1991), p. 59.
102. Quoted in Kelly, *The Humane Comedy,* p. 28.
103. Alfred de Musset, *A Modern Man's Confession,* G. F. Monkshood, trans. (London, 1908 [1836]), p. 8.
104. Ibid., p. 7.
105. Robert M. Adams, *Stendhal: Notes on a Novelist* (New York, 1959), p. 152.

106. Stendhal, *Lucien Leuwen,* H. L. R. Edwards, trans. (London, 1991), p. 143.
107. Ibid., p. 440.
108. Cited in Stendhal, *The Red and the Black,* Robert M. Adams, trans. (New York, 1969), p. 76.
109. Ibid., p. 58.

3. Ruins

1. Quoted in James J. Sheehan, *German History, 1770–1866* (New York, 1989), p. 311.
2. Caroline Herder to Georg Müller, 9 Nov. 1808, in Günter Jäckel, ed., *Das Volk braucht Licht: Frauen zur Zeit des Aufbruchs 1790–1848 in ihren Briefen* (Darmstadt, 1970), p. 137. See also Caroline Böhmer to Pauline Gotter, 24 Aug. 1807, p. 238.
3. Rudolf Ibbeken, *Preussen 1807–1813. Staat und Volk als Idee und Wirklichkeit* (Cologne, 1971), p. 190.
4. Germaine de Staël, *Ten Years in Exile,* Doris Beik, ed. (New York, 1972), p. 163. On the proposed trip to the United States, Mortiz Schlegel to August Wilhelm Schlegel, 14 July 1810, in Josef Körner, ed., *Krisenjahre der Frühromantik: Briefe aus dem Schlegelkreis,* 3 vols. (Brünn, 1936), 2: 147–48.
5. Dorothea to Friedrich Schlegel, 12 Aug. 1809, Dorothea von Schlegel, *Dorothea von Schlegel und deren Söhne Johannes und Philipp Veit. Briefwechsel,* 2 vols. (Mainz, 1881), 1: 368–69.
6. On this theme, Reinhart Koselleck, *Futures Past: On the Semantics of Historical Time* (Cambridge, Mass., 1985). For specific German and Austrian responses, Jörg Echternkamp, *Der Aufstieg des deutschen Nationalismus 1770–1840* (Frankfurt, 1998), pp. 171–72; and also W. K. Blessing, "Umbruchkrise und 'Verstörung:' Die 'Napoleonische' Erschütterung und ihre sozialpsychologische Bedeutung (Bayern als Beispiel)," *Zeitschrift für Bayerische Landesgeschichte* 42 (1979), pp. 75–106.
7. Letter to Sulpiz Boisserée dated end of Dec. 1809, Dorothea von Schlegel, *Briefwechsel,* 1: 396–99.

8. Dorothea Schlegel to Sulpiz Boisserée, 23 Aug. 1809, *Briefwechsel,* 1: 374–75.
9. For a similar argument on Ireland and Scotland, see Katie Trumpener, *Bardic Nationalism: The Romantic Novel and the British Empire* (Chicago, 1998).
10. Cited in Jean-François Bayart, *L'Illusion identitaire* (Paris, 1996), p. 75. The original French reads: "La culture est une nuit incertaine où dorment les révolutions d'hier . . . mais des lucioles, et quelquefois de grands oiseaux nocturnes, la traversent, surgissements et créations qui tracent la chance d'un autre jour."
11. Dorothea Schlegel to Caroline Paulus in Heidelberg, 10 Apr. 1813, Dorothea von Schlegel, *Briefwechsel,* 2: 155.
12. François-René de Chateaubriand, *The Memoirs of François René Vicomte de Chateaubriand,* Alexander Teixeria de Mattos, trans., 6 vols. (London, 1902), 1: 172.
13. Catherine Boulot, Jean de Cayeux, and Hélène Moulin, *Hubert Robert et la Révolution* (Paris, 1989); Roland Mortier, *La Poétique des ruines en France: Ses origines, ses variations de la Renaissance à Victor Hugo* (Geneva, 1974), pp. 158–62.
14. Philippe Raxhon, *La mémoire de la Révolution française: Entre Liège et Wallonie* (Brussels, 1996).
15. Quoted in Günter Hartmann, *Die Ruine im Landschaftsgarten: Ihre Bedeutung für den frühen Historismus und die Landschaftsmalerei der Romantik* (Worms, 1981), p. 129.
16. On the eighteenth-century ruin landscape, see Ingrid G. Daemmrich, "The Ruins Motif in French Literature," Ph.D diss. (Wayne State University, 1970); Laurence Goldstein, *Ruins and Empire: The Evolution of a Theme in Augustan and Romantic Literature* (Pittsburgh, 1977); Hartmann, *Die Ruine im Landschaftsgarten;* Mortier, *La Poétique des ruines en France;* Christopher Woodward, *In Ruins* (New York, 2001), pp. 93–94.
17. Ian Ousby, *The Englishman's England: Taste, Travel and the Rise of Tourism* (Cambridge, 1990), pp. 117–25.
18. Stephen Bann, *The Clothing of Clio* (Cambridge, 1984), p. 86.
19. François-René de Chateaubriand, "Herculaneum, Portici, Pompeii,"

dated 11 Jan. 1804, in *Travels in America and Italy,* 2 vols. (London, 1828), 2: 253–54.

20. Germaine de Staël *Corinne, or Italy* (Oxford, 1998 [1807]), p. 198 [11.IV].
21. Hugh Honour, *Romanticism* (New York, 1979), p. 208.
22. François-René de Chateaubriand, *The Genius of Christianity,* Charles I. White, trans. (Philadelphia, 1856), pp. 467–68, 517.
23. Goldstein, *Ruins and Empire,* pp. 153–54. See also Gerald N. Izenberg, *Impossible Individuality: Romanticism, Revolution, and the Origins of Modern Selfhood, 1787–1802* (Princeton, 1992).
24. Jean Mallion, *Victor Hugo et l'art architectural* (Paris, 1962), pp. 513–14.
25. M. H. Abrams, *Natural Supernaturalism: Tradition and Revolution in Romantic Literature* (New York, 1971), pp. 36–37, 66–67.
26. Klaus Behrens, *Friedrich Schlegels Geschichtsphilosophie (1794–1808): Ein Beitrag zur politischen Romantik* (Tübingen, 1984), pp. 87, 145.
27. Trumpener, *Bardic Nationalism,* pp. 27–28, but also Mortier, *La Poétique des ruines,* pp. 212–16, 225.
28. Karl Mannheim, *Conservatism: A Contribution to the Sociology of Knowledge,* David Kettler, Volker Mejr, and Nico Stehr, eds. (London, 1986), pp. 52, 194n22.
29. Joseph Leo Koerner, *Caspar David Friedrich and the Subject of Landscape* (New Haven, 1990), p. 25.
30. Trumpener, *Bardic Nationalism,* pp. 149, 111; Harriet Beecher Stowe, *Oldtown Folks* (Boston, 1869), pp. 165–66. See also Avery F. Gordon, *Ghostly Matters: Haunting and the Sociological Imagination* (Minneapolis, 1997).
31. Mortier, *La Poétique des ruines,* p. 212. See also Victor Hugo, "Guerre aux démolisseurs," *Revue des Deux Mondes* 5 (1832).
32. Hartmann, *Ruine im Landschaftsgarten,* p. 304.
33. Susan Crane, *Collecting and Historical Consciousness in Early Nineteenth-Century Germany* (Ithaca, 2000), p. 35.
34. Michel Foucault, *The Order of Things: An Archaeology of the Human Sciences* (New York, 1970), p. 251; Benedict Anderson, *Imagined Communities: Reflections on the Origin and Spread of Nationalism,* rev. ed. (New York, 1991), p. 198.

35. *Briefe eines reisenden Franzosen über Deutschland an seinen Bruder zu Paris* (1784), cited in Josef Bayer, ed., *Köln und die Wende des 18. und 19. Jahrhunderts 1770–1830. Geschildert von Zeitgenossen* (Cologne, 1912), p. 22.
36. Joseph Görres, "Der Dom in Köln" [*Rheinischer Merkur* (November 1814)], in *Ausgewählte Werke,* 2 vols., Wolfgang Frühwald, ed. (Freiburg, 1978), 1: 257; Steffens quoted by Eduard Trier, "Der vollendete Dom," in Hugo Borger, ed., *Der Kölner Dom im Jahrhundert seiner Vollendung: Essays zur Austellung der Historischen Museen in der Josef-Haubrich-Kunsthalle* (Cologne, 1980), p. 44.
37. Sulpiz Boisserée, "Fragmente einer Selbstbiographie," *Tagebücher,* vol. I, *1808–1823,* Hans-J. Weitz, ed. (Darmstadt, 1978), p. 9.
38. Schlegel quoted in Behrens, *Friedrich Schlegels Geschichtsphilosophie,* p. 167.
39. Boisserée, "Fragmente einer Selbstbiographie," pp. 19–20.
40. Friedrich Schlegel, "Reise nach Frankreich," *Europa* (1803), pp. 7–38.
41. Dorothea Schlegel to Schleiermacher, 21 Nov. 1802, in Dorothea von Schlegel, *Briefwechsel,* 1: 110.
42. Boisserée, "Fragmente einer Selbstbiographie," p. 22.
43. Sulpiz Boisserée, *Tagebücher,* 1: 43, 44, 47, 51.
44. Josef Bayer, *Die Franzosen in Köln. Bilder aus den Jahren 1794–1814* (Cologne, 1925), pp. 115–35; Wilhelm Joseph Heinen, *Der Begleiter auf Reisen durch Deutschland* (Cologne, 1808), quoted in Bayer, *Köln,* p. 133.
45. Dorothea Veit-Schlegel to Helmina von Hastfer, 19 Sept. 1804, in Jäckel, *Das Volk braucht Licht,* p. 260.
46. Boisserée to Goethe, 29 Apr. 1814, quoted in Eduard Firmenich-Richartz, *Die Brüder Boisserée: Sulpiz und Melchior Boisserée als Kunstsammler. Ein Beitrag zur Geschichte der Romantik* (Jena, 1916), p. 196.
47. Bertram Boisserée to Sulpiz, 13 July 1819, in Mathilde Boisserée, ed., *Sulpiz Boisserée,* 2 vols. (Stuttgart, 1862), 1: 366.
48. Supliz to Melchior Boisserée in May 1811, quoted in Firmenich-Richartz, *Die Brüder Boisserée,* p. 129.
49. Diary entry for 15 Aug. 1815, in Boisserée, *Tagebücher,* p. 1: 244.

50. Goethe to Reinhard, 22 July and 7 Oct. 1810, quoted in Firmenich-Richartz, *Die Brüder Boisserée,* pp. 126–27.
51. Sulpiz Boisserée to Goethe, 23 June 1817, quoted in ibid., pp. 292–93.
52. Sulpiz Boisserée to Goethe, 8 May 1810, quoted in ibid., pp. 123–25.
53. See, for example, Boisserée's notes for April 1814, *Tagebücher,* 1: 139–42.
54. Diary entry for 9 Jan. 1814, in Boisserée, *Tagebücher,* pp. 1: 108–09. See also Sulpiz to Melchior Boisserée, 12 Nov. 1813, Mathilde Boisserée, ed., *Sulpiz Boisserée,* 1: 190–91.
55. Notes for 18 Jan. 1814, in Boisserée, *Tagebücher,* 1: 131.
56. Sulpiz to Melchior Boisserée, 18 June 1814, in *Tagebücher,* pp. 1: 157–58.
57. Notes for 18 Jan. 1814, in Boisserée, *Tagebücher,* p. 1: 131.
58. Dorothea von Schlegel to Friedrich de la Motte Fouqué, 15 Jan. 1814, in *Briefe an Friedrich Baron de la Motte Fouqué,* ed. Elbertine Baronin de la Motte Fouqué (Bern, 1968 [Berlin 1848]), p. 376.
59. Sulpiz to Melchior Boisserée, 29 Oct., 2 Nov., 4 Nov., and 9 Nov. 1824, in Mathilde Boisserée, ed., *Sulpiz Boisserée,* pp. 445–52.
60. Sulpiz Boisserée to Köster, 12 June 1848, in ibid., p. 858.
61. Gerhard Schulz, *Die deutsche Literatur zwischen Französischer Revolution und Restauration* (Munich, 1989), pp. 143–44. On the French visitors, Victor Hugo, *Le Rhin* (Paris, 1842); Alexandre Dumas, *Excursions sur les bords du Rhin* (Paris, 1841); and Théophile Gautier, *Ce qu'on peut voir en six jours. IV. Le Rhin* (Paris, 1858). See also Edgar Quinet, to his mother, letter cxlvi, dated 26 Sept. 1827, Edgar Quinet, *Lettres à sa Mère,* vol. 2, in *Oeuvres complètes* (Paris, 1905), p. 51. Astolphe de Custine wanted to go too, and this is what Rahel Varnhagen exclaimed in reply: "And you wanted to go and see *Cologne!* That crazy place. A petrified colossus of old frankish follies and inconveniences that they now want to make so famous!" Rahel to Astolphe de Custine, 17 Feb. 1819 in Rahel Varnhagen, *Briefwechsel,* 4 vols. (Munich, 1979), 4: 190–91.
62. Ulrike Pretzel, *Die Literaturform Reiseführer im 19. und 20. Jahrhundert. Untersuchungen am Beispiel des Rheins* (Frankfurt, 1995), p. 46; J. A. Klein, *Rheinreise* (Koblenz, 1843) [1828]), pp. x–xi.

63. Rudy Koshar, *German Travel Cultures* (New York, 2001), p. 22.
64. Brent Maner, "The Search for the Buried Nation: Prehistorical Archeology in Central Europe, 1750–1932," Ph.D diss. (University of Illinois, 2002).
65. Celia Applegate, *A Nation of Provincials: The German Idea of Heimat* (Berkeley, 1990).
66. See the argument in Peter Märker, "Caspar David Friedrich zur Zeit der Restauration. Zum Verhältnis von Naturbegriff und geschichtlicher Stellung," in Berthold Hinz et al., eds., *Bürgerliche Revolution und Romantik: Natur und Gesellschaft bei Caspar David Friedrich* (Giessen, 1976).
67. Friedrich Ludwig Jahn, *Deutsches Volkstum* (Leipzig, 1817 [1810]), pp. 344–46.
68. Peter Märker, "Caspar David Friedrich zur Zeit der Restauration. Zum Verhältnis von Naturbegriff und geschichtlicher Stellung," in Berthold Hinz et al., eds., *Bürgerliche Revolution und Romantik,* p. 66.
69. I owe this insight to Brent Maner, "The Search for the Buried Nation."
70. Arndt to to Georg Andreas Reimer, 2 Aug. 1815, in Ernst Moritz Arndt, *Briefe,* A. Dühr, ed., 3 vols. (Darmstadt, 1972–75), 1: 466.
71. Goethe to Grossherzog Karl August, 3 Sept. 1815, in Firmenich-Richartz, *Die Brüder Boisserée,* pp. 225–26.
72. *Variscia. Mitteilungen aus dem Archive des Voigtländischen Alterthums-forschenden Vereins* 2 (1830), p. 53, quoted in Maner, "Prehistoric Answers to the German Question: Fridolfing as a Site of Archeological Excavation, 1834–1850," unpubl. ms.
73. Arndt to Friedrich von Schlichtegroll, 28 Apr. 1814, in Arndt, *Briefe,* 1: 368.
74. Arndt to Franz Hermann Hegewisch, 12 Mar. 1817, in Arndt, *Briefe,* 1: 552–53.
75. Winfried Speitkamp, "Kulturpolitik unter dem Einfluss der Französischen Revolution: Die Anfänge der modernen Denkmalpflege in Deutschland," *Tel Aviver Jahrbuch für deutsche Geschichte* 28 (1989), pp. 129–59, here pp. 131–32.
76. See also Applegate, *A Nation of Provincials;* Alon Confino, *The Nation as a Local Metaphor: Württemberg, Imperial Germany, and National Memory, 1871–1918* (Chapel Hill, 1997); and Rudy Koshar, *Germany's Tran-*

sient Pasts: Preservation and National Memory in the Twentieth Century (Chapel Hill, 1998).

77. Thomas Nipperdey, "Der Kölner Dom als Nationaldenkmal," in *Nachdenken über die deutsche Geschichte* (Munich, 1986).
78. Mannheim, *Conservatism,* p. 54.
79. Isidor Taylor et al., eds. *Voyages pittoresques et romantiques dans l'ancienne France,* 20 vols. (Paris, 1820–1878). See also Beth S. Wright, *Painting and History during the French Revolution; Abandoned by the Past* (Cambridge, 1997); A. Richard Oliver, *Charles Nodier: Pilot of Romanticism* (Syracuse, 1964); and M. Christine Boyer, *The City of Collective Memory: Its Historical Imagery and Architectural Entertainments* (Cambridge, Mass., 1994), pp. 239–40.
80. Anderson, *Imagined Communities,* pp. 202–06.
81. Quoted in Jean Mallion, *Victor Hugo et l'art architecturel* (Paris, 1962), p. 27.
82. Graham Robb, *Victor Hugo* (New York, 1997), p. 161.
83. Thomas Dibdin, *A Bibliographical, Antiquitarian and Picturesque Tour in France and Germany,* 3 vols. (London, 1829), 1: 29, 69.
84. Chateaubriand, *Genius,* pp. 524–25, 730–31npp; *Memoirs,* 2: 85, 155–56. See also Ernst Steinmann, "Die Zerstörung der Königsdenkmäler in Paris," *Monatshefte für Kunstwissenschaft* 10 (1917), pp. 337–80.
85. F. Schlegel, "Reise nach Frankreich," *Europa* (1803), pp. 17–18. See also John Scott, *A Visit to Paris in 1814* (London, 1815), pp. 9, 110.
86. Friedrich von Schlegel, "Principles of Gothic Architecture: Notes of a Journey through the Netherhlands, the Rhine Country, Switzerland, and a part of France in the Years 1804, 1805," *The Aesthetic and Miscellaneous Works of Friedrich von Schlegel,* E. J. Millington, trans. (London, 1875), pp. 198–99.
87. Friedrich to Marie von Raumer, 13 Sept. 1827, Friedrich von Raumer, *Lebenserinnerungen und Briefwechsel* (Leipzig, 1861), 2: 225.
88. Gregory Jusdanis, *The Necessary Nation* (Princeton, 2001), p. 22.
89. Barbara Breysach, *Die Persönlichkeit ist uns nur geliegen: Zu Briefwechseln Rahel Levin Varnhagens* (Göttingen, 1989), p. 178. Generally, see Karen Hagemann, *Mannlicher Muth und Teusche Ehre: Nation, Militär, und Geschlecht zur Zeit der Antinapoleonischen Kriege Preussens* (Paderborn, 2001).

90. Rahel to Pauline Wiesel, 26 June 1816, in Barbara Hahn, *"Antworten Sie Mir," Rahel Levin Varnhagens Briefwechsel* (Basel, 1990), p. 60.
91. Letter of 23 May 1813, cited in Hahn, *"Antworten Sie Mir,"* p. 141n27.
92. Rahel to Brede, 11 Nov. 1819, in Hahn, *"Antworten Sie Mir,"* p. 181.
93. Rahel to Astolphe de Custine, 17 Feb. 1819 in Rahel Varnhagen, *Briefwechsel,* 4 vols. (Munich, 1979), 4: 191.

4. Along the Hedges

1. Judith Butler, *Bodies That Matter: On the Discursive Limits of "Sex"* (New York, 1993), pp. 9, 12. See also David Campbell, *National Deconstruction: Violence, Identity, and Justice in Bosnia* (Minneapolis, 1998).
2. Arndt to Georg Andreas Reimer, 25 Dec. 1815, Ernst Moritz Arndt, *Briefe,* A. Dühr, ed., 3 vols. (Darmstadt, 1972–75), 1: 489.
3. Brent Maner, "The Search for the Buried Nation: Prehistorical Archeology in Central Europe, 1750–1932," Ph.D diss. (University of Illinois, 2002), ch. 5.
4. Letters to to Franz Hermann Hegewisch, 21 Mar. and 1 May 1817, in Arndt, *Briefe,* 1: 552–53, 560.
5. Zygmunt Bauman, *Life in Fragments* (London, 1995), pp. 136–37.
6. Anne Janowitz, *England's Ruins: Poetic Purpose and the National Landscape* (Cambridge, 1990), pp. 54–56.
7. Katie Trumpener, *Bardic Nationalism: The Romantic Novel and the British Empire* (Chicago, 1998), pp. xii–xiii, 6, 29.
8. Janowitz, *England's Ruins,* p. 63.
9. Entries for Windsor Forest, 31 Oct. 1822; Hambledon, 19–23 Nov. 1822; Salisburg, 30 Aug. 1826; Berghclere, 30 Oct. 1821; Bollitree, 13 Nov. 1821; Old Hall, 15 Nov. 1821, in William Cobbett, *Rural Rides* (London, 1830), 1: 123–24, 134; 2: 47; 1: 5–6, 28–29, 31. The "'Change" is the London stock exchange.
10. William Derry, "William Cobbett: A Sentimental Radical," in Derry, *The Radical Tradition: Tom Paine to Lloyd George* (London, 1967), p. 46, quoted in Ian Dyck, *William Cobbett and Rural Popular Culture* (Cambridge, 1992), p. 125.
11. Dyck, *William Cobbett,* p. 125.

12. Cobbett's entries for Folkestone, 1 Sept. 1823, and Ryall, 29 Sept. 1826; Cobbett, *Rural Rides,* 1: 237–38, 2: 121.
13. Leonora Nattrass, *William Cobbett: The Politics of Style* (Cambridge, 1995), pp. 208–09.
14. Jon P. Klancher, *The Making of the English Reading Audiences, 1790–1832* (Madison, 1987), p. 128.
15. Elisabeth Helsinger, *Rural Scenes and National Representation: Britain, 1815–1850* (Princeton, 1997), p. 133.
16. Alice Chandler, *A Dream of Order: The Medieval Ideal in Nineteenth-Century English Literature* (Lincoln, 1970), p. 60.
17. Helsinger, *Rural Scenes,* pp. 26–28. See also Laurence Goldstein, *Ruins and Empire: The Evolution of a Theme in Augustan and Romantic Literature* (Pittsburgh, 1977), pp. 126–29.
18. James Chandler, *England in 1819: The Politics of Literary Culture and the Case of Romantic Historicism* (Chicago, 1998), pp. 18, 89.
19. Quoted in Butler, *Romantics,* p. 62.
20. See, for example, Helsinger, *Rural Scenes.*
21. Ibid., p. 151. A very similar repertoire was assembled by the Silesian writer Joseph von Eichendorff. Set to music by Robert Schuman, his poems became part of the standard German songbook. Irish writers also excavated the sorts of things that Clare uncovered in the corners of fields in the undeveloped bogs that had been passed over by Britain's agricultural development. See Trumpener, *Bardic Nationalism,* p. 54.
22. John Clare, "The Nightingale's Nest" (1835).
23. John Lucas, "Clare's Politics," in Hugh Haughton, Adam Phillips, and Geoffrey Summerfield, eds., *John Clare in Context* (Cambridge, 1994), pp. 156–59.
24. John Barrell, *The Idea of Landscape and the Sense of Place, 1730–1840: An Approach to the Poetry of John Clare* (Cambridge, 1972), p. 175.
25. Barrell, *The Idea of Landscape,* p. 126.
26. See also Jonathan Boyarin, "Space, Time, and the Politics of Memory" in Boyarin, ed., *Remapping Memory: The Politics of TimeSpace* (Minneapolis, 1995).
27. Hugh Haughton and Adam Phillips, "Introduction: Relocating John Clare," in Haughton, *John Clare in Context,* p. 5.

28. Bob Heyes, "'Triumphs of Time': John Clare and the Uses of Antiquity," *John Clare Society Journal* 16 (1997).
29. Cited in Helmut Jendreiek, *Hegel und Jacob Grimm: Ein Beitrag zur Geschichte der Wissenschaftstheorie* (Berlin, 1975), p. 53. See also Friedrich Schlegel's contemptuous dismissal, quoted in Christa Kamenetsky, *The Brothers Grimm & Their Critics: Folktales and the Quest for Meaning* (Athens, Ohio, 1992), p. 187.
30. On this antiquarian sensibility, see Trumpener, *Bardic Nationalism,* pp. 27–28.
31. Jack Zipes, *The Brothers Grimm: From Enchanted Forests to the Modern World* (New York, 1988), pp. 2–3.
32. Cited in Gabriele Seitz, *Die Brueder Grimm: Leben—Werk—Zeit* (Munich, 1984), p. 15.
33. Wilhelm Grimm to Amalie Hassenpflug, 4 Mar. 1849, in Wilhelm Schoof, ed., *Unbekannte Briefe der Brueder Grimm* (Bonn, 1960), p. 393.
34. Wilhelm to Jacob Grimm, 28 Aug. 1809 in Hermann Grimm, Gustav Hinrichs, and Wilhelm Schoof, eds., *Briefwechsel zwischen Jacob und Wilhelm Grimm aus der Jugendzeit* (Weimar, 1963 [1881]), p. 148.
35. Ludwig Emil Grimm, *Erinnerungen aus meinem Leben,* cited in Seitz, *Die Brueder Grimm,* p. 27.
36. Cited in Seitz, *Die Gebrueder Grimm,* p. 123.
37. Jacob to Wilhelm Grimm, 1 Mar. 1814, in Grimm et al., eds., *Briefwechsel,* p. 267.
38. Wilhelm to Jacob Grimm, 18 Jan. 1814, in ibid., p. 238.
39. Ibid., p. 240.
40. Zipes, *The Brothers Grimm,* p. 37.
41. Jacob to Wilhelm Grimm, 25 June 1809, in Grimm et al., eds., *Briefwechsel,* p. 15, translated in Zipes, *The Brothers Grimm,* p. 36.
42. Jacob to Wilhelm Grimm, 26 Mar. 1814, in Grimm et al., eds., *Briefwechsel,* p. 286.
43. Zipes, *The Brothers Grimm,* pp. 55–59.
44. Paul Wigand quoted in Seitz, *Die Brueder Grimm,* p. 39.
45. Zipes, *The Brothers Grimm,* p. 37.
46. Jacob and Wilhelm Grimm, "Vorrede," 3 July 1819, *Kinder- und Hausmaerchen,* Heinz Roelleke, ed. (Stuttgart, 1980), p. 15.

47. Jacob Grimm, "Vorrede," *Deutsche Sagen* (1816), cited in Seitz, *Die Brueder Grimm,* p. 118.
48. Seitz, *Brueder Grimm,* p. 14.
49. "Aufforderung an die gesammte Freunde deutscher Poesie und Geschichte erlassen" (1811), in Heinz Roelleke, *Die Maerchen der Brueder Grimm* (Munich, 1985), p. 64.
50. Jacob to Wilhelm Grimm, 21 June 1814, in Grimm et al., eds., *Briefwechsel,* p. 341.
51. Carola L. Gottzmann, ed., *Briefwechsel der Brueder Grimm mit Hans Georg von Hammerstein-Equord* (Marburg, 1985), pp. 38–39.
52. Jacob and Wilhelm Grimm, "Vorrede," 3 July 1819, p. 15.
53. "Aufforderung an die gesammte Freunde deutscher Poesie und Geschichte erlassen" (1811), in Roelleke, *Maerchen,* pp. 63–69, here p. 65.
54. George Williamson, "The Longing for Myth in Germany: Culture, Religion, and Politics, 1790–1878," Ph.D. diss. (Yale University, 1996), p. 134.
55. "Aufforderung an die gesammte Freunde," in Roelleke, *Maerchen,* p. 64.
56. Jacob and Wilhelm Grimm, "Vorrede," p. 15.
57. M. M. Grimm, *German Popular Stories* (London, 1823), pp. vi, viii.
58. Jacob and Wilhelm Grimm, "Vorrede," p. 19.
59. Seitz, *Die Brueder Grimm,* pp. 57–58.
60. Jacob to Wilhelm Grimm, 17 May 1809, in Grimm et al., eds., *Briefwechsel,* p. 101. On Grimm scholarship see Roelleke, *Maerchen.*
61. Jacob to Wilhelm Grimm, 17 May 1809, in Grimm et al., eds., *Briefwechsel,* p. 101.
62. See, for example, Jacob Grimm to Paul Wigand, 1 July 1809, cited in Wilhelm Schoof, *Zur Entstehungsgeschichte der Grimmischen Maerchen* (Hamburg, 1959), p. 19.
63. "Aufforderung an die gesammte Freunde," in Roelleke, *Maerchen,* pp. 64–65.
64. Jendreiek, *Hegel und Jacob Grimm,* p. 309.
65. Zipes, *Brothers Grimm,* p. 14. See also Ulrike Bastian, *Die Kinder- und Hausmaerchen der Brueder Grimm in der literaturpaedagogischen Diskussion des 19. und 20. Jahrhunderts* (Frankfurt, 1981), pp. 31–37.

66. Wilhelm Grimm to Goerres, 3 Sept. 1812, cited in Schoof, *Zur Entstehungsgeschichte,* p. 18.
67. See Bastian, *Kinder- und Hausmaerchen,* pp. 50–53; Kamenetsky, *The Brothers Grimm,* pp. 61–68.
68. Zipes, *Brothers Grimm,* p. 15. See also Heinz Roelleke, "Nachwort," Jacob and Wilhelm Grimm, *Kinder- und Hausmaerchen,* Roelleke, ed. vol. 3 (Stuttgart, 1980), pp. 590–91.
69. Ingeborg Weber-Kellermann, "Hessen als Maerchenland der Brueder Grimm," in Charlotte Oberfeld and Andreas C. Bimmer, eds., *Hessen—Maerchenland der Brueder Grimm* (Kassel, 1984), pp. 93–103.
70. Quoted in Aleida Assmann, *Erinnerungsräume: Formen und Wandlungen des kulturellen Gedächtnisses* (Munich, 1999), p. 207.
71. See Hilmar Kallweit, "Zur 'anthropologischen' Wende in der zweiten Hälfte des 18. Jahrhunderts—aus der Sicht des 'Archäologen' Michel Foucault," in Wolfgang Küttler, Jörn Rüsen, and Ernst Schulin, eds., *Geschichtsdiskurs,* vol. 2, *Anfänge modernen historischen Denkens* (Frankfurt, 1994); and Albert Poetzsch, *Studien zur frühromantischen Politik und Geschichtsauffassung,* Beiträge zur Kultur und Universalgeschichte, no. 3 (Leipzig, 1907).

5. Household Fairies

1. Quoted in Susan A. Crane, "Collecting and Historical Consciousness: New Forms for Collective Memory in Early 19th-Century Germany," Ph.D diss. (University of Chicago, 1992), pp. 106–07.
2. Washington Irving, "Rural Life in England," *The Sketch Book of Geoffrey Crayon, Gent.,* vol. 8 in Richard Dilworth Rust, ed., *The Complete Works of Washington Irving* (Boston, 1978), p. 50. See also James Chandler, *England in 1819: The Politics of Literary Culture and the Case of Romantic Historicism* (Chicago, 1998), pp. 148–50.
3. Joan D. Hedrick, *Harriet Beecher Stowe: A Life* (New York, 1994), pp. 77–82.
4. Jack Larkin, *The Reshaping of Everyday Life, 1790–1840* (New York, 1988), pp. 206–07.
5. Joyce Appleby, *Inheriting the Revolution: the First Generation of Americans* (Cambridge, Mass., 2000), pp. 64–66.

6. Hedrick, *Harriet Beecher Stowe,* pp. 77–82.
7. See, for example, Ann C. Colley, *Nostalgia and Recollection in Victorian Culture* (New York, 1998), p. 33.
8. Hedrick, *Harriet Beecher Stowe,* p. 79.
9. Katherine C. Grier, "The Decline of the Memory Palace: The Parlor after 1890," in Jessica H. Foy and Thomas J. Schlereth, eds., *American Home Life, 1880–1930: A Social History of Spaces and Services* (Knoxville, 1992). See also John R. Gillis, *A World of Their Own Making: Myth, Ritual, and the Quest for Family Values* (New York, 1996), p. 16; and Louise L. Stevenson, *The Victorian Homefront: American Thought and Culture, 1860–1880* (Ithaca, 2001).
10. Georg Lukacs, *The Historical Novel* (Lincoln, 1983), p. 23.
11. Francis H. Underwood, *Quabbin: The Story of a Small Town with Outlooks on Puritan Life* (Boston, 1986 [London, 1893]), p. 43.
12. Appleby, *Inheriting the Revolution,* pp. 23–24, 164–65.
13. Cited in Jon P. Klancher, *The Making of the English Reading Audiences, 1790–1832* (Madison, 1987), p. 27.
14. Cited in Peter Gay, *The Naked Heart* (New York, 1995), p. 57.
15. Aleida Assmann, *Erinnerungsräume: Formen und Wandlungen des kulturellen Gedächtnisses* (Munich, 1999), p. 49.
16. On the autobiographical genre, see Jerome Hamilton Buckley, *The Turning Key: Autobiography and the Subjective Impulse since 1800* (Cambridge, Mass., 1984); George P. Landow, ed., *Approaches to Victorian Autobiography* (Athens, 1979); and Karl J. Weintraub, "Autobiography and Historical Consciousness," *Critical Inquiry* 1 (1975), pp. 821–48.
17. The line but not the context is from Liisa H. Malkki, *Purity and Exile: Violence, Memory, and National Cosmology among Hutu Refugees in Tanzania* (Chicago, 1995), p. 197.
18. Franz Xaver Freiherrn von Andlaw-Birseck, *Mein Tagebuch: Auszüge aus Aufschreibungen der Jahre 1811 bis 1861* (Frankfurt, 1862), p. 1. See also Willibald Alexis, *Erinnerungen* (Berlin, 1900), p. 1.
19. Ernst Wilhelm Martius, *Erinnerungen aus meinem neunzigjährigen Leben* (Leipzig, 1847), p. 284. See also Edgar Quinet, *The Story of a Child* (London, 1995), pp. 41, 51–53.
20. Hew Strachan, "The Nation in Arms," in Geoffrey Best, *The Permanent*

Revolution: The French Revolution and Its Legacy, 1789–1989 (London, 1988), p. 60.

21. Dorothea Schlegel to Sulpiz Boisserée, 4 Aug. 1808, in Mathilde Boisserée, ed., *Sulpiz Boisserée,* 2 vols. (Stuttgart, 1862), 1: 53.
22. Ibid., pp. 53–54.
23. Clive Emsley, *British Society and the French Wars, 1793–1815* (London, 1979), pp. 172–73. See also Gustav René Hocke, *Das europäische Tagebuch* (Wiesbaden, 1963), pp. 67, 201–02; and Peter Gay, *The Naked Heart* (New York, 1995), p. 109.
24. See, for example, Edward Costello, *The Peninsular and Waterloo Campaigns,* Antony Brett-James, ed. (London, 1967 [1839]); Emile Erckmann and Alexandre Chatrian, *The Conscript: A Story of the French War of 1813* (New York, 1912); John Green, *The Vicissitudes of a Soldier's Life* (Louth, 1827); *Memorials of the Late War,* 2 vols. (Edinburgh, 1828); E. Gridel and Richard, eds., *Cahiers de vieux soldats de la Révolution et de l'Empire* (Paris, 1902); B. H. Liddell Hart, ed., *The Letters of Private Wheeler* (Boston, 1952).
25. François-René de Chateaubriand, *The Memoirs of François René Vicomte de Chateaubriand,* Alexander Teixeira de Mattos, trans., 6 vols. (London, 1902), 3: 149.
26. Elizabeth Deeds Ermarth, *Realism and Consensus in the English Novel* (Princeton, 1983), p. 82.
27. Adalbert Stifter, "Die Mappe meines Urgrossvaters" (1840), in *Adalbert Stifter Studien* (Leipzig, n.d. [1920]), 1: 428, 437, 461. Incidentally, I am reading my grandfather's copy, which he signed and dated "Herbert Lauffer 1920." See also the English surgeon Sir Charles Bell on Waterloo and on his notebooks quoted in Susan Buck-Morss, *Dreamworld and Catastrophe: The Passing of Mass Utopia in East and West* (Cambridge, Mass., 2000), p. 102.
28. See Alf Lüdtke, "Introduction: What Is the History of Everyday Life and Who Are Its Practitioners," in Lüdtke, ed., *The History of Everyday Life: Reconstructing Historical Experiences and Ways of Life,* trans. William Templer (Princeton, 1995), pp. 20–21. See also Lüdtke, "Cash, Coffee Breaks, Horseplay: *Eigensinn* and Politics among Factory Workers in Germany circa 1900," in Michael Hanagan and C. Stephenson, eds.,

Confrontation, Class Consciousness, and the Labor Process (New York, 1986), pp. 65–95; and idem, "Organizational Order or *Eigensinn?* Workers' Privacy and Workers' Politics in Imperial Germany," in Sean Wilentz, ed., *Rites of Power: Symbolism, Ritual, and Politics since the Middle Ages* (Philadelphia, 1985).

29. Lukacs, *The Historical Novel,* pp. 20, 23, 33, 37, 47.
30. James Chandler, *England in 1819: The Politics of Literary Culture and the Case of Romantic Historicism* (Chicago, 1998), pp. 150, 262–63.
31. Marilyn Butler, *Romantics, Rebels, and Reactionaries: English Literature and Its Background, 1760–1830* (Oxford, 1981), p. 111.
32. Chandler, *England in 1819,* p. 107.
33. Petra ten-Doesschate Chu, "Pop Culture in the Making: The Romantic Craze for History," in Chu and Gabriel P. Weisberg, eds., *The Popularization of Images: Visual Culture under the July Monarchy* (Princeton, 1994), pp. 166–88. See also Beth S. Wright, *Painting and History during the French Restoration: Abandoned by the Past* (Cambridge, 1998).
34. See, for example, Frederika Bremer, *The Home; or Family Cares and Family Joys,* E. A. Friedländer, trans. (London, 1845), p. 31.
35. "Sylvie," in *Selected Writings of Gérard de Nerval,* trans. and introduced by Geoffrey Wagner (New York, 1957), pp. 50–76. The piece was first published in *Revue des Deux Mondes,* 15 Aug. 1853.
36. See also Geoffrey Wagner's comment in Wagner, *Selected Writings of Gérard de Nerval,* p. 53n5.
37. Buckley, *The Turning Key,* pp. 28–29. See also Aleida Assmann, "Die Wunden der Zeit: Wordsworth und die romantische Erinnerung," in Anselm Haverkamp and Renate Lachmann, eds., *Memoria: Vergessen und Erinnern* (Munich, 1993), pp. 359–82.
38. Assmann, *Erinnerungsräume,* pp. 98–99.
39. Richard N. Coe, *When the Grass Was Taller: Autobiography and the Experience of Childhood* (New Haven, 1984), p. 65. See also Rudolf Dekker, *Childhood, Memory, and Autobiography in Holland: From the Golden Age to Romanticism* (New York, 1999), pp. 3, 109–10, 122–24; Rosemary Lloyd, *The Land of Lost Content: Children and Childhood in Nineteenth-Century French Literature* (New York, 1992); Carolyn Steedman, *Strange Dislocations: Childhood and the Idea of Human Interiority, 1780–1930*

(London, 1995); Irene Hardach-Pinke, *Kinderalltag: Aspekte von Kontinuität und Wandel der Kindheit in autobiographischen Zeugnissen 1700 bis 1900* (Frankfurt, 1981), pp. 14, 16–17; and Joseph F. Kett, "Adolescence and Youth," in Theodore K. Rabb and Robert L. Rorberg, eds., *The Family in History* (New York, 1973), p. 98.

40. Steedman, *Strange Dislocations,* p. ix.
41. Susan Stewart, *On Longing: Narratives of the Miniature, the Gigantic, the Souvenir, the Collection* (Baltimore, 1984), p. 23. See also Svetlana Boym, *Common Places: Mythologies of Everyday Life in Russia* (Cambridge, Mass., 1994), p. 284. Just how uninteresting the actual past is and how alluring the idea of a lost past has become can be seen in the tendency for time capsules to be frequently buried, but rarely opened.
42. Julia Kristeva, *Strangers to Ourselves* (New York, 1991), p. 7.
43. James Clifford, *Routes: Travel and Translation in the Late Twentieth Century* (Cambridge, Mass., 1997), p. 28.
44. Karl-Heinz Bohrer, "Zeit der Revolution—Revolution der Zeit. Die Hermeneutik revolutionärer Gegenwart bei Friedrich Schlegel (1795–1800) und Heinrich Heine (1831–1855)," in Forum für Philosophie, ed., *Die Ideen von 1789 in der deutschen Rezeption* (Frankfurt, 1989), p. 32.
45. Jon Vanden Heuvel, "A German Life in the Age of Revolution: Joseph Görres," Ph.D diss. (Columbia, 1996), p. 2, citing Görres himself.
46. On aristocratic autobiography, see Marcus Funck and Stephan Malinowski, "Masters of Memory: The Strategic Use of Autobiographical Memory by the German Nobility," in Alon Confino and Peter Fritzsche, eds., *The Work of Memory: New Directions in the Study of German Society and Culture* (Urbana, 2002).
47. Kleist to Wilhelmine von Zenge, 13 Nov. 1800, quoted in Karl Heinz Bohrer, *Der romantische Brief. Die Entstehung ästhetischer Subjektivität* (Munich, 1987), p. 98.
48. Entries for 20 Nov. 1812 and 16 June 1814, quoted in René Bourgeois, "Fonctions du journal intime, d'après le journal inédit d'Antoine Métral," Vittorio Del Litto, ed., *Le Journal intime et ses formes littéraires* (Paris, 1978), pp. 184–85.
49. Anne Martin-Fugier, "Bourgeois Rituals," in Michelle Perrot, ed., *A History of Private Life: From the Fires of Revolution to the Great War* (Cam-

bridge, Mass., 1990), pp. 265–66. On "graphomania," Boym, *Common Places,* p. 169.

50. Gay, *The Naked Heart,* p. 109. On "right angles," M. H. Abrams, *Natural Supernaturalism: Tradition and Revolution in Romantic Literature* (New York, 1971), pp. 36–37.
51. Gillis, *A World,* pp. xvi–xviii.
52. Martin-Fugier, "Bourgeois Rituals," pp. 261–64, 337.
53. Dorothy Ross, "Historical Consciousness in Nineteenth-Century America," *American Historical Review* 89 (October 1984), p. 912. See also Michael Kammen, *Mystic Chords of Memory: The Transformation of Tradition in American Culture* (New York, 1991).
54. Harriet Beecher Stowe, *Oldtown Folks* (Boston, 1869), p. 1. See also Laurel Thatcher Ulrich, *The Age of Homespun: Objects and Stories in the Creation of an American Myth* (New York, 2001), pp. 343–64. On the "inevitable extermination," see "The Frontpiece," *The Family Magazine* (1834), pp. 407–08.
55. Elizabath A. Perkins, *Border Life: Experience and Memory in the Revolutionary Ohio Valley* (Chapel Hill, 1998), p. 168.
56. Michael Davitt Bell quoted in Renée L. Bergland, *The National Uncanny: Indian Ghosts and American Subjects* (Hanover, N.H., 2000), p. 35.
57. Chateaubriand, *Travels in America and Italy,* 2 vols. (London, 1828), 1: 98, 112, 123–34, 167; 2: 101.
58. Sarah Orne Jewett, *The Country Doctor* (New York, 1986 [1884]), pp. 42–43; preface, Sarah Orne Jewett, *Deephaven* (Boston, 1894 [1877]), p. 1; also p. 34.
59. Jewett, "An Autumn Holiday," in *Country Byways* (Boston, 1881), p. 142.
60. Jewett, *Deephaven,* p. 74; "The Village Grave Yard," *Godey's Lady's Book* 7 (1833), p. 95.
61. F. A. Durivage in "The Old Mansion: A Sketch from Domestic History," in *Godey's Lady's Book* 24 (1842), pp. 276–79.
62. Stowe, *Oldtown Folks,* pp. 165–66. See also "The Haunted House," *Godey's Lady's Book* 3 (1831), p. 253; and Jewett, *The Country Doctor,* pp. 7, 13.
63. "The Legend of Sleepy Hollow," in *The Sketch Book of Geoffrey Crayon,*

Gent., p. 8: 273. See also John Greenleaf Whittier, *Legends of New England* (Gainesville, 1965 [Hartford, 1831]); and Bergland, *The National Uncanny.*

64. Jane C. Nylander, *Our Own Snug Fireside: Images of the New England Home, 1760–1860* (New York, 1993). See also Rodris Roth, "The New England, or 'Olde Tyme,' Kitchen Exhibit at Nineteenth-Century Fairs," in Alan Axelrod, ed., *The Colonial Revival in America* (New York, 1985).
65. "A Villager," "'Moving' in the Country," *Godey's Lady's Book* 44 (1852), pp. 204–11.
66. Nylander, *Our Own Snug Fireside,* p. 97, and also p. 32.
67. Ibid., p. 14. See also Perla Korosec-Serfaty, "The Home from Attic to Cellar," *Journal of Environmental Psychology* 4 (1984), pp. 303–21.
68. Helen Maitland, "Autobiography of an Old Sofa," *Godey's Lady's Book* 28 (1844), pp. 278–80; Mary Davenant, "The Old Arm-Chair," ibid., 34 (1847), pp. 290–97.
69. Maitland, "Autobiography of an Old Sofa," p. 279.
70. Harriet Beecher Stowe, *House and Home Papers* (Boston, 1890 [1864]), pp. 22, 60, 120–21. See also Melanie V. Dawson, "From Carnival to Nostalgia: The Play of Cultural Literacy in the Nineteenth-Century Parlor," Ph.D diss. (University of Pittsburgh, 1997), p. 207.
71. Richard L. Bushman, *The Refinement of America: Persons, Houses, Cities* (New York, 1992), pp. 17, 231.
72. Agnes Heller, "Where Are We at Home?" *Thesis Eleven* 41 (1995), p. 15.
73. Stowe, *House and Home Papers,* p. 120.
74. See the remarkable opening to Avery F. Gordon, *Ghostly Matters: Haunting and the Sociological Imagination* (Minneapolis, 1997), pp. 3–4.
75. Celia Betsky, "Inside the Past; The Interior and the Colonial Revival in American Art and Literature," in Axelrod, *The Colonial Revival,* p. 248.
76. Louisa May Alcott, *Little Women* (New York, 1953 [1868]), p. 220; *An Old Fashioned Girl* (New York, 1991 [1870]), pp. 84, 101. See also Jane W. Frazer, "Some Passages in the Life of My Great Aunt," *Godey's Lady's Book,* 28 (1844), p. 234; the episode of the "The Old Cedar Chest" in Edith Woodley's serialization, "Aunt Tabitha's Fireside," in *Godey's Lady's Book* 44 (1852), p. 12; as well as "The Old Time Grand-

father," ibid., 56 (1858), pp. 320–21; and "The Dear Old Grandmother," ibid., pp. 435–37.

77. Mary E. Nealy, "The Old Bureau," *Godey's Lady Book* 77 (1868), pp. 226–27. See also H. B. Wildman, "My Grandmother's Stand," ibid., 48 (1854), p. 65.
78. Gillis, *A World,* p. 127.
79. Ibid., p. 16. See also "Katherine C. Grier, "The Decline of the Memory Palace: The Parlor after 1890," in Jessica H. Foy and Thomas J. Schlereth, eds., *American Home Life, 1880–1930: A Social History of Spaces and Services* (Knoxville, 1992).
80. Roth, "The New England, or 'Olde Tyme," Kitchen Exhibit."
81. Todd Steven Gernes, "Recasting the Culture of Ephemera: Young Women's Literary Culture in Nineteenth-Century America," Ph.D diss. (Brown University, 1992), p. 39.
82. Raphael Samuel, *Theatres of Memory: Past and Present in Contemporary Culture* (London, 1994), p. 161.
83. See Harold Fisher Wilson, *The Hill Country of Northern New England: Its Social and Economic History, 1790–1930* (New York, 1936), pp. 270–73; and Dona Brown, *Inventing New England: Regional Tourism in the Nineteenth Century* (Washington, D.C., 1995); as well as Thomas Anderson, "'Old-Home Week' in New England," *New England Magazine* 34 (August, 1906), pp. 673–85.
84. Mrs. D. P. S., "Aunt Esther's Warming Pan, *Godey's Lady's Book* 67 (1863), pp. 127–34, brings together two separated lovers. See also Jane W. Frazer, "Some Passages in the Life of My Great Aunt," *Godey's Lady's Book,* 28 (1844), p. 234; and Jewett, *Deephaven,* p. 25.
85. Gernes, "Recasting the Culture of Ephemera," pp. 38–39. See also Charles Francis Potter, "Round Went the Album," *New York Quarterly* 4 (1948), pp. 5–14.
86. Ulrich, *Age of Homespun,* p. 412.
87. Nylander, *Our Own Snug Fireside,* p. 171–72. See also Ruth E. Finley, *Old Patchwork Quilts* (1929).
88. Patsy and Myron Orlofksy, *Quilts in America* (New York, 1974), p. 44.
89. Patricia Cooper and Norma Bradley Buferd, *The Quilters: Women and Domestic Art* (New York, 1978), p. 17.
90. "The Autograph Bedquilt," *Godey's Lady Book* 68 (1864), p. 396.

91. Ricky Clark, "Quilt Documentation: A Case Study" in Marilyn Ferris Motz and Pat Browne, eds., *Making the American Home: Middle-Class Women and Domestic Material Culture 1840–1940* (Bowling Green, 1988), p. 173.
92. Elaine Hedges, "The Nineteenth-Century Diarist and Her Quilts," *Feminist Studies* 8 (1982), p. 297.
93. Susan S. Arpad, "'Pretty Much to Suit Ourselves': Midwestern Women Naming Experience Through Domestic Arts," in Motz and Browne, ed., *Making the American Home,* p. 20.
94. Gillis, *A World,* p. 77; Martin-Fugier, "Bourgeois Rituals," p. 263.
95. Patricia Holland, "Introduction: History, Memory, and the Family Album," in Jo Spence and Patricia Holland, *Family Snaps: The Meanings of Domestic Photography* (London, 1991), p. 9. See also Don Slater, "Consuming Kodak," in the same collection.
96. See the general theorizing in Katie Trumpener, *Bardic Nationalism: The Romantic Novel and the British Empire* (Chicago, 1998), pp. 201–04.
97. Martin-Fugier, "Bourgeois Rituals," pp. 263–64. See also Anne L. Bower's analysis of Joyce Carol Oates' poem "Celestial Timepiece," in "Reading Lessons," in Cheryl B. Torsney and Judy Elsley, *Quilt Culture: Tracing the Pattern* (Columbia, 1994).
98. Marilyn F. Motz, "Visual Autobiography: Photograph Albums of Turn-of-the-Century Midwestern Women," *American Quarterly* 41 (1989), pp. 63–92. See also Marianne Hirsch, *Family Frames: Photography, Narrative, and Postmemory* (Cambridge, Mass., 1997); and Annette Kuhn, *Family Secrets: Acts of Memory and Imagination* (London, 1995).

Conclusion

1. Cited in Reinhold Aris, *History of Political Thought in Germany from 1789 to 1815* (New York, 1965), p. 270.
2. F. Ancillon quoted in Reinhart Koselleck, *Futures Past: On the Semantics of Historical Time* (Cambridge, 1985), p. 251.
3. Johannes Fabian, *Time and the Other: How Anthropology Makes Its Object* (New York, 1983). See also Dipesh Chakrabarty, *Provincializing Europe: Postcolonial Thought and Historical Difference* (Princeton, 2000), pp. 31–32.

4. Franco Moretti, *Atlas of the European Novel 1800–1900* (London, 1998), p. 176.
5. François-René de Chateaubriand, *The Memoirs of François René Vicomte de Chateaubriand,* Alexander Teixeira de Mattos, trans., 6 vols. (London, 1902), 3: 149.
6. "History," writes Michel-Rolph Trouillot, in *Silencing the Past: Power and the Production of History* (Boston, 1995), p. xix, "is the fruit of power, but power itself is never so transparent that its analysis becomes superfluous. The ultimate mark of power may be its invisibility; the ultimate challenge, the exposition of its roots."
7. Thucydides, *History of the Peloponnesian War,* Rex Warner, trans. (London, 1954), i, 70.
8. On the boundaries of identity, see Richard Handler, "Is 'Identity' a Useful Cross-Cultural Concept?" in John R. Gillis, ed., *Commemorations: The Politics of National Identity* (Princeton, 1994), pp. 29–30.
9. Timothy Brennan, "The National Longing for Form," in Homi Bhabha, ed., *Nation and Narration* (London, 1990).
10. See, for example, the national configurations mapped out by David Bright, *Race and Renion: The Civil War in American Memory* (Cambridge, 2001).
11. Eichendorff to Jegor von Sivers, 14 Nov. 1853, in *Sämtliche Werke des Freiherrn Joseph von Eichendorff,* Sybille von Steinsdorff, ed. (Stuttgart, 1992) vol. 12, pp. 313–14.
12. Helmut Koopman, "Serielles in Eichendorffs Lyrik," in Michael Kessler and Koopman, eds., *Eichendorffs Modernität* (Tübingen, 1989), p. 94 Bergengruen cited in Koopman, "Eichendorff, das Schloss Duerande, und die Revolution," in Alfred Riemen, ed., *Ansichten zu Eichendorff* (Sigmaringen, 1988), p. 120.
13. Scott, *Waverly* (New York, 1986), p. 3; and Theodor Fontane, *Vor dem Storm* (Munich, 1994 [1878], p. 725 in notes; Storm, *The Dykemaster* (London, 1996 [1888]), p. 13. See also Aleida Assmann, *Erinnerungsräume: Formen und Wandlungen des kulturellen Gedächtnisses* (Munich, 1999).
14. In contemporary theory, memory work is often associated with the revisualization of difference. See, for example, the special issue on "Alter/Native Modernities," *Public Culture* 27 (1999). Katie Trumpener's

Bardic Nationalism: The Romantic Novel and the British Empire (Chicago, 1998) anticipates these issues as well.

15. See also Trumpener, *Bardic Nationalism,* p. 29.
16. Susan Crane, *Collecting and Historical Consciousness in Early Nineteenth-Century Germany* (Ithaca, 2000), p. iii.
17. Chateaubriand, *Memoirs,* 1: 231.
18. Charles Taylor, *Sources of the Self: The Making of the Modern Identity* (Cambridge, Mass., 1989). In this respect, Joyce Appleby, *Inheriting the Revolution: The First Generation of Americans* (Cambridge, Mass., 2000), is a superb case study.

Acknowledgments

This book has taken me eight years to complete. It began with ideas about "nostalgia," and ended with arguments about historical consciousness and the idea of subjectivity. Traveling such a long road, the book has benefited from and been shaped by many different believers, critics, and helpers. In the first place, I would like to thank Modris Eksteins, Geoff Eley, Michael Geyer, Jürgen Kocka, and Robert Wohl. Their support made it possible for me to have a year in Berlin in 1999–2000, during which I wrote the first draft of the book, funded generously by the John Simon Guggenheim Memorial Foundation, the Alexander von Humboldt Stiftung, and the Institut für vergleichende Gesellschaftsgeschichte at the Free University, Berlin. That I actually wrote the book in the time alloted that winter I owe to the kind indulgence of Karen, Eric, and Lauren, who put up with a writer with no room of his own. I had wonderful conversations about this book with Aleida Assmann, Matti Bunzl, Antoinette Burton, Clare Crowston, Ute Frevert, Michael Geyer, Beatriz Jaguaribe, Konrad Jarausch, Diane Koenker, Christoph Konrad, Reinhart Koselleck, Harry Liebersohn, Alf Lüdtke, John Lynn, Brent Maner, Kathy Oberdeck, Glenn Penny, Joe Perry, Leslie Reagan, Adelheid von Saldern, Mark Steinberg, and Bernd Widdig. I wish to acknowledge the generous support of the Research Board and the William and Flora Hewlett Summer International Research Grants of the University of Illinois at Urbana-Champaign, which provided early support for research assistants and a semester off. I have been lucky to be at Illinois since August 1987: it is a great university with great colleagues and great students. Indeed, I profited immensely from the research assistance of Amanda Brian, Jason Hansen, Michele May, and Molly Wilkinson Johnson. Harvard University Press has been supportive of my ideas while overlooking my delays, and I am tremendously grateful to Aida Donald and Kathleen McDermott for their advice and help along the way and thankful to Anita Safran for her clear-sighted editorial suggestions. Thanks also to Jim Brophy, John Gillis, Jean-Philippe Mathy, and John Whittier-Furgeson for their encouragement at crucial junctures.

Index